SCIENCE FICTION

This is a volume in the
Arno Press collection

SCIENCE FICTION

ADVISORY EDITORS

R. Reginald

Douglas Menville

See last pages of this volume
for a complete list of titles

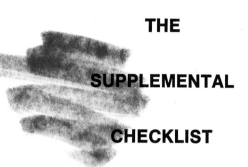

THE SUPPLEMENTAL CHECKLIST OF FANTASTIC LITERATURE

Edited by

Bradford M. Day

ARNO PRESS
A New York Times Company
New York — 1975

[redacted]

Reprint Edition 1974 by Arno Press Inc.

Reprinted from a copy in
The Newark Public Library

SCIENCE FICTION
ISBN for complete set: 0-405-06270-2
See last pages of this volume for titles.

Publisher's Note: The pagination between pages 96-99 is incorrect. The book is complete as published here. This book was reprinted from the best available copy.

Manufactured in the United States of America

Library of Congress Cataloging in Publication Data

Day, Bradford M
The supplemental checklist of fantastic literature.

(Science fiction)
Reprint of the ed. published by Science-Fiction & Fantasy Publications, Denver, N. Y.
1. Fantastic fiction--Bibliography. 2. Science fiction--Bibliography. I. Title. II. Series.
[Z5917.F3D35 1975] 016.80883'876 74-15962
ISBN 0-405-06327-X

THE

SUPPLEMENTAL CHECKLIST

OF

FANTASTIC LITERATURE

Compiled and Edited by

Bradford M. Day

SCIENCE-FICTION & FANTASY PUBLICATIONS

DENVER, NEW YORK

THE SUPPLEMENTAL CHECKLIST OF FANTASTIC LITERATURE

Dedicated to Dr. J. Lloyd Eaton. He answered my request for information about books not listed in "The Checklist of Fantastic Literature" by sending several hundred titles, with bibliographic data.

My sincere thanks for much additional information to John C. Nitka, D. Sc. F., and to many other people who furnished bits and pieces.

Every bibliophile who attempts to compile an index wishes to make it as complete, as all encompassing, as possible. My experience at this task shows no such completion can be achieved. An index of books in the English language listing works of fiction with varying content of the supernatural and the super-scientific is obsolete on the day of publication. Many additional titles will be brought to my attention soon after this appears. Wonderful! Be certain to write legibly, or use a typewriter, and include all necessary publishing data.

I started to read science fiction in 1928, the August issue of Amazing Stories with the first installment of THE SKYLARK OF SPACE by Edward Elmer Smith. The super-imaginative adventure, the terrific distances traversed, and the horrific forces unleashed made me a life-long reader of science fiction.

Dr. Smith continued this series with SKYLARK THREE and THE SKYLARK OF VALERON, evolving mightier forces, and sending his characters on longer/faster journeys to even stranger adventures. The "Lensmen" series began in our own backyard, the Solar System, in, TRIPLANETARY and began to span the galaxy in GALACTIC PATROL. The super-hero, Kimball Kinnison, flourished in GRAY LENSMAN, SECOND STAGE LENSMAN, and CHILDREN OF THE LENS.

Edmond Hamilton and Murray Leinster were active writers at this time. Hamilton gained the name and fame of "world-wrecker" from his many "space operas." Leinster Contributed the original concept of parallel time-tracks with the story, SIDEWISE IN TIME, which later appeared in the collection of that title. Jack Williamson and Stanton A. Coblentz also contributed to science fiction magazines of that period. Williamson wrote a truly fine tale of an Earth invasion, THE LEGION OF SPACE, and among others to see book publication, DARKER THAN YOU THINK, a modern werewolf story, proved his versatility. Avalon has published two good satires by Coblentz, THE BLUE BARBARIANS, and, HIDDEN WORLD. Collectors will discover that Avalon books when out of print are quite difficult to find. The earlier books, at least, were published in small (2500 copies) editions, and over half were bought by libraries. If we estimate there are 2000 collectors in this country, the remaining amount will spread rather thin.

John W. Campbell produced several excellent super-science fiction books in the few years he was writing before assuming the editor's chair of Astounding (now Analog). THE BLACK STAR PASSES, ISLANDS OF SPACE, and, INVADERS FROM THE INFINITE detail the amazing adventures of a group of super-scientists; their development and use of monstrous forces and weapons to battle invading entities in the far reaches of our island universe. THE MOON IS HELL is a battle of men against the barren and lifeless Moon as they attempt to wrest air, water and food from a satellite that has never supported life. THE INCREDIBLE PLANET tells of a wandering planet lost in the utterly remote depths of space between the galaxies. We lost one excellent teller of tallest tales when Mr. Campbell became editor of Astounding, but, in ultimate effect, gained many very fine authors who were discovered and encouraged to explore new frontiers in science fiction.

Some of the authors who followed Campbell:
Isaac Asimov: many short stories (EARTH IS ROOM ENOUGH, NINE TOMORROWS); time travel(THE END OF ETERNITY); the "Foundation" series (FOUNDATION, FOUNDATION AND EMPIRE, SECOND FOUNDATION) describe the fall of man's galactic empire, the long interregnum with squabbling war-lords warring on empire remnants, and the eventual rise of the Foundation to dominance and peace.
Robert A. Heinlein: a fine descriptive power to give the reader the feeling of the future. He wrote a "future history" series, THE MAN WHO SOLD THE MOON (the near future struggle to get there), THE GREEN HILLS OF EARTH(to the rest of the Solar System), REVOLT IN 2100 (against non-science tyranny), METHUSELAH'S CHILDREN (reaching the stars). 29 books - novels, and collections of short stories. One short story, "By His Bootstraps" (in THE MENACE FROM EARTH) is the prime example of paradox possible in time-travel
A. E. van Vogt: excellent tales of the future. He has a fine ability to project the image of alien entities in, THE VOYAGE OF THE SPACE BEAGLE, THE WAR AGAINST THE RULL. Space opera, THE MIXED MEN. Super-science, DESTINATION UNIVERSE, AWAY AND BEYOND. Future civilization, EMPIRE OF THE ATOM.
James Blish: an excellent future history series, A LIFE FOR THE STARS, THEY SHALL HAVE STARS, EARTHMAN COME HOME, A CLASH OF CYMBALS. The adventures of a city (New York) wrenched from off the Earth, enclosed in a field of force, and plying the far reaches of our galaxy.

Other fine authors of future and science fiction stories:
George O. Smith, space-opera and super-science.
Hal Clement, alien planets and strange life forms.
Stanley G. Weinbaum, adventure in our Solar System.
Frederic Brown, future and space-opera.
L. Ron Hubbard, future science fiction, and good fantastic adventure.
Poul Anderson, space-opera, and good fantastic adventure.
Arthur C. Clarke, future science fiction.
Andre Norton, future and far planet adventure.
Henry Kuttner (Vance, Padgett), future science fiction.
Clifford D. Simak, Raymond F. Jones, Eric Frank Russell, future science fiction.

Anthologists: Groff Conklin, and Bleiler and Dikty, for science fiction
Weird tales: August W. Derleth. Also a good number in science fiction.

L. Sprague de Camp and Fletcher Pratt singly, and together, wrote good science fiction, and good fantastic adventure. Regretfully for science fiction, Mr. de Camp decided steak is better than beans and now writes excellent historical novels.

Fantastic adventure: three authors on seperate pedestals. Robert E. Howard told the tale of Conan the super-hero of battle, blood and blondes. Mervyn Peake built the incredible castle Gormenghast and recounts the struggle of Titus Groan for mastery in truly sparkling prose. J. R. R. Tolkien created an entire mythical world in the superlative "Lord of the Ring" trilogy.

We specialize in retail sales of science fiction and fantasy books. Regretfully, only part of the following listing is in stock.

Abdullah, Achmed
DELIVER US FROM EVIL Putnam New York 1939 248
NIGHT DRUMS McCann New York 1921 329
About, Edmond
THE NOTARY'S NOSE Holt New York 1886 237
Adair, Hazel and Marriott, Ronald
STRANGER FROM SPACE Weidenfeld & Nicolson London 1953 191
Adams, Frederick Upham
THE KIDNAPPED MILLIONAIRES Lothrop Boston 1901 11-504
Adams, H. C.
TRAVELER'S TALES Boni & Liveright New York 1927 334
Adler, Allen
MACH I; A STORY OF THE PLANET IONUS Farrar, Strauss & Cudahy New York 1957 212
Akutagawa, Ryunosuke
KAPPA Akitaya Osaka, Japan 1947 3-154
RASHOMON AND OTHER STORIES Tuttle Rutland, Vt. 1951 95
TALES GROTESQUE AND CURIOUS Hakussaida Press Tokyo 1930 166
Alden, W. L.
AMONG THE FREAKS Longmans, Green London and New York 1896 195
VAN GAWENER'S WAYS Pearson London 1898 204
Aldiss, Brian (Wilson)
STARSHIP Criterion Press New York 1959 256
Alethitheras
TRAVELS BY SEA AND LAND J. Miller New York 1868 390
Alexander, R. W.
BACK TO NATURE S. Paul London nd 5-192
Alington, Adrian
DONALDSON Chatto & Windus London 1933 192
Allen, Dexter
JAGUAR AND THE GOLDEN STAG Coward, McCann New York 1954 340
Ambler, Eric
THE DARK FRONTIER Hodder & Stoughton London 1936 320
Ames, Huse and Hayter, Flora
THE BOOK OF THE GOLDEN KEY Kegan, Paul, Trench & Traubner London 1909 348
Amis, Kingsley and Conquest, Robert (Editors)
SPECTRUM Harcourt, Brace & World New York 1962 304
SPECTRUM II Harcourt, Brace & World New York 1963 271
An Adept
CHRYSAL; OR, THE ADVENTURES OF A GUINEA Becket London 1764 2 vol
Anderson, Poul
BRAIN WAVE Ballantine New York 1954 164
THE BROKEN SWORD Abelard-Schuman New York 1954 274
THE ENEMY STARS Lippincott Philadelphia 1959 189
THE HIGH CRUSADE Doubleday Garden City, N. Y. 1960 192
STAR WAYS Avalon New York 1956 224
THREE HEARTS AND THREE LIONS Doubleday Garden City, N. Y. 1961 191
TWILIGHT WORLD Dodd, Mead New York 1961 181
VAULT OF THE AGES Winston Philadelphia 1952 210
VIRGIN PLANET Avalon New York 1959 224
Anderson, Poul and Dickson, Gordon
EARTHMAN'S BURDEN Gnome Press New York 1957 185
Andrews, Frank Emerson
GRUGAN'S GOD Muhlenberg Press Philadelphia 1955 196

Andreyev, Leonid
THE SEVEN WHO WERE HANGED Boni & Liveright New York 1919 194

Anonymous
AURIFONDA; OR, ADVENTURES IN THE GOLD REGIONS Baker & Scribner New York 1849 3-103
BEYOND THE SUNRISE Lovell New York 1883 7-247
CHANCES AND CHANGES; OR, LIFE AS IT IS ILLUSTRATED IN THE HISTORY OF A STRAW HAT Appleton New York 1865 158
CHRISTMAS EVE WITH THE SPIRITS; OR, THE CANON'S WANDERINGS THROUGH WAYS UNKNOWN Bull, Simmons London 1870 90 ill.
THE CURSE OF INTELLECT Roberts Bros. Boston 1895 177
A DEAD MAN'S DIARY Ward, Lock London 1890 218
THE DREAM OF RAVAN Theosophical Pub Co London 1895 248
THE FLAMING SWORD Digby, Long London 1894 309
GHOST STORIES Carey & Hart Philadelphia 1846 192
THE HISTORY OF BENJAMIN KENNICOTT Rider London nd 143
AN INTERNATIONAL INTERLUDE Exposition Press New York 1956 66
THE ISLAND OF ATLANTIS no publisher given 1871 59
JOHN WHOPPER, THE NEWSBOY Roberts, Bros. Boston 1871 128
THE LAST EGYPTIAN Stern Philadelphia 1908 9-287
THE MAHATMA Downey London 1895 284
MAN ABROAD Dillingham New York 1886 114
THE MAN WHO KILLED HITLER Laurie London 1939 113
A NEW ALICE IN THE OLD WONDERLAND Lippincott Philadelphia 1895 309 (by Anna M. Richards, Jr.)
NOCTURNAL REVELS Noble, Wright, Stichall London 1749 320
PETER SCHLEMIHL IN AMERICA Carey & Hart Philadelphia 1848 494 (by Adalber Von Chamisso)
THE REMARKABLE LIFE OF DR. FAUSTUS, A GERMAN ASTROLOGER AND ENCHANTER T & J Allman London 1829 24
ROBINSON THE GREAT Christopher London 1929 149 (by Ramsay Muir)
THE SCIENCE FICTIONAL SHERLOCK HOLMES Science Fiction Assoc. Denver 1960 168
THE SECOND ARMADA; A CHAPTER OF FUTURE HISTORY AND A REPLY TO THE GERMAN CONQUEST OF ENGLAND IN 1875 AND BATTLE OF DORKING Porter & Coates Philadelphia 1879 58 wraps
THE SPAEWIFE; A TALE OF THE SCOTTISH CHRONICLES Oliver & Boyd Edinburgh 1823 3 vol (by John Galt)
THE SPECTRE OF THE PRIORY; OR, MYSTERY OF THE IRON TOMB Mason London 1800? 35
THE SURPRISING TRAVELS AND ADVENTURES OF BARON MUNCHAUSEN, ALSO AN ACCOUNT O A VOYAGE INTO THE MOON AND DOG STAR J Allman London 1830 28

Anonymous Anthologies
"COME NOT, LUCIFER" Westhouse London 1945 13-267
THE CONTINENTAL CLASSICS - VOLUME 14 - SPANISH, ITALIAN AND ORIENTAL TALES Harper New York and London 1890 368
THE CONTINENTAL CLASSICS - VOLUME 15 - MODERN GHOSTS Harper New York and London 1890 364
DREAM WARNINGS AND MYSTERIES Redway London nd 318
FIFTY ADVENTURES INTO THE UNKNOWN Odhams London nd 703
FIFTY STRANGEST STORIES EVER TOLD Odhams London nd 704
GERMAN TALES OF TERROR. WONDERFUL AND THRILLING TALES FOR WINTER EVENINGS Shepard, Clark & Brown Boston nd (1850) 178, 119 2 vol in 1

Anonymous Anthologies
GHOST STORIES AND OTHER QUEER TALES Pearson London nd 256
GHOST STORIES AND PRESENTIMENTS Redway London nd (1904) 308
LAURIE'S SPACE ANNUAL: 1953 Laurie London 1953 86 juv
MINIATURE ROMANCES FROM THE GERMAN WITH OTHER PROLUSIONS OF LIGHT LITERATURE Little, Brown Boston 1841 13-324
MORE UNCANNY STORIES Pearson London 1918 110
MYSTERY Hulton London 1952 437
NOVELS, SKETCHES AND ESSAYS Herbert London 1888 432
PANORAMA OF MODERN LITERATURE Doubleday, Doran Garden City, N. Y. 1920 344
STORIES BY AMERICAN AUTHORS - VOLUME 5 Scribner New York 1884 191
STORIES BY AMERICAN AUTHORS - VOLUME 8 Scribner New York 1884 206
STORIES BY ENGLISH AUTHORS - IRELAND Scribner New York 1896 180
STORIES BY ENGLISH AUTHORS - THE SEA Scribner New York 1896 161
STORIES BY FOREIGN AUTHORS - FRENCH Scribner New York 1898 163
STRANGE DOINGS IN STRANGE PLACES Cassell London 1890 310
STRANGES TALES FROM "BLACKWOOD" Blackwood Edinburgh and London 1950 521
TALES OF MYSTERY AND ADVENTURE Allied Newspapers Manchester, Eng nd 416 ill
TALES OF THE DEAD White, Cochrane London 1813 248
THRILLS, CRIMES AND MYSTERIES Assoc Newspapers London nd 864
UNCANNY STORIES Pearson London 1916 125
WEIRD TALES BY AMERICAN WRITERS Dent London 1896 188
WORLD'S GREAT ADVENTURE STORIES Blue Ribbon New York 1929 676

antoniorrobles (Robles, Antonio)
THE REFUGEE CENTAUR Twayne New York 1952 245

Apple, A. A.
MR. CHANG'S CRIME RAY Chelsea House New York 1928 249

Appleton, Victor, II (Pseud)
TOM SWIFT AND HIS ATOMIC EARTH BLASTER Grosset & Dunlap New York 1954 210
TOM SWIFT AND HIS DEEP SEA HYDRODOME Grosset & Dunlap New York 1958 184 juv
TOM SWIFT AND HIS DIVING SEACOPTER Grosset & Dunlap New York 1956 214 juv
TOM SWIFT AND HIS ELECTRONIC RETROSCOPE Grosset & Dunlap New York 1959 184
TOM SWIFT AND HIS FLYING LAB Grosset & Dunlap New York 1954 219 juv
TOM SWIFT AND HIS GIANT ROBOT Grosset & Dunlap New York 211 juv
TOM SWIFT AND HIS JETMARINE Grosset & Dunlap New York 1954 208 juv
TOM SWIFT AND HIS OUTPOST IN SPACE Grosset & Dunlap New York 1955 210 juv
TOM SWIFT AND HIS ROCKET SHIP Grosset & Dunlap New York 1954 208 juv
TOM SWIFT AND HIS SPACE SOLARTRON Grosset & Dunlap New York 1958 183 juv
TOM SWIFT AND HIS SPECTROMARINE SELECTOR Grosset & Dunlap New York 1960 184
TOM SWIFT AND HIS ULTRASONIC CYCLOPLANE Grosset & Dunlap New York 1957 182
TOM SWIFT AND THE COSMIC ASTRONAUTS Grosset & Dunlap New York 1960 184 juv
TOM SWIFT AND THE PHANTOM SATELLITE Grosset & Dunlap New York 1956 214 juv
TOM SWIFT IN THE CAVES OF NUCLEAR FIRE Grosset & Dunlap New York 1956 214
TOM SWIFT IN THE RACE TO THE MOON Grosset & Dunlap New York 1958 180 juv
TOM SWIFT AND THE VISITOR FROM PLANET X Grosset & Dunlap New York 1961 184

Arch, E. L.
BRIDGE TO YESTERDAY Avalon New York 1963 192

Ariss, Bruce
FULL CIRCLE Avalon New York 1963 224

Armstrong, Anthony
THE STRANGE CASE OF MR. PELHAM Methuen London 1957 224

Armstrong, Charlotte
THE CASE OF THE WEIRD SISTERS Coward-McCann New York 1943 279

Arne, Aaron
FEET OF CLAY; A FANTASY Vantage Press New York 1958 276
Arnold, Andrew W.
THE ATTACK ON THE FARM White London 1899 312 Front
Arnold, Edwin
THE VOYAGE OF ITHOBAL Dillingham New York 1901 226 Nar. poem
Aronin, Ben
THE LOST TRIBE Simons Press New York and Chicago 1934 9-352
THE MOOR'S GOLD Argus Chicago 1935 7-271
Ashbee, C. R.
THE BUILDING OF THELEMA Dent London 1910 361
Ashton, Francis
ALAS, THAT GREAT CITY Dakers London nd 395
Ashton, Francis and Stephen
WRONG SIDE OF THE MOON Boardman London and New York 1952 5-191
Asimov, Isaac
THE CAVES OF STEEL Doubleday Garden City, N. Y. 1954 13-224
THE CURRENTS OF SPACE Doubleday Garden City, N. Y. 1952 217
EARTH IS ROOM ENOUGH Doubleday Garden City, N. Y. 1957 192
THE END OF ETERNITY Doubleday Garden City, N. Y. 1955 191
FOUNDATION Gnome Press New York 1951 11-255
FOUNDATION AND EMPIRE Gnome Press New York 1952 7-247
I, ROBOT Gnome Press New York 1950 13-253
THE MARTIAN WAY Doubleday Garden City, N. Y. 1955 222
THE NAKED SUN Doubleday Garden City, N. Y. 1957 187
NINE TOMORROWS Doubleday Garden City, N. Y. 1959 236
PEBBLE IN THE SKY Doubleday Garden City, N. Y. 1950 9-223
SECOND FOUNDATION Gnome Press New York 1953 210
THE STARS, LIKE DUST Doubleday Garden City, N. Y. 1951 13-218
TRIANGLE (see ibid, The Currents of Space, Pebble in the Sky, The Stars Like Dust)
Asquith, Cynthia
A BOOK OF MODERN GHOSTS (see ibid, The Second Ghost Book)
THE SECOND GHOST BOOK Barrie London 1952 236
Assollant, Alfred
THE FANTASTIC HISTORY OF THE CELEBRATED PIERROT Low, Marston, Searle London 1875 262
Astor, W. W.
PHARAOH'S DAUGHTER AND OTHER STORIES Macmillan London 1900 235
Aswell, Mary Louise
THE WORLD WITHIN McGraw-Hill New York 1947 371
Atkey, Philip
HEIRS OF MERLIN Cassell London 1945 192
Atkinson, T. C.
LAST OF THE GIANT KILLERS Macmillan London 1891 244
Author of, "The Haunted Priory"
THE CASTLE OF INCHVALLY T. Kelly London 1820 522
Author of, "The Holiday Book"
THE LADY OF LOWFORD AND OTHER CHRISTMAS STORIES Pott New York and Miss Knigh Troy, N. Y. 1891 334
Author of, "The Island of Atlantis"
THE EMIGRANTS; OR, THE ISLAND OF ESMERALDA no publisher given 1879 64

Author of, "Secret Memoirs and Manners of Several Persons of Quality from the New Atlantis" (by Mrs. Manley)
COURT INTRIGUES IN A COLLECTION OF ORIGINAL LETTERS FROM THE ISLAND OF THE NEW ATLANTIS Morphew London 1711 220
Ayme, Marcel
THE GREEN MARE Harper New York 1955 234
THE MAGIC PICTURES: MORE ABOUT THE WONDERFUL FARM Harper New York 1954 117 juv
THE SECOND FACE Harper New York 1951 182
THE WONDERFUL FARM Harper New York 1951 190 juv
Babcock, Dwight W.
THE GORGEOUS GHOUL United Authors London 1947 5-256
Bacon, Alice Muriel
IN THE LAND OF THE GODS Houghton, Mifflin Boston and New York 1905 265
Bahnson, Agnew H. Jr.
THE STARS ARE TOO HIGH Random House New York 1959 250
Baillie-Saunders, Margaret
THE CANDLE VIRGINS Hutchinson London nd 286
Bair, Patrick
FASTER! FASTER! Viking Press New York 1950 11-251
Baker, Denys Val
WORLDS WITHOUT END Sylvan Press London 1945 7-168
Baker, Frank
THE DOWNS SO FREE Dakers London 1948 366
Baker, Gordon
NONE SO BLIND N. Wolsey London and Leicester 1946 9-207
Baker, G. P.
THE MAGIC TALE OF HARVANGER AND YOLANDE Mills & Boon London 1914 346
THE ROMANCE OF PALOMBRIS AND PALLOGRIS Mills & Boon London 1915 451
Balchin, Nigel
THE SMALL BACK ROOM Houghton Mifflin Boston 1945 192
Balint, Emery
DON'T INHALE IT Gaer Assoc New York 1949 13-222
Ball, John Jr.
OPERATION SPACE Hutchinson London 1960 208
OPERATION SPRINGBOARD Duell, Sloane & Pearce New York 1958 168 juv
Balzac, Honore de
ELIXIR OF LIFE Macmillan New York 1901 332
THE QUEST OF THE ABSOLUTE Dent London 1910 226
Banister, Manly
CONQUEST OF EARTH Avalon New York 1957 224
Barclay, Florence L.
THE UPAS TREE Putnam New York 1912 13-287
Barcynska, Countess (pseud of Margaret Caradoc Evans)
THE CONJUROR Rich & Cowan London nd 7-236
Baring-Gould, S(abine)
THE BOOK OF WERE-WOLVES Smith Elder London 1865 265
LEGENDS OF THE PATRIARCHS AND PROPHETS Holt & Williams New York 1872 380
Barker, Elsa
LETTERS FROM A LIVING DEAD MAN Kennerley New York 1916 291
THE SON OF MARY BETHEL Duffield New York 1902 549
Barker, Nugent
WRITTEN WITH MY LEFT HAND Marshall London 1951 233

Barker, Shirley (Frances)
PEACE, MY DAUGHTERS Crown New York 1949 248
SWEAR BY APOLLO Random New York 1958 306
Barlow, J. Swindells
A MIGHTY EMPIRE Ward, Lock London 1902 311
Barlow, James
ONE HALF THE WORLD Harper New York 1957 277
Barnard, Allan
THE HARLOT KILLER Dodd, Mead New York 1953 236
Barnard, Patricia
THE CONTEMPORARY HOUSE Coward-McCann New York 1954 47
Barnes, Arthur K.
INTERPLANETARY HUNTER Gnome Press New York 1956 231
Barnett, Ada
THE JOYOUS ADVENTURER Putnam New York and London 1924 497
Barney, Natalie Clifford
THE ONE WHO IS LEGION Partridge London 1930 158
Barnhouse, Perl T.
MY JOURNEYS WITH ASTARGO Bell Denver 1952 212
Baron, Walter
DEVIL-BROTHER Hurst & Blackett London 1935 286
Barr, Densil Neve
THE MAN WITH ONLY ONE HEAD Rich & Cowan London 1955 192
Barrett, William Edward
THE EDGE OF THINGS Doubleday Garden City, N. Y. 1960 335
Barrie, (Sir) James
PETER PAN AND WENDY Hodder & Stoughton London nd 317
Barrow, Percy James
THE MAN WHO WENT BACK Unwin London 1925 288
Barry, William
THE PLACE OF DREAMS Sands London 1901 274
Bartlett, Vernon
TOMORROW ALWAYS COMES Macmillan New York 1943 128
Barton, Donald R.
ONCE IN ALEPPO Scribner New York 1955 234
Barzman, Ben
TWINKLE, TWINKLE LITTLE STAR Putnam New York 1960 261
Baudelaire, Charles
PROSE AND POETRY Boni & Liveright New York 1919 248
Baum, L(yman) Frank
DOROTHY AND THE WIZARD IN OZ Reilly & Britton Chicago 1908 256 juv
THE EMERALD CITY OF OZ Reilly & Britton Chicago 1910 295 juv
THE ENCHANTED ISLAND OF YEW Bobbs-Merrill Indianapolis 1903 242 juv
GLINDA OF OZ Reilly & Lee Chicago 1920 279 juv
JACK PUMPKINHEAD AND THE SAWHORSE OF OZ, also, TIK-TOK AND THE GNOME KING OF OZ Rand, McNally Chicago 1939 61 juv
THE LAND OF OZ; A SEQUEL TO THE WIZARD OF OZ Reilly & Lee Chicago 1939 286
LITTLE WIZARD STORIES OF OZ Reilly & Britton Chicago 1914 198 juv
THE LOST PRINCESS OF OZ Reilly & Lee Chicago 1917 312 juv
THE MAGIC OF OZ Reilly & Lee Chicago 1919 265 juv
THE MARVELLOUS LAND OF OZ Reilly & Britton Chicago 1904 287 juv
THE NEW WIZARD OF OZ Bobbs-Merrill Indianapolis 1903 259 juv
A NEW WONDERLAND Russell New York 1900 189 juv

Baum, L(yman) Frank (continued)
OZMA OF OZ Reilly & Britton Chicago 1907 270 juv
THE PATCHWORK FIRL OF OZ Reilly & Britton Chicago 1913 340 juv
QUEEN ZIXI OF IX Century New York 1905 303 juv
RINKITINK IN OZ Reilly & Britton Chicago 1916 314 juv
THE ROAD TO OZ Reilly & Britton Chicago 1909 261 juv
THE ROYAL BOOK OF OZ Reilly & Lee Chicago 1921 312 juv
THE SCARECROW OF OZ Reilly & Britton Chicago 1915 288 juv
THE SEA FAIRIES Reilly & Britton Chicago 1911 239 juv
SKY ISLAND Reilly & Britton Chicago 1912 287 juv
THE SURPRISING ADVENTURES OF THE MAGICAL MONARCH OF MO AND HIS PEOPLE Bobbs-Merrill Indianapolia 1903 236 juv
TIK-TOK OF OZ Reilly & Britton Chicago 1914 271 juv
THE TIN WOODMAN OF OZ Reilly & Britton Chicago 1918 287 juv
THE WIZARD OF OZ (see ibid, The Wonderful Wizard of Oz)
THE WONDERFUL WIZARD OF OZ Hill New York and Chicago 1900 259 juv

Baumgartl, I.
SEA GODS. A JAPANESE FANTASY IN FIVE PARTS Kroch's Bookstores Chicago 1937 110 500 copy edition

Bayldon, Arthur Alfred Dawson
THE TRAGEDY BEHIND THE CURTAIN AND OTHER STORIES Townsend Sydney, Australia 1910 342

Bazhov, Pavel
THE MALACHITE CASKET Hutchinson London nd 5-192

Beagle, Peter S.
A FINE AND PRIVATE PLACE Viking Press New York 1960 272

Beamish, Noel de Vic
THE KING'S MISSAL Jenkins London 1934 312

Beaton, David C.
THE MAGICIAN Pilgrim Press Boston and Chicago 1898 286 ill.

Beaumont, Charles
THE HUNGER, AND OTHER STORIES Putnam New York 1957 234

Bechdolt, Jack
THE TORCH Prime Press Philadelphia 1948 11-228

Beck, L. Adams
THE GARDEN OF VISION Cosmopolitan New York 1929 421

Becke, Louis
RIDAN THE DEVIL Unwin London 1899 330

Beddoes, Willoughby T. H.
A GODDESS FROM THE SEA Drane London nd 9-387 Front

Bede, Cuthbert
THE WHITE WIFE S. Low, Son & Marston London 1868 252

Bedford-Jones, H.
THE DRUMS OF DAMBALLA Covici-Friede New York 1929 295

Beer, Alec
GHOST STORIES Australia Broadcasting Comm Sydney 1935 138

Beerbohm, Max
THE DREADFUL DRAGON OF HAY HILL Heinemann London 1928 113

Bell, Neil (pseud of Stephen Southwold)
ALPHA AND OMEGA Hale London 1946 326
LIFE COMES TO SEATHORPE Eyre & Spottiswoode London 1946 7-302
THE SECRET LIFE OF MISS LOTTINGER Redman London and Sydney 1953 320

Bell, Robert
IN REALMS UNKNOWN Vantage Press New York 1954 194

Bellamy, Francis Rufus
    ATTA Wyn New York 1953 216
Belloc, Hillaire
    MR. PETRE Arrowsmith London 1925 310
Benet, Stephen Vincent
    O'HALLORAN'S LUCK & OTHER SHORT STORIES Murray Hill Books New York 1940 247
Bengtsson, Frans G.
    THE LONG SHIPS Knopf New York 1954 503
Bennett, Alfred Gordon
    THE SEA OF DREAMS Macauley New York 1926 316
Bennett, John
    THE DOCTOR TO THE DEAD Rinehart New York 1946 260
    MADAME MARGOT Century New York 1921 3-110 150 copy edition
Bennett, Ken(ys Deverall)
    THE FABULOUS WINK Pellegrini & Cudahy New York 1951 244
Bennett, Margot
    THE LONG WAY BACK Coward-McCann New York 1954 248
Benson, A(rthur) C(hristopher)
    BASIL NETHERBY Hutchinson London nd 211
Benson, Theodora
    THE MAN FROM THE TUNNEL, AND OTHER STORIES Appleton-Century-Crofts New York 1950 271
Beresford, J(ohn) D(avys)
    THE MEETING PLACE & OTHER STORIES Faber & Faber London 1929 410
    PECKOVER Putnam New York 1935 276
Beresford, J. D. and Tyson; Esme Wynne
    THE GIFT Hutchinson London nd (1957) 224
Beresford, Leslie
    THE GREAT IMAGE Odhams London nd 288
Berneri, Marie Louise
    JOURNEY THROUGH UTOPIA Beacon Press Boston 1951 350
Berrow, Norman
    IT HOWLS AT NIGHT Ward, Lock London and Melbourne 1937 9-320
Berry. Bryan
    BORN IN CAPTIVITY Hamilton London 1952 192
    FROM WHAT FAR STAR? Hamilton London 1953 143
    THE VENOM SEEKERS Hamilton London 1953 160
Bessand-Massenet, Pierre
    AMOROUS GHOST Abelard-Schuman New York 1958 126
Bester, Alfred
    THE DEMOLISHED MAN Shasta Chicago 1953 250
    TIGER, TIGER Sidgwick & Jackson London nd (1955) 232
Beuf, Carlo (Maria Luigi)
    THE INNOCENCE OF PASTOR MULLER Duell, Sloan & Pearce New York 1951 156
Beyer, William Grey
    MINIONS OF THE MOON Gnome Press New York 1950 9-190
Bhattacharya, Bhabani
    A GODDESS NAMED GOLD Crown New York 1960 280
    HE WHO RIDES A TIGER Crown New York 1954 245
Biemiller, Carl L.
    THE MAGIC BALL FROM MARS Morrow New York 1953 127 juv
    STARBOY Holt New York 1956 158 juv
Bien, H. M.
    BEN BEOR Friedenwald Baltimore 1892 528

Bierce, Ambrose (Gwinnet)
THE COLLECTED WRITINGS OF AMBROSE BIERCE Citadel Press New York 1946 830
Bierce, Ambrose with Danziger, G. A.
THE MONK AND THE HANGMAN'S DAUGHTER Shulte Chicago 1892 166
Bierstadt, E. H.
SATAN WAS A MAN Doubleday, Doran Garden City, N. Y. 1935 292
Biggs, John (Jr.)
DEMI-GODS Scribner New York 1926 230
SEVEN DAYS WHIPPING Scribner New York 1928 219
Bilbo, Jack
OUT OF MY MIND. STRANGE STORIES Modern Art Gallery London 1946 124
Binder, Eando (Ernest and Otto)
THE LORDS OF CREATION Prime Press Philadelphia 1949 232
Binns, Jack
THE FLYING BUCCANEER Brown New York 1923 311
Birkin, Charles Lloyd
THE DEVIL'S SPAWN Allen London 1936 9-252
Bishop, Zealia
THE CURSE OF YIG Arkham House Sauk City, Wisc 1953 175
Black, Frank Burn
CHRONICLES OF KANUL THE KUTE Putnam London 1918 102
Blackburn, John
A SCENT OF NEW-MOWN HAY Mill New York 1958 224
A SOUR APPLE TREE Mill New York 1959 189
Blackstock, Charity
THE EXORCISM Hodder & Stoughton London 1961 222
Blackwood, Algernon
IN THE REALM OF TERROR Pantheon New York 1957 312 (reprints)
TALES OF THE UNCANNY AND SUPERNATURAL British Book Co. New York 1950 426 (reprints)
Blair, Adrian
COSMIC CONQUEST arren London 1953 159
Blake, Nicholas
THE SMILER WITH THE KNIFE Harper New York 1939 303
Blamires, Harry
BLESSING UNBOUNDED; A VISION Longmans New York 1956 185
COLD WAR IN HELL Longmans New York 1955 207
THE DEVIL'S HUNTING-GROUNDS Longmans New York 1954 162
Bleiler, Everett and Dikty, Theodore E. (editors)
THE BEST SCIENCE FICTION STORIES: 1949 Fell New York 1949 314
THE BEST SCIENCE FICTION STORIES: 1950 Fell New York 1950 341
THE BEST SCIENCE FICTION STORIES: 1951 Fell New York 1951 351
THE BEST SCIENCE FICTION STORIES: 1952 Bell New York 1952 288
THE BEST SCIENCE FICTION STORIES: 1953 Fell New York 1953 279
THE BEST SCIENCE FICTION STORIES: 1954 Fell New York 1954 316
IMAGINATION UNLIMITED Farrar, Strauss & Young New York 1952 443
YEAR'S BEST SCIENCE FICTION NOVELS: 1952 Fell New York 1952 351
YEAR'S BEST SCIENCE FICTION NOVELS: 1953 Fell New York 1953 315
YEAR'S BEST SCIENCE FICTION NOVELS: 1954 Fell New York 1954 317
Blish, James
A CLASH OF CYMBALS Faber & Faber London 1959 204
EARTHMAN, COME HOME Putnam New York 1955 252
JACK OF EAGLES Greenberg New York 1952 246
A LIFE FOR THE STARS Putnam New York 1962 224

Blish, James (continued)
THE SEEDLINGS STARS Gnome Press New York 1957 185
THE STAR DWELLERS Putnam New York 1961 224
THEY SHALL HAVE STARS Faber & Faber London 1956 184
Blish, James and Lowndes, Robert W.
THE DUPLICATED MAN Avalon New York 1959 222
Bloch, Bertram
THE LITTLE LAUNDRESS AND THE FEARFUL KNIGHT Doubleday Garden City, N. Y. 1954 122
Bloch, Robert
PLEASANT DREAMS Arkham House Sauk City, Wisc 1960 233
THE SCARF Dial New York 1947 9-247
Blodgett, Mabel Fuller
AT THE QUEEN'S MERCY Lamson, Wolfe Boston, New York, London 1897 261
Bloom, Ursula
THE JUDGE OF JERUSALEM Harrap London 1926 303
Blore, Trevor
THE HOUSE OF LIVING DEATH Aldor London 1946 155
Blundell, Peter
THE STAR OF THE INCAS Milford - Oxford Univ Press London 1926 304 juv
Blyth, James
THE WEIRD SISTERS Ward, Lock London 1918 304
Boileau, Pierre and Narcejac, Thomas
THE WOMAN WHO WAS NO MORE Rinehart New York 1954 202
Boland, John
NO REFUGE M. Joseph London 1956 254
WHITE AUGUST M. Joseph London 1956 268
Bombal, Maria-Louisa
THE SHROUDED WOMAN Cassell London 1950 145
Bond, Nelson, F.
THE EXILES OF TIME Prime Press Philadelphia 1949 183
LANCELOT BIGGS: SPACEMAN Doubleday Garden City, N. Y. 1950 224
31st OF FEBRUARY Gnome Press New York 1949 13-272
Borodin, George
THE BOOK OF JOANNA Staples Press London 1947 7-198
PILLAR OF FIRE McBride New York 1948 320
SPURIOUS SUN Laurie London 1948 7-282
Borgese, Elizabeth
TO WHOM IT MAY CONCERN Braziller New York 1960 167
Bosschere, Jean de
WEIRD ISLANDS McBride New York 1922 210
Botkin, B. A. (editor)
A TREASURY OF AMERICAN FOLKLORE Crown New York 1944 932
Boucher, Anthony and McComas, J. Francis (editors)
THE BEST FROM FANTASY AND SCIENCE FICTION Little, Brown Boston 1952 227
THE BEST FROM FANTASY AND SCIENCE FICTION: Second series Little, Brown Boston 1953 270
THE BEST FROM FANTASY AND SCIENCE FICTION: Third series Doubleday Garden City, N. Y. 1954 252
Boucher, Anthony (editor) (pseud of White, William Anthony Parker)
THE BEST FROM FANTASY AND SCIENCE FICTION: Fourth series Doubleday Garden City, N. Y. 1955 250
THE BEST FROM FANTASY AND SCIENCE FICTION: Fifth series Doubleday Garden City, N. Y. 1956 256

Boucher, Anthony (continued)
THE BEST FROM FANTASY AND SCIENCE FICTION: Sixth series Doubleday Garden City, N. Y. 1957 255
THE BEST FROM FANTASY AND SCIENCE FICTION: Seventh series Doubleday Garden City, N. Y. 1958 264
FAR AND AWAY Ballantine New York 1955 166
A TREASURY OF GREAT SCIENCE FICTION Doubleday Garden City, N. Y. 1959 2 vol
Bouie, Frederic Vernon
GOOD-BYE WHITE MAN Exposition Press New York 1953 241
Bounds, S. J.
DIMENSION OF HORROR Hamilton London 1953 160
Bova, Ben
THE STAR CONQUERORS Winston Philadelphia 1959 215
Bowen, John
AFTER THE RAIN Faber & Faber London 1958 203
Bowen, Marjorie (pseud of Gabrielle M. V. Long)
THE BISHOP OF HELL Lane London 1949 11-230
FIVE WINDS Hodder & Stoughton London 1927 317
Boyd, Halbert J.
STRANGE TALES OF THE BORDERS Moray Edinburgh 1948 238
Bozman, E. F.
THE TRAVELLER'S RETURN Dent London 1938 13-313
Brackett, Leigh
THE LONG TOMORROW Doubleday Garden City, N. Y. 1955 222
THE STARMEN Gnome Press New York 1952 213
Bradbury, Ray(mond Douglas)
THE ANTHEM SPRINTERS Dial Press New York 1962 128
DANDELION WINE Doubleday Garden City, N. Y. 1957 281
THE DAY IT RAINED FOREVER Rupert Hart-Davis London 1959 254
FAHRENHEIT 451 Ballantine New York 1953 199
THE GOLDEN APPLES OF THE SUN Doubleday Garden City, N. Y. 1953 250
THE ILLUSTRATED MAN Doubleday Garden City, N. Y. 1951 256
THE MARTIAN CHRONICLES Doubleday Garden City, N. Y. 1950 13-222
A MEDICINE FOR MELANCHOLY Doubleday Garden City, N. Y. 1959 240
THE OCTOBER COUNTRY Ballantine New York 1955 306
R IS FOR ROCKET Doubleday Garden City, N. Y. 1962 233
THE SILVER LOCUSTS (see ibid, The Martian Chronicles)
SOMETHING WICKED THIS WAY COMES Simon & Schuster New York 1962 317
Braddy, Nella
MASTERPIECES OF ADVENTURE. STORIES OF THE SEA AND SKY Doubleday, Page New York 1921 168
Bradley, H. Dennis
TOWARD THE STARS Laurie London 1924 331
Brady, Cyrus Townsend
AND THUS HE CAME Putnam New York and London 1916 103
THE ISLAND OF SURPRISE McClurg Chicago 1915 371
Brahms, Caryl and Simon, S. J. (pseud of Abrahams, Doris Caroline and Skidelsky, Simon Jasha)
TITANIA HAS A MOTHER Joseph London 1944 7-194
Bramah, Ernest
THE SECRET OF THE LEAGUE Nelson London 1907 287
Bramson, Karen
DR. MOREL Greenberg New York 1927 211

Bramwell, James (Guy)
GOING WEST Cobden-Sanderson London 1935 263
Brand, Millen
THE OUTWARD ROOM Simon & Schuster New York 1937 309
Brand, Neville
THE SLEEPING QUEEN Lane London 1926 308
Brandon, Henry
THE AFTER DEATH Theosophical Pub Co London 1911 224
Branley, Franklyn M.
LODESTAR - ROCKET SHIP TO MARS Crowell New York 1951 248
Brayley, Berton
THE ENCHANTED FLIVVER Century New York 1925 255
Brennan, Joseph Payne
THE DARK RETURNERS Macabre House New Haven, Conn 1959 110 150 copy edition
NINE HORRORS Arkham House Sauk City, Wisc 1958 120
SCREAM AT MIDNIGHT Macabre House New Haven, Conn 1963 124 250 copy edition
Bremner, Blanche Irbe
THE HUT IN THE FOREST no publisher given 1917 106
Brett, Sylvia
PAN AND THE LITTLE GREEN GATE Hodder & Stoughton London 1908 237
Bretnall, George H.
BULO AND LELE Comet Press New York 1954 208
Bridge, Ann
AND THEN YOU CAME Macmillan New York 1948 306
Bridges, Roy
A MIRROR OF SILVER Hutchinson London nd 280
Bridges, T. C.
THE CITY OF NO ESCAPE Newnes London nd 255 juv
THE HIDDEN CITY Collins Press London and Glasgow nd 7-320 juv
Brighouse, Harold
SIX FANTASIES French New York 1931 155
Bristow, Gwen and Manning, Bruce
THE INVISIBLE HOST Mystery League New York 1930 286
Brodie-Innes, J. W.
THE GOLDEN ROPE Lane London and New York 1919 3-311
MORAG, THE SEAL Ribman London 1908 323
Brooke, Jocelyn
THE IMAGE OF A DRAWN SWORD Lane London 1950 9-183
THE SCAPEGOAT Harper New York 1949 3-209
Brooks, Walter R(ollin)
ERNESTINE TAKES OVER Morrow New York 1935 265
FREDDY AND THE BASEBALL TEAM FROM MARS Knopf New York 1955 241 juv
FREDDY AND THE MEN FROM MARS Knopf New York 1954 246 juv
FREDDY AND THE SPACE SHIP Knopf New York 1953 240 juv
Brophy, Brigid
HACKENFELLER'S APE Random New York 1954 177
Broster, D(orothy) K.
A FIRE OF DRIFTWOOD Heinemann London 1932 348
Brown, Fredric
ANGELS AND SPACESHIPS Dutton New York 1954 224
THE LIGHTS IN THE SKY ARE STARS Dutton New York 1953 9-222
MARTIANS, GO HOME Dutton New York 1955 174
PROJECT JUPITER (see ibid, The Lights in the Sky Are Stars)
ROGUE IN SPACE Dutton New York 1957 189

Brown, Fredric (continued)
SPACE ON MY HANDS Shasta Chicago 1951 224
WHAT MAD UNIVERSE? Dutton New York 1949 9-255
Brown, Fredric and Reynolds, Mack (editors)
SCIENCE FICTION CARNIVAL Shasta Chicago 1953 315
Brown, F. H.
ONE DOLLAR'S WORTH Privately Printed Chicago 1893 5-177
Brown, Lewis
SEE WHAT I MEAN? Random New York 1943 245
Brown, Slater
SPACEWARD BOUND Prentice-Hall New York 1955 213 juv
Brown, Vinson
BLACK TREASURE Little, Brown Boston 1951 209
Browne, Barum
THE DEVIL AND X Y Z Doubleday, Doran Garden City, N. Y. 1931 310
Browne, Howard
RETURN OF THARN Grandon Providence, R. I. 1956 253
Browne, Reginald
THE SCHOOL IN SPACE Swan London 1947 5-189 juv
Bruce, Mary Grant
THE STONE AXE OF BURKAMUKK Ward, Lock London 1922 256
Bryant, Marguerite
THE HEIGHTS Duffield New York 1924 13-285
Buchan, John
THE COURTS OF THE MORNING Houghton Mifflin Boston and New York 1929 384
PRESTER JOHN Houghton Mifflin Boston and New York 1928 11-272 juv
Buchanan, Muriel
THE WHITE WITCH Jenkins London 1913 336
Buchanan, Robert
THE DEVIL'S CASE Buchanan London nd 169
Buchanan, Thomas G.
THE UNICORN Sloane Assoc New York 1960 223
Buck, Charles W.
UNDER THE SUN; OR, THE PASSING OF THE INCAS Sheltman Louisville, Ky. 1902 413
Bull, Albert E.
THE MYSTERY OF THE HIDDEN CITY Federation Press London 1925 11-256
Bull, Lois
THE CAPTIVE GODDESS Macauley New York 1935 253
Bull, R. C. (editor)
PERTURBED SPIRITS Assoc Booksellers Westport, Conn. 1955 287
Bulmer, H. K.
EMPIRE OF CHAOS Hamilton London 1953 153
GALACTIC INTRIGUE Hamilton London 1953 160
THE STARS ARE OURS Hamilton London 1953 158
Burbridge, Juanita Cassil
CHEATING THE DEVIL Brown New York 1925 272
Burdekin, Kay
THE REBEL PASSION Morrow New York 1929 306
Burke, Jonathan
THE DARK GATEWAY Hamilton London 1953 223
THE ECHOING WORLDS Hamilton London 1953 159
HOTEL COSMOS Panther London 1954 142

Burke, Jonathan (continued)
PATTERN OF SHADOWS Museum Press London 1954 128
PURSUIT THROUGH TIME Ward, Lock, London 1956 187
Burks, Arthur J.
LOOK BEHIND YOU Shroud Buffalo, N. Y. 1954 73 hinged boards
Burland, Harris (John B. Harris-Burland)
THE FINANCIER Dillingham New York 1906 11-352
Burman, Ben Lucien
HIGH WATER AT CATFISH BEND Messner New York 1952 121
SEVEN STARS FOR CATFISH BEND Funk & Wagnalls New York 1956 133
Burnand, F. C.
MOKEANNA! Bradbury, Agnew London 1873 273 Ill.
Burnett, Frances Hodgson
IN THE CLOSED ROOM McClure, Phillips New York 1904 3-130
Burnshaw, Stanley
THE SUNLESS SEA Davies London 1948 192
Burr, Hanford M(ontrose)
AROUND THE FIRE; STORIES OF BEGINNINGS Assoc Press New York 1912 238
Burrage, A. Harcourt
HURTLERS THROUGH SPACE Warne London and New York 1951 255 juv
Burrage, A. M.
DON'T BREAK THE SEAL Swan London 1946 159
Burroughs, Edgar Rice
BEYOND THIRTY and THE MAN-EATER Science-Fiction & Fantasy Pub S. Ozone Park, N. Y. 1957 11-229
LLANA OF GATHOL Burroughs Tarzana, Calif. 1948 9-317
TARZAN AND THE FOREIGN LEGION Burroughs Tarzana, Calif. 1947 11-314
Burton, Miles
DEVIL'S RECKONING Doubleday Garden City, N. Y. 1949 190
Burton, Richard F. (translator)
VIKRAM AND THE VAMPIRE Tylston and Edwards London 1870 243
Bushnell, Adelyn
STRANGE GIFT Coward-McCann New York 1951 309
Butler, Ewan
TALK OF THE DEVIL Moxon London 1948 7-128
Butler, Joan
DEEP FREEZE Paul London 1952 256
SPACE TO LET Paul London 1955 191
Butterfield, Roger (editor)
THE SATURDAY EVENING POST TREASURY Simon & Schuster New York 1954 544
Butts, Mary
ARMED WITH MADNESS Boni New York 1928 238
Cabell, James Branch
THE DEVIL'S OWN DEAR SON Lane London 1950 11-198
DOMNEI McBride New York 1920 218
THE EAGLE'S SHADOW McBride New York 1923 280
GALLANTRY Harper New York and London 1907 323
THE KING WAS IN HIS COUNTING HOUSE Farrar & Ronehart New York 1938 304
THE SOUL OF MELICENT (see ibid, Domnei)
STRAWS AND PRAYERBOOKS McBride New York 1924 302
THERE WERE TWO PIRATES Farrar, Strauss New York 1946 121
THE WITCH WOMAN Farrar, Strauss New York 1948 161
Cadell, Elizabeth
BRIMSTONE IN THE GARDEN Morrow New York 1950 236

Cadell, Elizabeth (continued)
CRYSTAL CLEAR Morrow New York 1953 250
Caidin, Martin
THE LONG NIGHT Dodd, Mead New York 1956 242
Caldecott, Sir Andrew
FIRES BURN BLUE Arnold London 1948 9-222
Caldwell, Taylor
THE DEVIL'S ADVOCATE Crown New York 1952 375
YOUR SINS AND MINE Caxton Caldwell, Idaho 1959 181
Callender, Julian
ST. DINGAN'S BONES Vanguard Press New York 1958 178
Cameron, Berl
SOLAR GRAVITA Warren London 1953 159
Cameron, Eleanor
MR. BASS'S PLANETOID Little, Brown Boston 1958 228 juv
STOWAWAY TO THE MUSHROOM PLANET Little, Brown Boston 1956 226 juv
THE WONDERFUL FLIGHT TO THE MUSHROOM PLANET Little, Brown Boston 1954 214
Campbell, Donald
THE GOLDEN SNAKE Federation Press London 1924 155
Campbell, (Sir) Gilbert
WILD AND WEIRD. TALES OF IMAGINATION AND MYSTERY Ward, Lock London and New York 1889 162, 143, 175
Campbell, H. J.
ANOTHER SPACE, ANOTHER TIME Hamilton London 1953 158
BEYOND THE VISIBLE Hamilton London 1952 189
BRAIN ULTIMATE Hamilton London 1953 157
THE RED PLANET Hamilton London 1953 158
Campbell, John W(ood) Jr.
THE BLACK STAR PASSES Fantasy Press Reading, Pa. 1953 254
THE CLOAK OF AESIR Shasta Chicago 1952 255
THE INCREDIBLE PLANET Fantasy Press Reading, Pa. 1949 344
INVADERS FROM THE INFINITE Gnome Press Hicksville, N. Y. 1961 189
ISLANDS OF SPACE Fantasy Press Reading, Pa. 1954 292
THE MOON IS HELL! Fantasy Press Reading, Pa. 1951 7-256
WHO GOES THERE? Shasta Chicago 1948 3-230
Campbell, John W. Jr. (editor)
THE ASTOUNDING SCIENCE FICTION ANTHOLOGY Simon & Schuster New York 1952 585
FROM UNKNOWN WORLDS Atlas London 1952 124
Campbell, Reginald
THE ABOMINABLE TWILIGHT Cassell London 1948 232
DEATH BY APPARITION Cassell London 1949 249
Campbell, Sarah
THIRTY MILLION GAS MASKS Daviess London 1937 313
Capes, Bernard
LOAVES AND FISHES Collins Press London and Glasgow nd 7-286
Capon, Paul
DOWN TO EARTH Heinemann London 1954 196
LOST: A MOON Bobbs-Merrill Indianapolis 1956 222
THE OTHER HALF OF THE PLANET Heinemann London 1952 255
THE OTHER SIDE OF THE SUN Heinemann London 1950 321
THE WORLD AT BAY Winston Philadelphia 1954 219 juv
Capote, Truman
OTHER VOICES, OTHER ROOMS Heinemann London 1948 192
A TREE OF NIGHT Random New York 1949 209

Carlson, Esther
MOON OVER THE BACK FENCE Doubleday Garden City, N. Y. 1947 9-191 juv
Carlton, Mary Shaffer
THE GOLDEN PHOENIX Vantage Press New York 1958 69
Carmer, Carl Lanson
THE SCREAMING GHOST Knopf New York 1956 146
Carnell, E. J(ohn)
NO PLACE LIKE EARTH Boardman London 1952 255
Carolin, Q. O.
THE VERGE OF TWILIGHT Hurst & Blackett London 1911 336
Carpenter, Bishop W. B.
TWILIGHT DREAMS Macmillan London and New York 1893 225
Carr, John Dickson
THE DEVIL IN VELVET Harper New York 1951 335
FIRE, BURN Hamilton London 1957 287
Carr, Robert Spencer
BEYOND INFINITY Fantasy Press Reading, Pa. 1951 11-236
THE ROOM BEYOND Appleton-Century-Crofts New York 1948 427
Carrel, Frederic
THE ADVENTURES OF JOHN JOHNS Laurie London 1897 302
Carrington, Hereward (editor)
THE WEEK-END BOOK OF GHOST STORIES Washburn New York 1953 288
Carroll, Lewis (pseud of Charles L. Dodgson)
SYLVIE AND BRUNO Macmillan London 1890 395 juv Ill.
SYLVIE AND BRUNO CONCLUDED Macmillan London 1899 411 juv Ill.
Carson, Robin
PAWN OF TIME Holt New York 1957 442
Carter, Bruce
INTO A STRANGE LOST WORLD (see ibid, The Perilous Descent)
THE PERILOUS DESCENT Lane London 1952 179 juv
Carter, Dee
BLUE CORDON Warren London 1952 128
PURPLE ISLANDS Warren London 1953 159
Carter, John F. Jr.
THE DESTROYERS Neale Washington and New York 1907 5-350
Casey, Robert J.
CAMBODIAN QUEST Elkins Mathiews & Marriot London 1937 268
Casewit, Curtis W.
THE PEACEMAKERS Avalon New York 1960 224
Caspary, Vera
STRANGER THAN TRUTH Eyre & Spottiswoode London 1947 218
Casserly, Gordon
THE TIGER GIRL Allan London 1934 252
Castle, Jeffery Lloyd
SATELLITE E ONE Dodd, Mead New York 1954 223
VANGUARD TO VENUS Dodd, Mead New York 1957 212
Caven, Stewart
THE GREEN ENIGMA Latimer London nd 9-354
Cecil, Henry
FULL CIRCLE Chapman & Hall London 1948 9-235
Chamberlain, Elinor
SNAPE FOR WITCHES Dodd, Mead New York 1948 240
Chamber, Robert W.
THE HIDDEN CHILDREN Appleton New York 1914 651

Chambers, W. Jerome
THE OPAL MATRIX Salisbury Hill Press Worcester, Mass. 1937 247
Chandler, A. Bertram
THE RIM OF SPACE Avalon New York 1961 220
Chaney, J. M.
POLIOPOLIS AND POLIOLAND; A TRIP TO THE NORTH POLE J. M. Chaney, Jr. Kansas City, Mo. 1900 172
Channing, Mark
INDIA MOSAIC Lippincott Philadelphia 1936 295
Chanter, Granville
THE WITCH OF WITHYFORD; A STORY OF EXMOOR Macmillan New York and London 1896 187
Chapin, Maud Hudnut
THE LOST STAR AND OTHER STORIES Falmonst Portland, Maine 1948 79
Chappell, Connery
THE ARRIVAL OF MASTER JINKS Falcon Press London 1949 7-220
Charbonneau, Louis
NO PLACE ON EARTH Doubleday Garden City, N. Y. 1958 184
Charles, Neil
THE LAND OF ESA Warren London 1952 128
PLANET THA Warren London 1953 159
TWENTY FOUR HOURS Warren London 1952 128
Charlot, Jean
DANCE OF DEATH Sheed & Ward New York 1951 no pagination
Charques, Dorothy
THE DARK STRANGER Coward-McCann New York 1957 352
Charteris, Leslie
THE HAPPY HIGHWAYMAN Triangle New York 1939 273
SAINT ERRANT Doubleday Garden City, N. Y. 1948 192
Chase, Adam
THE GOLDEN APE Avalon New York 1959 221
Chatelain, Madame de
THE SEDAN CHAIR AND SIR WILFRED'S SEVEN FLIGHTS Routledge London 1866 302
Chetwynd, Bridgett
FUTURE IMPERFECT Hutchinson London 1953 174
Child, Washburn
THE HANDS OF NARA Dutton New York 1922 326
Chilton, Charles
JOURNEY INTO SPACE Jenkins London 1954 220
Chilton, Eleanor Carroll
SHADOWS WAITING Day New York 1927 289
Chipman, Charles P(hillips)
THE LAST CRUISE OF THE ELECTRA Saalfield Akron, Ohio 1902 268
Christian, Emeline Fate
THE DAMS CAN BREAK Storm New York 1951 216
Christie, Agatha
SO MANY STEPS TO DEATH Dodd, Mead New York 1955 212
Christie, Robert
INHERIT THE NIGHT Farrar, Strauss New York 1949 209
Christopher, John
THE LONG WINTER Simon & Schuster New York 1962 253
NO BLADE OF GRASS Simon & Schuster New York 1957 218
THE YEAR OF THE COMET Joseph London 1956 256
Christopher, John (editor)
THE TWENTY SECOND CENTURY Grayson & Grayson London 1954 23

Clarke, Arthur C(harles)
ACROSS THE SEA OF STARS (see ibid, Earthlight, Childhood's End, & short stories) Harcourt, Brace New York 1959 596
AGAINST THE FALL OF NIGHT Gnome Press New York 1953 223
CHILDHOOD'S END Ballantine New York 1953 214
THE CITY AND THE STARS Harcourt, Brace New York 1956 318 (an expanded and completely re-written version of Against the Fall of Night)
THE DEEP RANGE Harcourt, Brace New York 1957 238
EARTHLIGHT Ballantine New York 1955 155
EXPEDITION TO EARTH Ballantine New York 1953 165
A FALL OF MOONDUST Harcourt, Brace & World New York 1961 248
FROM THE OCEAN, FROM THE STARS (see ibid, The City and the Stars, The Deep Range, The Other Side of the Sky)
ISLANDS IN THE SKY Winston Philadelphia 1952 202
THE OTHER SIDE OF THE SKY Harcourt, Brace New York 1958 245
PRELUDE TO SPACE Gnome Press New York 1954 166
REACH FOR TOMORROW Ballantine New York 1956 166
THE SANDS OF MARS Sidgwick & Jackson London 1951 219
Clarke, Francis H.
MORGAN ROCKEFELLER'S WILL Clarke-Cree Portland, Ore. 1909 306
Clarke, Ida Clyde
MEN WHO WOULDN'T STAY DEAD Ackerman New York 1945 288
Clason, Clyde B.
ARK OF VENUS Knopf New York 1955 181
Claus, Hugo
THE DUCK HUNT Random New York 1955 183
Clement, Hal (pseud of Harry Clement Stubbs)
ICEWORLD Gnome Press New York 1953 216
MISSION OF GRAVITY Doubleday Garden City, N. Y. 1954 9-224
NEEDLE Doubleday Garden City, N. Y. 1950 222
Clewes, Howard
THE MASK OF WISDOM Dutton New York 1949 7-346
Clifton, Mark
EIGHT KEYS TO EDEN Doubleday Garden City, N. Y. 1960 187
WHEN THEY COME FROM SPACE Doubleday Garden City, N. Y. 1962 192
Clifton, Mark and Riley, Frank
THEY'D RATHER BE RIGHT Gnome Press New York 1957 189
"Clotilda"
COLYMBIA Trubner London 1873 320
Clowes, (Sir) W. Laird and Burgoyne, Alan H.
TRAFALGAR REFOUGHT Nelson London 1905 328
Coates, John
HERE TODAY Methuen London 1949 7-264
Coatsworth, Elizabeth Jane (pseud of Mrs. Henry Beston)
THE ENCHANTED Pantheon New York 1951 157
MOUNTAIN BRIDE Pantheon New York 1954 154
Cobb, Michael
SIR PETER'S ARM Chapman & Hall London 1929 281
Cobban, James Maclaren
THE KING OF ANDAMAN Appleton New York 1895 342
Coblentz, Stanton A(rthur)
AFTER 12,000 YEARS Fantasy Pub Co Los Angeles 1950 9-295
THE BLUE BARBARIANS Avalon New York 1958 233

Coblentz, Stanton A. (continued)
HIDDEN WORLD Avalon New York 1957 224
NEXT DOOR TO THE SUN Avalon New York 1960 223
THE RUNAWAY WORLD Avalon New York 1961 224
THE SUNKEN WORLD Fantasy Pub Co Los Angeles 1948 3-184
UNDER THE TRIPLE SUNS Fantasy Press Reading, Pa. 1955 224
Cock, Capt. Samuel
A VOYAGE TO LITHO Congbears London 1741 43
Cocteau, Jean
THE BLOOD OF A POET Bodley Press New York 1949 53
Cody, C. S. (pseud
THE WITCHING NIGHT World Cleveland and New York 1952 11-252
Coggs, (Dr.)
TEDDY IN DARKEST AFRICA Privately printed Chicago 1910 345 map Front
Cohn, Emil Bernhard
STORIES AND FANTASIES FROM THE JEWISH PAST Jewish Pub Soc Philadelphia 1951 262
Colcord, Lincoln
THE DRIFTING DIAMOND Macmillan New York 1912 279
Cole, Burt
SUBI: THE VOLCANO Macmillan New York 1957 220
Cole, Everett B.
THE PHILOSOPHICAL CORPS Gnome Press Hicksville, N. Y. 1961 187
Coleman, Charles G. Jr.
THE SHINING SWORD Loizeau Bros. New York 1956 181
Coles, Manning (pseud of Manning, Adelaide Frances and Cyril Henry Coles)
BRIEF CANDLES Doubleday Garden City, N. Y. 1954 252
COME AND GO Doubleday Garden City, N. Y. 1958 236
HAPPY RETURNS Doubleday Garden City, N. Y. 1955 224
Collier, Dwight A.
KATHY'S VISIT TO MARS Exposition Press New York 1955 53 juv
Collier, John
DEFY THE FOUL FIEND Knopf New York 1934 388
FANCIES AND GOODNIGHTS Doubleday Garden City, N. Y. 1951 364
PICTURES IN THE FIRE Rupert Hart-Davis London 1958 190
Collins, Errol
SUBMARINE CITY Lutterworth London 1946 247
Collins, Hunt
TOMORROW'S WORLD Avalon New York 1956 223
Colmore, George
A BROTHER OF THE SHADOW Douglas London 1926 5-320
Colp, Harry D.
THE STRANGEST STORY EVER TOLD Exposition Press New York 1953 46
Colum, Padraic
THE FOUNTAIN OF YOUTH Macmillan New York 1927 206
Colvin, Ian
DOOMSDAY VILLAGE Falcon Press London 1948 126
Comfort, Will Levington
THE YELLOW LORD Doran New York 1919 311
Comfort, Will Levington and Ki Dost, Zamin
SON OF POWER Doubleday, Page Garden City, N. Y. 1920 350
Conklin, Groff (editor)
THE BIG BOOK OF SCIENCE FICTION Crown New York 1950 545

Conklin, Groff (editor) (continued)
INVADERS OF EARTH Vanguard Press New York 1952 346
THE OMNIBUS OF SCIENCE FICTION Crown New York 1952 562
POSSIBLE WORLDS OF SCIENCE FICTION Vanguard Press New York 1951 372
SCIENCE FICTION ADVENTURES IN DIMENSION Vanguard Press New York 1953 369
SCIENCE FICTION ADVENTURES IN MUTATION Vanguard Press New York 1955 316
SCIENCE FICTION TERROR TALES Gnome Press New York 1955 272
SCIENCE FICTION THINKING MACHINES Vanguard Press New York 1954 380
A TREASURY OF SCIENCE FICTION Crown New York 1948 517
Conklin, Groff and Lucy (editors)
THE SUPERNATURAL READER Lippincott Philadelphia 1953 349
Connolly, Cyril (editor)
THE GOLDEN HORIZON British Book Centre New York 1954 596
Connelly, J. R.
NEILA SEN AND MY CASUAL DEATH U S Book Co New York 1890 5-345
Connolly, Myles
THE BUMP ON BRANNIGAN'S HEAD Macmillan New York 1950 157
Conquest, Robert
A WORLD OF DIFFERENCE Ward, Lock London 1956 186
Coolidge-Rask, Marie
LONDON AFTER MIDNIGHT Grosset & Dunlap New York 1928 261
Cooper, Edward H.
• CHILDREN, RACEHORSES AND GHOSTS Duckworth London 1899 260
Cooper, J(ames) Fenimore
THE MONIKINS: A LAND OF CIVILIZED MONKEYS Bentley London 1835 3 vol
Coppard, A(lfred) E(dgar)
THE COLLECTED TALES OF A. E. COPPARD Knopf New York 1948 532
Corbett, James
THE AIR KILLER Jenkins London 1941 254
Cornelius, Mary R.
THE WHITE FLAME Stockham Chicago 1900 402 Front
Correy, Lee (pseud of G. Harry Stine)
ROCKET MAN Holt New York 1955 224 juv
STARSHIP THROUGH SPACE Holt New York 1954 241 Ill.
Corwin, Norman (Lewis)
DOG IN THE SKY Simon & Schuster New York 1952 156
Cost, March (pseud of Margaret M. Morrison)
THE DARK STAR Collins London 1939 384
Courtney, L. T.
TRAVELS IN THE INTERIOR; OR, THE WONDERFUL ADVENTURES OF LUKE AND BELINDA
Ward and Downey London 1887 316 Ill.
Coury, Phil
ANNO DOMINI 2000 Vantage Press New York 1959 147
Cousins, E. G.
"I WILL NOT CEASE" Archer London 1933 286
Cowan, William Joyce
THE FIFTH MIRACLE Longmans, Green New York 1954 214
Cowie, Donald
THE RAPE OF MAN Tantivy Press Malvern, Eng. 1947 224
Cowles, Frederick I. (editor)
THE HORROR OF ABBOTT'S GRANGE AND OTHER STORIES Muller London 1936 256
Cowles, John D(lifford)
THE WHISPERING BUDDHA Hollyway Pub Los Angeles 1932 460

Cox, A. B.
THE FAMILY WITCH Jenkins London 1925 312
Cox, William Edward
THE PURPLE PROPHET Humphries Boston 1953 103
Cradock, Phyllis
THE ETERNAL ECHO Dakers London nd 276
THE GATEWAY TO REMEMBRANCE Dakers London 1949 361
Craigie, David
DARK ATLANTIS Heinemann London 1951 221 juv
THE VOYAGE OF THE LUNA I Eyre & Spottiswoode London 1948 9-272
Craine, E. J.
FLYING TO AMY-RAN FASTNESS World Synd Pub Cleveland and New York 1930 9-243
Crane, Robert
HERO'S WALK Ballantine New York 1954 196
Crawford, Merwin Richard
AZTIMC Dorrance Philadelphia 1945 130
Crawshay-Williams, Eliot
BORDERLINE Long London nd 176
HEAVEN TAKES A HAND Long London nd 5-256
THE MAN WHO MET HIMSELF Long London 1947 223
NIGHT IN NO TIME Long London nd 5-240
THE WOLF FROM THE WEST Long London nd 5-224
Cripps, A. S.
LION MAN Sheldon Press London 1928 127
Crispin, Edmund (editor)
BEST S F: SCIENCE FICTION STORIES Faber & Faber London 1955 7-368
BEST S F II Faber & Faber London 1957 7-342
Criswell, Charles
NOBODY KNOWS WHAT THE STORK WILL BRING McDowell, Obolensky New York 1958 180
Crockett, S(amuel R(utherford)
THE GRAY MAN Harper New York 1896 406
THE LIGHT OUT OF THE EAST Doran New York 1920 254
Cromie, Robert
EL DORADO Ward, Lock London 1904 308
A NEW MESSIAH Digby, Long London 1903 320
Crompton, Richmal (Richmal Crompton Lamburn)
WILLIAM AND THE MOON ROCKET Transatlantic Arts Hollywood-by-the-sea, Fla. 1954 248 juv
Cronin, Edward
TOAD Hodder & Stoughton London nd 320
Cross, John Keir
THE RED JOURNEY BACK Coward-McCann New York 1954 252 juv
THE STOLEN SPHERE Dutton New York 1953 220 juv
Cross, John Keir (editor)
BEST BLACK MAGIC STORIES Faber & Faber London 1960 269
Crossen, Kendall Foster
ONCE UPON A STAR Holt New York 1953 246
Crossen, Kendall Foster (editor)
ADVENTURES IN TOMORROW Greenberg New York 1951 278
FUTURE TENSE Greenberg New York 1952 364
Crottet, Robert
STRANDED IN HEAVEN Richards Press London 1952 95
Crowcroft, Peter
THE FALLEN SKY P. Nevill London 1954 222

Crowquil, Alfred (pseud
THE STRANGE AND SURPRISING ADVENTURES OF THE VENERABLE GOOROO SIMPLE Trubner London 1861 322 juv
Crump, J. Irving
MOG, THE MOUND BUILDER Dodd, Mead New York 1931 228
Cruso, Solomon
MESSIAH ON THE HORIZON Audubon Pub Co New York 1940 5-288
Cullingford, Guy (pseud of Constance Lindsay Taylor)
POST MORTEM Lippincott Philadelphia 1953 192
Cummings, Ray
THE PRINCESS OF THE ATOM Boardman London and New York 1951 7-191
Cunningham, E. V.
PHYLLIS Doubleday Garden City, N. Y. 1962 214
Cupples, George
HINCHERIDGE HAUNTED Nimmo - Edinburgh Simpkin, Marshall - London 1849 422
Curtin, Jeremiah
TALES OF THE FAIRIES AND OF THE GHOST WORLD Little, Brown Boston 1895 198
Curtis, George William
PRUE AND I Crowell New York 1899 234
Cushing, Tom
THE DEVIL IN THE CHEESE French New York and London 1927 180 Play
Dabbs, George H. R., M. D.
"UGLY," A HOSPITAL DOG Nutt London 1908 200
Dahl, Roald
DOMEONE LIKE YOU Knopf New York 1953 359
SOMETIME NEVER Collins London 1949 5-255
Dali, Salvador
HIDDEN FACES Dial Press New York 1947 413
Dallas, Paul
THE LOST PLANET Winston Philadelphia 1956 207
Dalmaine, James
THE VENGEANCE OF SCIENCE Stockwell London nd 240
Dana, Julian
LOST SPRINGTIME Macmillan New York 1938 279
Dardanelle, Louise
WORLD WITHOUT RAIMENT Valiant New York 1943 260
Daughter of Eve
A WOMAN'S UTOPIA Benn London 1931 11-92
D'Aurevilly, Jules Barbey
THE DIABOLIQUES Knopf New York 1925 275
Davenport, Basil (editor)
DEALS WITH THE DEVIL Dodd, Mead New York 1958 349
GHOSTLY TALES TO BE TOLD Faber & Faber London 1952 320
TALES TO BE TOLD IN THE DARK Dodd, Mead New York 1953 345
David-Neel, Alexandra and The Lama Yongden
THE SUPERHUMAN LIFE OF GESAR OF LING Kendall New York 1934 390
Davidson, John
THE PILGRIMAGE OF STRONGSOUL AND OTHER STORIES Ward & Downey London 1896 2
Davies, Valentine
IT HAPPENS EVERY SPRING Farrar, Strauss New York 1949 224
THE MIRACLE ON 34th STREET Harcourt, Brace New York 1947 3-120
Davis, E. Adams
OF THE NIGHT WIND'S TELLING Univ of Oklahoma Norman, Okla. 1946 269

Davis, William Stearns
BELSHAZAR Macmillan New York 1929 427
Dawe, Carleton
THE GOLDEN LAKE, OR, THE MARVELLOUS HISTORY OF A JOURNEY THROUGH THE GREAT LONE LAND OF AUSTRALIA Trischler London 1890 384 Ill.
Dawe, Carlton
A STRANGE DESTINY Ward, Lock London and Melbourne 1937 320
Dawson, Carley
DRAGON RUN Houghton Mifflin Boston 1955 282 Juv
THE SIGN OF THE SEVEN SEAS Houghton Mifflin Boston 1954 287 juv
Dawson, Conningsby
AUCTIONING OF MARY ANGEL Doubleday, Doran Garden City, N. Y. 1930 307
Dawson, Forbes
A SENSATIONAL TRANCE Downey London 1895 176
Dawson, Warrington
THE GREEN MOUSTACHE Bernard Pub Co Chicago 1924 315
THE GUARDIAN DEMONS Rider London 1928 9-287
Dawson, William J.
THE HOUSE OF DREAMS Marshall & Son London 1906 136
Dawson, William J. and Dawson, Coningsby W. (editors)
GREAT GHOST STORIES Harper New York 1910 313,337
Day, Langston
MAGIC CASEMENTS Rider London 1951 200
Day, Millard F.
DESTINATION HELL—STANDING ROOM ONLY Greenwich Pub New York 1957 100
LET'S ALL GO TO HEAVEN Exposition Press New York 1958 119
Deamer, Dulcie
AS IT WAS IN THE BEGINNING F. Wilmot, York House Melbourne, Australia nd 319 500 copy edition
HOLIDAY Johnson Sydney, Australia 1940 9-326
de Beauvoir, Simone
ALL MEN ARE MORTAL World Cleveland and New York 1955 345
de Bra, Lemuel
WAYS THAT ARE WARY Clode New York 1925 320
de Camp, L(yon) Sprague
THE CONTINENT MAKERS Twayne Pub New York 1952 272
DIVIDE AND RULE Fantasy Press Reading, Pa. 1948 9-241
THE GLORY THAT WAS Avalon New York 1960 223
ROGUE QUEEN Doubleday Garden City, N. Y. 1951 222
THE SEARCH FOR ZEI Avalon New York 1963 220
SOLOMON'S STONE Avalon New York 1957 224
SPRAGUE DE CAMP'S NEW ANTHOLOGY OF SCIENCE FICTION Hamilton London 1953 159
THE TOWER OF ZANID Avalon New York 1958 220
THE TRITONIAN RING Twayne Pub New York 1953 262
THE UNDESIRED PRINCESS Fantasy Pub Co Los Angeles 1951 248
THE WHEELS OF IF Shasta Chicago 1948 3-222
de Camp, L. Sprague and Miller, P. Schuyler
GENUS HOMO Fantasy Press Reading, Pa. 1950 9-225
de Camp, L. Sprague and Pratt, Fletcher
THE CARNELIAN CUBE Gnome Press New York 1948 7-230
CASTLE OF IRON Gnome Press New York 1950 7-224
TALES FROM GAVAGAN'S BAR Twayne Pub New York 1953 228
WALL OF SERPENTS Avalon New York 1960 224

Decourdemanche, J. A.
THE WILES OF WOMEN Dial Press New York 1929 225
Dee, Sylvia
DEAT GUEST AND GHOST Macmillan New York 1950 259
Deegan, Jon J.
ANTRO: THE LIFE GIVER Hamilton London 1953 144
BEYOND THE FOURTH DOOR Hamilton London 1953 158
CORRIDORS OF TIME Hamilton London 1953 159
THE GREAT ONES Hamilton London 1953 158
Deeping, arwich
UTHER AND IGRAINE Outlook New York 1903 385
De Fontmoll, E. V.
FORBIDDEN MARCHES Scholartis Press London 1929 241
de Koven, (Mrs.) Reginald
BY THE WATERS OF BABYLON Stone Chicago 1901 349
de la Mare, Walter
THE COLLECTED TALES OF WALTER DE LA MARE Knopf New York 1950 549
MEMOIRS OF A MIDGET Knopf New York 1922 436
THE OLD LION AND OTHER STORIES Faber & Faber London 1942 155
THE PICNIC Faber & Faber London 1941 154
de Lavigne, Jeanne
GHOST STORIES OF OLD NEW ORLEANS Rinehart New York 1946 374
de Loucanton, Baroness Alexandra
THE BELOVED OF SENNACHERIB Granton London nd 234
del Rey, Lester
...AND SOME WERE HUMAN Prime Press Philadelphia 1949 9-331
ATTACK FROM ATLANTIS Winston Philadelphia 1953 207 juv
DAY OF THE GIANTS Avalon New York 1959 224
MAROONED ON MARS Winston Philadelphia 1952 210 juv
MISSION TO THE MOON Winston Philadelphia 1956 218 juv
NERVES Ballantine New York 1956 153
OUTPOST OF JUPITER Holt New York 1963 191
STEP TO THE STARS Winston Philadelphia 1954 222 juv
THE YEAR AFTER TOMORROW Winston Philadelphia 1954 350
Delcarol, Marwin
FIRE AND WATER Duckworth London 1920 367
Demaitre, Edmund and Appleman, Mark J.
THE LIBERATION OF MANHATTAN Doubleday Garden City, N. Y. 1949 9-223
Dempster, Guy
THE AIRMEN OF SHEBA'S TEMPLE Lutterworth Press London 1952 143 juv
Dennis, Geoffrey
THE RED ROOM Simon & Schuster New York 1932 9-311
Dent, John Charles
THE GERRARD STREET MYSTERY AND OTHER WEIRD TALES Rose Pub Co Toronot 1888 206
Denwood, J. M. and Wright, S. Fowler
UNDER THE BRUCHSTONE Coward-McCann New York 1931 3-314
Derleth, August (William)
IN RE: SHERLOCK HOLMES Mycroft & Moran Sauk City, Wisc 1945 238
LONESOME PLACES Arkham House Sauk City, Wisc 1962 198
THE MASK OF CTHULHU Arkham House Sauk City, Wisc 1958 201
THE MEMOIRS OF SOLAR PONS Mycroft & Moran Sauk City, Wisc 1951 245
NOT LONG FOR THIS WORLD Arkham House Sauk City, Wisc 1948 3-321

Derleth, August W. (cont.)
REMINISCENCES OF SOLAR PONS Mycroft & Moran Sauk City, Wisc. 1961 199
THE TRAIL OF CTHULHU Arkham House Sauk City, Wisc. 1962 248
Derleth, August W. (editor)
BEACHHEADS IN SPACE Pellegrini & Cudahy New York 1952 320
BEYOND TIME AND SPACE Pellegrini & Cudahy New York 1950 643
DARK MIND, DARK HEART Arkham House Sauk City, Wisc. 1962 249
FAR BOUNDARIES Pellegrini & Cudahy New York 1951 290
FIRE AND SLEET AND CANDLELIGHT Arkham House Sauk City, Wisc. 1961 236 poetry
NIGHT'S YAWNING PEAL Pellegrini & Cudahy New York 1952 288
THE OTHER SIDE OF THE MOON Pellegrini & Cudahy New York 1949 458
THE OUTER REACHES Pellegrini & Cudahy New York 1951 351
PORTALS OF TOMORROW Rinehart New York 1954 383
STRANGE PORTS OF CALL Pellegrini & Cudahy New York 1948 390
TIME TO COME; SCIENCE-FICTION STORIES OF TOMORROW Farrar, Straus & Young New York 1954 317
WORLDS OF TOMORROW Pellegrini & Cudahy New York 1953 351
Dern, Dorothy Louise
THE DOCTOR'S SECRET Pageant Press New York 1954 116
De Rouen, Reed R.
SPLIT IMAGE Wingate London 1955 283
Desani, G. V.
ALL ABOUT H. HATTERR Farrar, Straus & Yongg New York 1951 300
Desent, George W.
GISLI THE OUTLAW Edmonston and Douglas Edinburgh 1866 123 Ill. Maps
Desmond, Hugh
THE TERRIBLE AWAKENING Wright & Brown London nd 7-220
Desmond, Shaw
DEMOCRACY Scribner New York 1919 327
INCARNATE ISIS Hutchinson London 1941 333
De Teramond, Guy
THE MYSTERY OF LUCIEN DELORME Appleton New York 1915 314
de Tourville, Anne
WEDDING DANCE Farrar, Straus & Young New York 1953 246
De Veer, W.
AN EMPEROR IN THE DOCK Lane London 1915 320
Devereux, Roy
WHEN THEY CAME BACK Cassell London 1938 9-281
de Wohl, Louis
THE LIVING WOOD Lippincott Philadelphia 1947 11-318
THE SECOND CONQUEST Lippincott Philadelphia 1954 239
Dexter, William
CHILDREN OF THE VOID P. Owen London 1955 195
WORLD IN ECLIPSE P. Owen London 1954 195
Dick, Philip K(indred)
THE MAN IN THE HIGH CASTLE Putnam New York 1962 239
TIME OUT OF JOINT Lippincott Philadelphia 1959 221
Dickson, Carter (pseud of Carr, John Dickson)
THE DEPARTMENT OF QUEER COMPLAINTS Morrow New York 1940 125
FEAR IS THE SAME Morrow New York 1956 284
Dickson, Gordon R.
NECROMANCER Doubleday Garden City, N. Y. 1962 191
Dikty, T(haddeus) E(ugene) (Editor)
THE BEST SCIENCE FICTION STORIES AND NOVELS: 1955 Fell New York 1955 544

Dikty, T. E. (cont.)
THE BEST SCIENCE FICTION STORIES AND NOVELS: 9th Series Advent Pub. Chicago 1958 258
EVERY BOY'S BOOK OF OUTER SPACE STORIES Fell New York 1960 283
Dilke, Lady (Emilie F.)
THE SHRINE OF LOVE Routledge Glasgow and New York 1891 3-187
Dimondstein, Boris
UTOPIA (THE VOLCANO ISLAND) Literashe Keftn Pub. Tujunga, Calif. 1958 196
Dinesen, Thomas
TWILIGHT ON THE BETZY Putnam London 1952 219
Dinnis, Endi M.
OUT OF THE EVERYWHERE Sands London and Edinburgh nd 9-210
Divine, Arthur D.
THEY BLOCKED THE SUEZ CANAL Green Circle New York 1936 252
Divine, David (Arthur Durham)
ATOM AT SPITHEAD Macmillan New York 1953 186
Dodge, Constance W.
IN ADAM'S FALL Macrae-Smith Philadelphia 1946 494
Dolbier, Maurice
THE HALF-PINT JINNI AND OTHER STORIES Random New York 1948 242
Dormer, Daniel
THE MESMERIST'S SECRET Haddon London 1891 335
Dorrington, Albert
THE HALF-GOD Wright & Brown London nd 251
Dougall, L.
THE MERMAID Appleton New York 1895 290
THE ZEIT-GEIST Appleton New York 1895 184
Dowding, Air Chief Marshall Lord
MANY MANSIONS Rider London nd 112
Doyle, (Sir) A(rthur) Conan
DREAMLAND AND GHOSTLAND Redway London 1888 3 vol. 318, 308, 320
Drake, (Henry) Burgess
HUSH-A-BY BABY Falcon Press London 1952 352
CHILDREN OF THE WIND (See ibid Hush-a-by Baby)
Drake, Catherine
THE SEANCE AT RADLEY MANOR Marshall London nd 88
Drake, Leah Bodine
A HORNBOOK FOR WITCHES Arkham House Sauk City, Wisc. 1951 3-270
Dranker, Charles
FARAWAY HILLS ARE GREEN Vantage New York 1953 235
Draper, Blanche A.
THE GREAT AWAKENING Vantage New York 1953 177
Dreifuss, Kurt
THE OTHER SIDE OF THE UNIVERSE Twayne Pub. New York 1961 224
Drury, Allen
ADVISE AND CONSENT Doubleday Garden City, N. Y. 1959 616
Du Bois, Theodora
THE DEVIL'S SPOON Stokes New York 1930 312
SARAH HALL'S SEA GOD Doubleday Garden City, N. Y. 1952 250
SOLUTION T-25 Doubleday Garden City, N. Y. 1951 218
Duff, Douglas V.
ATOMIC VALLEY Blackie London nd 224 juv.
PERIL ON THE AMAZON Blackie London nd 207 juv.

Duke, Ivo and Kolda, Helena (Ivo Duka pseud of Ivo Duchacek)
MARTIN AND HIS FRIEND FROM OUTER SPACE Harper New York 1955 95 juv.
Duke, Winifred
DIRGE FOR A DEAD WITCH Jarrolds London nd 256
du Maurier, Daphne (Pseud of Browning, Mrs. Frederick Arthur Montague)
KISS ME AGAIN, STRANGE Doubleday Garden City, N. Y. 1953 319
Du Maurier, George L.
THE MARTIAN Harper London 1898 471
Duncan, David
BEYOND EDEN Ballantine New York 1955 169
DARK DOMINION Ballantine New York 1954 206
THE MADRONE TREE Macmillan New York 1949 230
OCCAM'S RAZOR Gollancz London 1958 200
THE SHADE OF TIME Random New York 1946 244
Duncan, Ronald
THE LAST ADAM Dobson London 1947 93
Dunn, Gertrude
AND SO FOREVER Butterworth London 1929 286
Dunne, J(ohn) W(illiam)
ST. GEORGE AND THE WITCHES Holt New York 1939 206
Dunsany, Lord (Pseud of Plunkett, Edward John Moreton Drax)
THE FOURTH BOOK OF JORKENS Arkham House Sauk City, Wisc. 1948 3-184
THE LAST REVOLUTION Jarrolds London 1951 5-192
THE LITTLE TALES OF SMETHERS Jarrolds London 1952 188
LORD ADRIAN Golden Cockerell Press Lawrence, Berks., England 1929 76 325 copy edition
THE MAN WHO ATE THE PHOENIX Jarrolds London 1949 9-223
SEVEN MODERN COMEDIES Putnam New York and London 1929 204
THE STRANGE JOURNEYS OF COLONEL POLDERS Jarrolds London 1950 5-208
Durant, Theo
THE MARBLE FOREST Wingate London 1951 3-235
Duthie, Eric (Editor)
TALL SHORT STORIES Simon & Schuster New York 1959 716
Dutourd, Jean
A DOG'S HEAD Lehmann London 1951 143
Dwyer, James Francis
COLD EYES Methuen London 1937 277
THE LADY WITH FEET OF GOLD Jenkins London 1937 311
THE SPOTTED PANTHER Doubleday, Page Garden City, N. Y. 1913 293
Dye, Charles
PRISONER IN THE SKULL Abelard Press New York 1952 256
Dyrenforth, James and Kester, Max
ADOLF IN BLUNDERLAND Muller London 1939 60
Eager, Edward
HALF MAGIC Harcourt, Brace New York 1954 417 juv.
KNIGHT'S CASTLE Harcourt, Brace New York 1956 183 juv.
MAGIC BY THE LAKE Harcourt, Brace New York 1957 183 juv.
MAGIC OR NOT? Harcourt, Brace New York 1959 190 juv.
SEVEN DAY MAGIC Harcourt, Brace New York 1961 156 juv.
THE TIME GARDEN Harcourt, Brace New York 1958 188 juv.
THE WELL WISHERS Harcourt, Brace New York 1962 191 juv.
Earnest, Olga Dorothea Agnes
FAIRY TALES FROM THE LAND OF THE WATTLE Robertson Melbourne 1904 334
MAGIC SHADOW SHOW Robertson Melbourne 1913 208

Ebers, Georg
THE KING AND QUEEN OF MOLLEBUSCH Brown Boston 1899 124
UARDA Caldwell Boston and New York nd 471
Echard, Margaret
THE DARK FANTASTIC Doubleday Garden City, N. Y. 1947 312
Edmonds, Harry
THE ROCKETS Macdonald London 1951 5-286
Edmund, James
A JOURNALIST AND TWO BEARS Platypus Press Sydney 1913 431
Edon, Rob
GOLDEN GODDESS Locker Hanley, Stoke-on-Trent 1947 159
Edwards, David
NEXT STOP--MARS Greenwich Book Pub. New York 1960 113
Eels, Elsie S.
THE MAGIC TOOTH AND OTHER TALES FROM THE AMAZON Little, Brown Boston 1927 243
Efremov, I. (see also Yefremov, I.)
A MEETING OVER TUSCARORA Hutchinson London nd 9-124
Egbert, H. M. (Pseud of Emanuel, Victor Rousseau)
MY LADY OF THE NILE Hodder & Stoughton London nd 286
Ehrlich, Max
THE BIG EYE Doubleday Garden City, N. Y. 1949 9-221
Ehrmann, Max
THE MYSTERY OF MADELINE LE BLACE Cooperative Pub. Cambridge, Mass. 1900 107
Ekberg, C. Whitworth
THE STORY OF KASTAN Exposition Press New York 1954 104
Ekbergh, Ida Diana
THE MYSTERIOUS CHINESE MANDRAKE, AND OTHER STORIES Pageant Press New York 1954 52
Elam, Richard M., Jr. (Editor)
TEEN-AGE SCIENCE FICTION STORIES Lantern Press New York 1952 254
TEEN-AGE SUPER SCIENCE STORIES Lantern Press New York 1957 253
YOUNG VISITOR TO MARS Lantern Press New York 1953 256
Eldershaw, M. Barnard
TOMORROW AND TOMORROW Phoenix House London 1948 466
Eliat, Helene
SHEBA VISITS SOLOMON Cassell London 1932 223
Eliot, George Fielding
THE PURPLE LEGION Caslon New York 1936 255
Eliott, E. C.
KEMLO AND THE CRAZY PLANET Nelson New York 1954 207 juv.
KEMLO AND THE MARTIAN GHOSTS Nelson London 1954 191 juv.
KEMLO AND THE SKY HORSE Nelson London 1954 189 juv.
KEMLO AND THE ZONES OF SILENCE Nelson London 1954 201 juv.
Ellet, (Mrs.)
EVENINGS AT WOODLAWN Baker & Scribner New York 1849 9-348
Elliott, Lee
BIO-MUTON Warren London 1952 128
Elliott, H. Chandler
REPRIEVE FROM PARADISE Gnome Press New York 1955 256
Wlliott, William J.
TOMORROW'S SPECTACLES Swan London 1946 188

Elshemus, Louis M.
THE DEVIL'S DIARY Abbey New York 1901 271
Emersie, John
ALLISTO--A ROMANCE Williams New York 1884 327
Erckmann, Emile and Chatrian, Alexandre
FANTASTIC TALES OF THE RHINELAND Dicks London nd 158
Erlanger, Michael
SILENCE IN HEAVEN Atheneum New York 1961 169
Erskine, Douglas
A BIT OF ATLANTIS Chapman Montreal 1900 197
Erskine, John
CINDERELLA'S DAUGHTER Bobbs-Merrill Indianapolis 1930 305
VENUS: THE LONELY GODDESS Wingate London and New York 1950 5-175
Eshback, Lloyd Arthur
TYRANT OF TIME Fantasy Press Reading, Pa. 1955 253
Esteven, John
THE DOOR OF DEATH Century New York and London 1928 3-293
VOODOO Doubleday, Doran Garden City, N. Y. 1930 317
Estival
MANDRAGORA Staples London 1952 239
Evans, E(dward) E(verett)
ALIEN MINDS Fantasy Press Reading, Pa. 1955 223
MAN OF MANY MINDS Fantasy Press Reading, Pa. 1953 222
THE PLANET MAPPERS Dodd, Mead New York 1955 242
Evans, Gwyn
SATAN, LTD. Godwin New York nd 7-285
Evans, Henry Ridgeley
THE HOUSE OF THE SPHINX Neale New York and Washington 1907 7-219
Evans, I. O.
GADGET CITY Warne London 1944 256
Everitt, Nicholas
TOLD AT TWILIGHT Everitt London nd 9-266 Ill.
Ewers, Hanns Heinz
BLOOD Heron Press New York 1930 80
Ewers, John
WRITTEN IN SAND Dutton New York 1947 7-160
Ewing, (Mrs.) Juliana Horst
MELCHIOR'S DREAM Roberts Bros. Boston 1895 356
Eytinge, Margaret
THE BALL OF THE VEGETABLES AND OTHER STORIES Harper New York 1883 246
Falkner, John Meade
MOONFLEET Cape London 1934 256
Faralla, Dana
DREAM IN THE STONE Messner New York 1948 234
Farjeon, Benjamin Leopold
THE CLAIRVOYANTS Hutchinson London 1905 305
DEVLIN THE BARBER Ward & Downey London 1888 191
THE MESMERISTS Hutchinson London 1900 246
SAMUEL BOYD OF CATCHPOLE SQUARE Hutchinson London 1899 284
SOMETHING OCCURRED Routledge London 1893 331
A STRANGE ENCHANTMENT White London 1889 102
Farjeon, J. Jefferson
DEATH OF A WORLD Collins London 1948 5-192

Farley, Ralph Milne (Pseud of Hoar, Roger Sherman)
THE HIDDEN UNIVERSE Fantasy Pub. Co. Los Angeles 1950 11-134
THE OMNIBUS OF TIME Fantasy Pub. Co. Los Angeles 1950 9-315
THE RADIO MAN Fantasy Pub. Co. Los Angeles 1948 9-177
Farmer, Philip
THE GREEN ODYSSEY Ballantine New York 1957 152
Farrere, M.
THE KINGDOM OF A THOUSAND ISLANDS Lunn London 1947 208 Juv.
Farrow, G. E.
THE NEW PANJANDRUM Dutton New York nd 199 Ill.
Faucett, Francis
THOU MUST WRITE: A BUSHMAN'S STORY Canning Sydney 1886 142
Faure, Raoul Cohen
THE CAVE AND THE ROCK Morrow New York 1953 276
Favenc, Ernest
THE LAST OF SIX; TALES OF THE AUSTRALIAN TROPICS Bulletin Co. Sydney 1898 342
MY ONLY MURDER AND OTHER TALES Robertson Sydney and Melbourne 1899 334
Fawcett, F. Dubrez
HOLE IN HEAVEN Sidgwick & Jackson London 1954 244
Fearing, Kenneth
THE LONELIEST GIRL IN THE WORLD Harcourt, Brace New York 1951 238
Fearn, John Russell
THE AMAZON'S DIAMOND QUEST World's Work Kingswood, Surrey 1951 175
THE AMAZON STRIKES AGAIN World's Work Kingswood, Surrey 1953 174
THE GOLDEN AMAZON RETURNS World's Work Kingswood, Surrey 1948 133
THE GOLDEN AMAZON'S TRIUMPH World's Work Kingswood, Surrey 1953 192
TWIN OF THE AMAZON World's Work Kingswood, Surrey 1954 172
Feiner, Ruth
A MIRACLE FOR CAROLINE Coward-McCann New York 1950 314
Fennessey, J. C.
THE SONNET IN THE BOTTLE Jenkins London 1951 270
Fenwick, Kenneth
THE ISLES WERE DISTURBED Hutchinson London nd 240
Fergusson, Harvey
THE CONQUEST OF DON PEDRO Morrow New York 1954 250
Ferrar, William M.
THE DREAM OF UBERTUS Walsh Hobart Town, Tasmania 187- 220
Fessier, Michael
CLOVIS Dial New York 1948 7-189
Field, Marlo
ASTRO BUBBLES Four Seas Boston 1938 297
Finn, Ralph L.
TIME MARCHES SIDEWAYS Hutchinson London 1950 224
Finney, Jack
THE THIRD LEVEL Rinehart New York 1957 256
Fitzgerald, Ena
THE WITCH QUEEN OF KHAM Greening London 1909 316
Fitzgibbon, Constantine
WHEN THE KISSING HAD TO STOP Norton New York 1960 247
Fitz-Gibbon, Ralph (Edgerton)
THE MAN WITH TWO BODIES Vantage Press New York 1952 137

Fleischman, Theo
A MAN FROM THE PAST Gollancz London 1957 207
Fleming, Berry
THE SQUARE ROOT OF VALENTINE Norton New York 1932 282
Fleming, Ian
DOCTOR NO Macmillan New York 1958 256
MOONRAKER Macmillan New York 1955 220
Fleming, Peter
THE SIXTH COLUMN Hart-Davis London 1951 224
Fletcher, George U. (Pseud of Pratt, Fletcher)
THE WELL OF THE UNICORN Sloane New York 1948 338
Fletcher, H. L. V.
THE DEVIL HAS THE BEST TUNES Macdonald London 1947 5-253
Flight, Edward G.
THE TRUE LEGEND OF ST. DUNSTAN AND THE DEVIL Bell & Daldy London 1871 62
Foa, George
THE BLOOD RUSHED TO MY POCKETS Calder London 1957 90
Foley, Martha (Editor)
BEST AMERICAN SHORT STORIES OF 1943 World Cleveland 1943 394
Forbes, Duncan
THE ADVENTURES OF HATIM TAI Cherag Bombay 1911 309
Ford, Garrett (Editor)
SCIENCE AND SORCERY Fantasy Pub. Co. Los Angeles 1954 327
Forester, E. Lascelles
'WARE WOLF! Cassell London 1928 314
Forrest, A. E.
SILENT GUESTS Covici Chicago 1927 305
Foster, James R. (Editor)
THE WORLD'S GREAT FOLK TALES Harper New York 1953 330
Foulke, William Dudley
MAYA Putnam New York 1900 404
Fowler, Ellen Thorneycroft
SIRIUS AND OTHER STORIES Hodder & Stoughton London 1901 437
Fowler, Syndey (Pseud of Wright, S. Fowler)
THE ADVENTURE OF THE BLUE ROOM Rich & Cowan London nd 168
Fox, Richard A.
THE PEOPLE ON OTHER PLANETS Wetzel Los Angeles 1930 164
Frank, Pat
ALAS, BABYLON Lippincott Philadelphia 1959 253
FORBIDDEN AREA Lippincott Philadelphia 1956 232
7 DAYS TO NEVER Constable London 1957 252
Frankau, Gilbert
SON OF THE MORNING Macdonald London 1949 7-432
UNBORN TOMORROW Macdonald London 1953 302
Franklin, Jay (Pseud of Carter, John Franklin)
CHAMPAGNE CHARLIE Duell, Sloan & Pearce New York 1950 190
THE RAT RACE Fantasy Pub. Co. Los Angeles 1950 13-371
Fraser, Helen
FULFILMENT AT NOON Hutchinson London 1959 251
Fraser, Ronald
BEETLE'S CAREER Cape London 1951 160
JUPITER IN THE CHAIR Cape London 1958 190
SUN IN SCORPIO Cape London 1949 9-351
TROUT'S TESTAMENT Cape London 1960 191

Fraser, William Alexander
THE OUTCASTS Briggs Toronto 1901 138
Frazee, Steve
THE SKY BLOCK Ronehart New York 1953 247
Frazer, Douglas
PERSEVERANCE ISLAND, OR, THE ROBINSON CRUSOE OF THE 19th CENTURY Lee & Shepar Boxton 1885 373 Ill.
Frazer, Joseph
MELBOURNE AND MARS: MY MYSTERIOUS LIFE ON TWO PLANETS Pater & Knapton Melbourne 1889 278
French, Joseph Lewis (Editor)
MASTERPIECES OF MYSTERY. RIDDLE STORIES Doubleday, Page New York 1920 258
French, Paul (Pseud of Asimov, Isaac)
DAVID STARR: SPACE RANGER Doubleday Garden City, N. Y. 1952 186
LUCKY STARR AND THE BIG SUN OF MERCURY Doubleday Garden City, N. Y. 1956 191
LUCKY STARR AND THE MOONS OF JUPITER Doubleday Garden City, N. Y. 1957 192
LUCKY STARR AND THE OCEANS OF VENUS Doubleday Garden City, N. Y. 1954 186
LUCKY STARR AND THE PIRATES OF THE ASTEROIDS Doubleday Garden City, N. Y. 1953 188
LUCKY STARR AND THE RINGS OF SATURN Doubleday Garden City, N. Y. 1958 179
Freyer, Dermot
NIGHT ON THE RIVER AND OTHER STORIES Heffer Cambridge, Eng. 1923 85
Friend, Oscar J.
THE KID FROM MARS Fell New York 1949 9-270
Frith, Walter
THE SACK OF MONTE CARLO Harper New York and London 1898 244
Frobenius, Leo and Fox, Douglas C. (Editors)
AFRICAN GENESIS Faber & Faber London 1938 7-265
Frost, Conrad
EVIDENCE BEFORE GABRIEL Aldor London 1947 255
Fry, H. R.
AMATEUR GHOST STORIES Barclay & Fry London 1932 62
Fumento, Rocco
DEVIL BY THE TAIL McGraw-Hill New York 1954 250
Furnell, John
THE DARK PORTAL Skeffington London 1950 284
THE GOD ON THE MOUNTAIN Skeffington London 1951 288
Galgano, Ruth H.
THE WISHING STAR Pageant Press New York 1952 88 Juv.
Gallico, Paul
THE ABANDONED Knopf New York 1950 307
LOVE OF SEVEN DOLLS Doubleday Garden City, N. Y. 1954 125
Gallun, Raymond Z.
PEOPLE MINUS X Stimon & Schuster New York 1956 186
Gammon, David
SECRET OF THE SACRED LAKE Lutterworth Press London 1947 184 Juv.
Gamon, Richard B.
THE STRANGE THIRTEEN Drane's London nd 365
Gandon, Yves
THE LAST WHITE MAN Cassell London 1949 11-254
"Ganpat" (Pseud of Gompertz, Martin Louis Alan)
HIGH SNOW Doran New York 1927 11-338

"Ganpat" (cont.)
THE SECOND TIGRESS Hodder & Stoughton London 1933 320
SEVEN TIMES PROVEN Hodder & Stoughton London 1934 312
Gantz, Kenneth F.
NOT IN SOLITUDE Doubleday Garden City, N. Y. 1959 240
Gardner, G. B.
A GODDESS ARRIVES Stockwell London nd 382
Gardner, Maurice B.
BANTAN AND THE ISLAND GODDESS Meador Boston 1939 364
BANTAN DEFIANT Greenwich New York 1955 256
BANTAN FEARLESS Forum Boston 1963 349
BANTAN--GODLIKE ISLANDER Meador Boston 1936 395
BANTAN INCREDIBLE Forum Boston 1960 367
BANTAN OF THE ISLANDS (See ibid Bantan--Godlike Islander)
BANTAN PRIMEVAL Forum Boston 1961 373
BANTAN VALIANT Meador Boston 1957 357
BANTAN'S ISLAND PERIL Meador Boston 1959 332
HORRORS OF SMILING MANOR Forum Boston 1962 394
Gargilis, Stephen
THE PATH OF THE GREAT Athens Pub Boston 1945 480
Garner, Rolf
THE IMMORTALS Hamilton London 1953 158
THE INDESTRUCTIBLE Hamilton London 1954 159
RESURGENT DUST Hamilton London 1953 160
Garrett, Charles W.
AURILLY, THE VIRGIN ISLE Christopher Boston 1923 152
Garrett, Randall
UNWISE CHILD Doubleday Garden City, N. Y. 1962 215
Garver, Ronald G.
THE SAUCER PEOPLE Meador Boston 1957 132
Gask, Arthur
FALL OF A DICTATOR Jenkins London 1939 9-284
Gask, Lillian
THE QUEST OF THE WHITE MERLO Harrap London nd 282
Gaskell, Jane
STRANGE EVIL Dutton New York 1958 256
Gatch, Tom (Jr.)
KING JULIAN Vantage Press New York 1954 187
Gaunt, Jeffrey
THE HAUNTED MAN Eldon London nd 247
Gavassa, M.
IN THE FROCK OF A PRIEST Skeffington London nd 7-403
Gaylo, Harold
SPAWN OF THE VORTEX Comet Press New York 1957 138
Gazdanov, Gaito
BUDDHA'S RETURN Dutton New York 1951 224
Geach, Edwina Catherine
AN ELPHIN LAND Endacott Melbourne 1914 138
FROM THE SOUL OF THE TI-TREE Lothian Melbourne 1909 172
Gearon, John
THE VELVET WELL Pilot Press London 1947 267
Gee, H. L.
FOLK TALES OF YORKSHIRE Nelson London and Edinburgh 1952 152
Gerard, Francis

Gerard, Francis
THE MARK OF THE MOON Macdonald London 1952 224
PRINCE OF PARADISE Rich & Cowan London 1938 319
SORCEROR'S SHAFT Macdonald London 1947 7-256
Gerhardi, William
RESURRECTION Macdonald London 1948 367
Germaine, Victor Wallace
COLONEL TO PRINCESS Methuen London 1936 327
CRUSOE WARBURTON Coward-McCann New York 1954 250
Gervais, Albert
GHOSTS OF SIN CHANG Hamilton London 1936 319
Ghosh, Sarah Kumar
VERDICT OF THE GODS Dodd, Mead New York 1905 307
Gibbon, Perceval
VROUW GROBELAAR AND HER LEADING CASES McClure, Phillips New York 1906 293
Gibbons, Stella
CONFERENCE AT COLD COMFORT FARM Longmans, Green London and New York 1949 167
Gibbs, George
THE SILVER DEATH Appleton-Century New York 1939 270
Gibbs, Henry
PAWNS IN ICE Jarrolds London 1947 222
Gibbs, Lewis
LATE FINAL Dent London 1951 216
Gibbs, (Sir) Philip
THE KEY OF LIFE Locke London nd 123
Gibran, Kahlil
NYMPHS OF THE VALLEY Heinemann London 1948 55
Gibson, Rev. Edmund H.
A. D. 2018 Greenwich New York 1958 62
Gibson, Jewel
HOSHUA BEENE AND GOD Eyre & Spottiswoode London 1948 7-224
Gide, Andre (Paull Guillaume)
MARSHLANDS, AND, PROMETHEUS MISBOUND New Directions Norfolk, Conn. 1953. 192
Gielgud, Val
THE BROKEN MEN Houghton Mifflin Boston 1933 288
Gilbert, Stephen
MONKEYFACE Faber & Faber London 1948 252
Gillmore, Parker
THE AMPHIBIOUS VOYAGE Allen London 1885 366
Gilmore, Anthony
SPACE HAWK Greenberg New York 1952 281
Gilmore, Louis
ROAD UNCONVENTIONAL Pageant Press New York 1955 88
Gilson, (Major) Charles
THE CITY OF THE SORCEROR Hutchinson London nd 219
THE LOST ISLAND Hodder & Stoughton London nd 210
THE REALM OF THE WIZARD KING Boy's Own Paper Office London nd 380
THE TREASURE OF THE RED TRIBE Cassell London 1926 380
Giraud, S. Louis
UNCANNY STORIES Fleetgate London nd 116
WARNINGS FROM BEYOND Fleetgate London nd 121

Glaskin, Gerald M.
A CHANGE OF MIND Doubleday Garden City, N. Y. 1960 232
Glovatsky, Alexander
THE PHARAOH AND THE PRIEST Little, Brown Boston 1903 696
Godden, Rumer
CHINESE PUZZLE Davies London 1936 149
Godwin, George
EMPTY VICTORY Long London nd 160
Godwin, Tom
THE SURVIVORS Gnome Press Hicksville, N. Y. 1957 190
Gold, H(orace) L.
THE OLD DIE RICH Crown New York 1955 250
Gold, H. L. (Editor)
BODYGUARD, AND FOUR OTHER SHORT NOVELS Doubleday Garden City, N. Y. 1960 312
THE GALAXY READER OF SCIENCE FICTION Crown New York 1952 576
THE SECOND GALAXY READER OF SCIENCE FICTION Crown New York 1954 509
THE THIRD GALAXY READER Doubleday Garden City, N. Y. 1958 262
THE FOURTH GALAXY READER Doubleday Garden City, N. Y. 1959 264
THE FIFTH GALAXY READER Doubleday Garden City, N. Y. 1961 260
THE SIXTH GALAXY READER Doubleday Garden City, N. Y. 1962 240
FIVE GALAXY SHORT NOVELS Doubleday Garden City, N. Y. 1959 287
MIND PARTNER Doubleday Garden City, N. Y. 1961 263
THE WORLD THAT COULDN'T BE Doubleday Garden City, N. Y. 1959 288
Golding, Louis
THE DOOMINGTON WANDERER--A BOOK OF TALES Gollancz London 1934 286
HONEY FOR THE GHOST Dial New York 1949 383
Golding, William
LORD OF THE FLIES Coward-McCann New York 1954 243
Goldring, Douglas and Nepean, Hubert
THE SOLVENT Daniel London 1920 256
Goldston, Robert C.
THE CATAFALQUE Rinehart New York 1958 314
Goodchild, George
DOCTOR ZIL'S EXPERIMENT Ward, Lock London 1953 206
THE EMPEROR OF HALLELUJAH ISLAND Hodder & Stoughton London nd 5-319
A MESSAGE FROM SPACE Jarrolds London nd 7-254
Goodrich, Arthur
YOU WOULDN'T BELIEVE IT Appleton-Century New York 1936 230
Goodrich, Charles
THE GENESIS OF NAM Dorrance Philadelphia 1956 136
Goodrich-Freer, A. (Editor)
THE PROFESSIONAL & OTHER PSYCHIC STORIES Hurst & Blackett London 1900 288
Gordon, Edward
CHRISTMAS GIFT AND OTHER STORIES Bolton Bros. Bendigo, Australia 1913 358
Gordeon, I. L. and Grueh, A. J.
THE LOG OF THE ARK BY NOAH Dutton New York 1915 147
Gordon, Neil (Pseud of Macdonnell, Archibald Gordon)
THE PROFESSOR'S POISON Harcourt, Brace New York 1928 280
Gordon, Rex
NO MAN FRIDAY Heinemann London 1956 201
UTOPIA 239 Heinemann London 1955 208
Gorska, Halina
PRINCE GODFREY Roy New York 1948 207

Gottlieb, Kinko
THE KEY TO THE GREAT GATE Simon & Schuster New York 1948 178
Goudge, Elizabeth
THE ELIZABETH GOUDGE READER Coward-McCann New York 1947 498
Gould, F. C.
EXPLORATIONS IN THE SIT-TREE DESERT Unwin London nd 130
Gould, Maggy
THE DOWRY Morrow New York 1949 244
Goyne, Richard
THE KISS OF THE PHARACH Stokes New York 1923 307
Graeme, Bruce
LORD BLACKSHIRT Hutchinson London 1942 136
TEN TRAILS TO TYBURN Hutchinson London nd (1944) 192
Graham, James M.
A WORLD BEWITCHED Harper London and New York 1898 357
Graham, Jamet Pollock
THE ENCHANTED WOOD Pageant Press New York 1954 102 Juv.
Graham, (Mrs.) John Ellsworth.
THE TOLTEC SAVIOR Dillingham New York 1901 7-294
Graham, Winifred (Pseud of Corey, Winifred)
THE FROZEN DEATH Hutchinson London nd 280
HALLOMAS ABBEY Hutchinson London nd 304
Graham-White, Claude and Harper, Harry
THE AIR KING'S TREASURE Cassell London 1913 312
Grant, Joan
THE LAIRD AND THE LADY Methuen London 1949 281
LORD OF THE HORIZON Methuen London 1943 291
RETURN TO ELYSIUM Methuen London 1947 317
Grant, Richard
LIVES IN A BOX Paul London 1951 224
Franville, Austyn and Knott, William Wilson
IF THE DEVIL CAME TO CHICAGO Bow Knot Pub Co Chicago 1894 7-352
Gratton-Smith, T. E.
THE CAVE OF A THOUSAND COLUMNS Hutchinson London 1938 288 Juv.
Graves, Robert
SEVEN DAYS IN NEW CRETE Cassell London 1949 281
WATCH THE NORTH WIND RISE (See ibis Seven Days in New Crete)
Gray, Berkeley
THE LOST WORLD OF EVEREST Collins London 1941 13-256 Ill.
Cray, Curme
MURDER IN MILLENIUM VI Shasta Chicago 1952 11-249
Gray, John
PARK; A FANTASTIC STORY Sheed & Ward London 1932 129 250 copy edition
Graydon, William Murray
THE RIVER OF DARKNESS; OR, UNDER AFRICA Thompson & Thomas Chicago 1902 296
Green, Frederick (Editor)
THE GRIM THIRTEEN Dodd, Mead New York 1917 385
Green, Henry
CONCLUDING Hogarth Press London 1948 5-254
Green, Julian
IF I WERE YOU Eyre & Spottiswoode London 1950 3-250
Green, Roger Lancelyn
FROM THE WORLD'S END Ward Leicester nd 9-127

Greenberg, Martin (Editor)
ALL ABOUT THE FUTURE Gnome Press New York 1955 374
COMING ATTRACTIONS Gnome Press New York 1956 254
FIVE SCIENCE FICTION NOVELS Gnome Press New York 1952 382
JOURNEY TO INFINITY Gnome Press New York 1951 381
MEN AGAINST THE STARS Gnome Press New York 1950 3-351
THE ROBOT AND THE MAN Gnome Press New York 1953 251
TRAVELERS OF SPACE Gnome Press New York 1951 400
Greene, Joseph
THE FORGOTTEN STAR Golden Press New York 1959 188 Juv.
Greener, Leslie
MOON AHEAD Viking New York 1951 256
Greenwood, James
THE ADVENTURES OF SEVEN FOUR FOOTED FORESTERS Ward, Lock London 1865 390
THE BEAR KING. A NARRATIVE CONFIDED TO THE MARINES Griffith & Farron
L London 1868 373 Juv.
THE PURGATORY OF PETER THE CRUEL Routledge London 1868 164
Gregory, H. B.
DARK SANCTUARY Rider London nd 288
Gregory, Jackson
DAUGHTER OF THE SUN Scribner New York 1921 271
Grendon, Stephen (Pseud of Derleth, August W.)
MR. George and other odd persons Arkham House Sauk City, Wisc. 1962 239
Grey, Charles
ENTERPRISE 2115 Milestone London 1953 160
Grey, Robert Malory
I, YAHWEH Willet, Clark Chicago and New York 1937 352
Grice, Frederick
FOLK TALES OF THE NORTH COUNTRY Nelson London and Edinburgh 1944 150
Griffith, George (Chetwynd)
GAMBLES WITH DESTINY White London 1899 232
Grimshaw, Robert
FIFTY YEARS HENCE Practical Pub Co New York 1892 89
Grindrod, E. E.
TALES IN THE SPEECH HOUSE Unwin London 1886 3-323 Ill.
Grinnell, David
ACROSS TIME Avalon New York 1957 223
DESTINY'S ORBIT Avalon New York 1961 224
EDGE OF TIME Avalon New York 1958 221
THE MARTIAN MISSILE Avalon New York 1959 224
Groom, Arthur
THE GHOST OF GORDON GREGORY Lunn London 1946 236 Juv.
Groom, Pelham
THE FOURTH SEAL Jarrolds London nd 9-208
THE PURPLE TWILIGHT Laurie London 1948 282
Guaraschi, Giovanni
DON CAMILLO'S DILEMMA Farrar, Straus Young New York 1954 255
THE LITTLE WORLD OF DON CAMILLO Grosset New York 1951 205
Guinn, Jack
THE CAPERBERRY BUSH Little, Brown Boston 1954 273
Gunn, James (Edward)
THIS FORTRESS WORLD Gnome Press New York 1955 216
Gunn, Neil M.
SECOND SIGHT Faber & Faber London 1940 327
YOUNG ART AND OLD HECTOR Stewart New York

Gwinn, D. Howard
THE GOLD OF OPHIR Neely New York and London 1898 335
Hadley, Arthur T(wining)
THE JOY WAGON Viking New York 1958 223
Haggard, (Capt.) Andrew
LESLIE'S FATE AND HILDA Arrowsmith Bristol 1891 214
THE KISS OF ISIS AND THE MYSTERY OF CASTLEBOURNE Hurst & Blackett London 1900 306
Haggard, Audrey
THE DOUBLE AXE Dent London 1929 289 Map
Haggard, H(enry) Rider
FINISHED Ward, Lock London 1917 9-320
Haggard, William
SLOW BURNER Little, Brown Boston 1958 192
Haldane, Charlotte
THE SHADOW OF A DREAM Weidenfeld & Nicolson London 1952 287
Hales, A. G.
THE MYSTERY OF WO-SING Long London 1929 318
Haley, Harry F.
IMMORTAL ATHALIA Dorrance Philadelphia 1922 310
Halford, John
HIDDEN SARIA Heritage London 1934 5-301
Halidom, M. Y.
THE LAST OF THE WONDER CLUB Burleigh London 1905 302
THE WIZARD'S MANTLE Burleigh London 1903 311
Hall, Austin
PEOPLE OF THE COMET Griffin Los Angeles 1948 9-131
Hall, Austin and Flint, Homer Eon
THE BLIND SPOT Prime Press Philadelphia 1951 293
Hall, Manly P.
SHADOW FORMS Hall Pub Co Los Angeles 1925 165
Hallack, Cecily E.
CANDLELIGHT ATTIC Benziger New York 1925 119
Hallam, Atlantis
STAR SHIP ON SADDLE MOUNTAIN Macmillan New York 1955 182 Juv.
Hallam, A. L.
ANGILIN: A VENITE KING Digby, Long London 1907 314
Halliday, Arthur (Editor)
SAVAGE CLUB PAPER FOR 1869 Tinsley Bros. London 1868 304
Hamilton, Edmond
BATTLE FOR THE STARS Dodd, Mead New York 1961 206
THE CITY AT WORLD'S END Fell New York 1951 239
THE HAUNTED STARS Dodd, Mead New York 1960 192
THE STAR KINGS Fell New York 1949 9-262
THE STAR OF LIFE Dodd, Mead New York 1959 192
Hamilton, Patrick
HANGOVER SQUARE Random New York 1941 308
Hancock, H. Irving
IN THE BATTLE FOR NEW YORK Altemus Philadelphia 1916 256 Juv.
THE INVASION OF THE UNITED STATES Altemus Philadelphia 1916 256 Juv.
Hansom, Mark
THE MASTER OF SOULS Wright & Brown London 1937 7-256
Harding, Ellison
THE DEMETRIAN Brentano New York 1907 7-315

Harding, John William
    A CONJUROR OF PHANTOMS Neely New York 1898 177
Hargrave, John
    HARBOTTLE, A MODERN PILGRIM'S PROGRESS FROM THIS WORLD TO THAT WHICH IS TO COME Lippincott Philadelphia 1924 347
Harkins, James W. (Jr.)
    A PRINCE OF THE EAST Abbey Press New York 1922 308
Harley, William Nicholas
    LITTLE JOURNEYS WITH MARTIN LUTHER Privately printed Columbus, Ohio 1916 354
Harness, Charles L.
    FLIGHT INTO YESTERDAY Bouregy & Curl New York 1953 256
Harper, Constance Ward
    BEYOND DEATH'S CURTAIN Vantage Press New York 1958 86
Harper, Harry
    WINGED WORLD Gifford London 1946 9-139
Harris A. L.
    THE SIN OF SALOME Greening London 1906 245
Harrison, Michael
    THE BRAIN Cassell London 1953 287
Hart, Edward
    THE SILICA GEL PSEUDOMORPH AND OTHER STORIES Chemical Easton, Pa. 1924 175
Hartley, L(eslie) P(oles)
    FACIAL JUSTICE Doubleday Garden City, N. Y. 1961 263
    THE GO-BETWEEN Knopf New York 1954 311
    THE TRAVELLING GRAVE Arkham House Sauk City, Wisc. 1948 3-235
Hartley, (Harry) Livingston
    YANKEE VIKING Exposition Press New York 1951 155
Harvey, Alexander
    THE TOE AND OTHER TALES Kennerley New York 1913 310
Harvey, William Fryer
    THE ARM OF MRS. EGAN, AND OTHER STRANGE STORIES Dent London 1951 256
Harwood, H. C.
    JUDGMENT EVE Constable London 1924 9-299
Hastings, A. C. G.
    VENOM Eldon Press London 1934 284
Hatch, Eric
    THE BEAUTIFUL BEQUEST Little, Brown Boston 1950 243
Hauff, Wilhelm
    THE LITTLE GLASS MAN Cassell New York 1893 176
Hauser, Marianne
    DARK DOMINION Random New York 1947 316
Hawker, Caleb
    THE GREAT PERIL Blackie London and Glasgow nd 255 Juv.
Hawkes, Jacquetta (Hopkins)
    PROVIDENCE ISLAND Random New York 1959 239
    A WOMAN AS GREAT AS THE WORLD, AND OTHER FABLES Random New York 1953 192
Hawkes, John
    THE GOOSE ON THE GRAVE New Directions Norfolk, Conn. 1954 207
Hawkinson, John L.
    WE, THE FEW Exposition Press New York 1952 376
Hawthorne, Julian
    JOHN PARMALEE'S CURSE Mershon New York 1896 9-270

Hawton, Hector
OPERATION SUPERMAN Ward, Lock London and Melbourne 1951 5-224
Hayes, Herbert Edward Elton
AN UNCONVENTIONAL FAIRY TALE FOR CHILDREN OF ALL AGES Ramsey Melbourne 1927 284
Hayes, Hiram W.
THE PEACEMAKERS Reid Boston 1909 420
Hayes, Lillian
THE THIRTIETH PIECE OF SILVER Macmillan New York 1924 9-326
Hayne, William P.
TALE OF TWO FUTURES Exposition Press New York 1958 160
Haynes, Dorothy K.
ROBIN RITCHIE Methuen London 1949 198
THOU SHALT NOT SUFFER A WITCH Methuen London 1949 200
Hazlitt, Henry
THE GREAT IDEA Appleton-Century-Crofts New York 1951 3-374
TIME WILL RUN BACK (See ibid The Great Idea)
Healy, Raymond J. (Editor)
NEW TALES OF SPACE AND TIME Holt New York 1951 307
NINE TALES OF SPACE AND TIME Holt New York 1954 317
Heard, Gerald (Henry F.)
THE BLACK FOX Cassell London 1950 234
GABRIEL AND THE CREATURES Harper New York 1952 244
THE LOST CAVERN Vanguard New York 1948 3-262
Hearn, Lafcadio
A JAPANESE MISCELLANY Little, Brown Boston 1901 305
KARMA Boni & Liveright New York 1918 11-183
KWAIDAN Houghton Mifflin Boston and New York 1904 240
SHADOWINGS Little, Brown Boston 1900 268
SOME CHINESE GHOSTS Roberts Bros. Boston 1887 185
Hecht, Ben
MIRACLE IN THE RAIN Knopf New York 1943 52
Hedges, Doris
DUMB SPIRIT Barker London 1952 224
Heinlein, Robert A(nson)
ASSIGNMENT IN ETERNITY Fantasy Press Reading, Pa. 1953 256
BETWEEN PLANETS Scribner New York 1951 222
BEYOND THIS HORIZON Fantasy Press Reading, Pa. 1948 242
CITIZEN OF THE GALAXY Scribner New York 1957 302
THE DOOR INTO SUMMER Doubleday Garden City, N. Y. 1957 188
DOUBLE STAR Doubleday Garden City, N. Y. 1956 186
FARMER IN THE SKY Scribner New York 1950 216
GLORY ROAD Putnam New York 1963 288
THE GREEN HILLS OF EARTH Shasta Chicago 1951 11-256
HAVE SPACE SUIT--WILL TRAVEL Scribner New York 1958 276
THE MAN WHO SOLD THE MOON Shasta Chicago 1950 9-288
THE MENACE FROM EARTH Gnome Press Hicksville, N. Y. 1959 255
METHUSELAH'S CHILDREN Gnome Press Hicksville, N. Y. 1958 188
THE PUPPET MASTERS Doubleday Garden City, N. Y. 1951 219
THE RED PLANET Scribner New York 1948 211
REVOLT IN 2100 Shasta Chicago 1954 317
THE ROLLING STONES Scribner New York 1952 276
SIXTH COLUMN Gnome Press New York 1950 9-256
SPACE CADET Scribner New York 1948 242

Heinlein, Robert A. (cont.)
THE STAR BEAST Scribner New York 1954 282
STARMAN JONES Scribner New York 1953 305
STARSHIP TROOPERS Putnam New York 1959 309
STRANGER IN A STRANGE LAND Putnam New York 1961 408
PODKAYNE OF MARS Putnam New York 1963 191
TIME FOR THE STARS Scribner New York 1956 244
TUNNEL IN THE SKY Scribner New York 1955 273
THE UNPLEASANT PROFESSION OF JONATHAN HOAG Gnome Press Hicksville, N. Y. 1959 256
WALDO & MAGIC, INC. Doubleday Garden City, N. Y. 1951 219
Heinlein, Robert A. (Editor)
TOMORROW THE STARS Doubleday Garden City, N.Y. 1952 249
Helfenstein, Ernest
THE SALAMANDER Putnam New York 1848 149
Heller, Frank
STRANGE ADVENTURES OF MR. COLLIN Crowell New York 1926 356
THE THOUSAND AND SECOND NIGHT Crowell New York 1925 333
Heming, Arthur
SPIRIT LAKE Musson Toronto 1923 3-280
Henderson, Zenna
PILGRIMAGE: THE BOOK OF THE PEOPLE Doubleday Garden City, N. Y. 1961 239
Henriques, Robert D. Q.
HOME FIRES BURNING Viking New York 1945 241
THE JOURNEY HOME (See ibid Home Fires Burning)
Henry, Dr. W. O.
EQUITANIA, OR THE LAND OF EQUITY Privately printed Omaha 1914 168 wraps
Herbert, A(lan) P(atrick)
NUMBER NINE, OR, THE MIND SWEEPERS Doubleday Garden City, N. Y. 1952 286
Herbert, Frank
THE DRAGON IN THE SEA Doubleday Garden City, N. Y. 1956 192
Hesse, Herman
STEPPENWOLF Holt New York 1929 309
Hewlett, Maurice
THE FOREST LOVERS Macmillan New York 1898 384
LORE OF PROSERPINE Scribner New York 1913 245
PAN AND THE YOUNG SHEPHERD Lane London and New York 1898 140
Heyse, Paul J. Von
THE FOREST LAUGH Dodd, Mead New York 1894 80
Hichens, Robert S.
AFTER THE VERDICT Doran New York 1924 532
THE PROPHET OF BERKELEY SQUARE Methuen London 1901 334
Higginson, Thomas Wentworth
TALES OF THE ENCHANTED ISLANDS OF THE ATLANTIC Macmillan New York 1989 259
Hill, Dorothy
THE LITTLE BLUE MAN Skeffington London nd 200
Hill, H. Haverstock (Pseud of Walsh, James Morgan)
THE SECRET OF THE CRATER Hurst London 1930 324
Hillam, S. A.
SHEYKH HASSAN; THE SPIRITUALIST Allen London 1888 223
Hillgarth, Alan
THE BLACK MOUNTAIN Knopf New York 1934 3-379
Hingley, Ronald
UP JENKINS! Longmans, Green London and New York 1956 226

Hilzinger, J. George
    THE SUNSTONE. A ROMANCE OF PREHISTORIC ARIZONA Neal London and New York 1899 281
Hind, C(harles) Lewis
    THE INVISIBLE GUIDE Lane New York 1917 11-208
Hitchcock, Alfred (Joseph) (Editor)
    ALFRED HITCHCOCK PRESENTS: STORIES THEY WOULDN'T LET ME DO ON T V Simon & Schuster New York 1957 380
Hobson, Harold
    THE DEVIL WOODFORD WELLS Longmans London 1946 188
Hocking, Silas K.
    THE STRANGE ADVENTURES OF ISRAEL PENDRAY Warne London 1899 429
Hodder-Williams, Christopher
    CHAIN REACTION Doubleday Garden City, N. Y. 1959 240
Hoelriegel, Arnold
    THE FOREST SHIP Viking New York 1931 5-284
Holbein, John
    THE DANCE OF DEATH Hamilton, Adams London 1887 no pages paintings
Holcombe, William Henry
    LAZARUS OF BETHANY: THE STORY OF HIS LIFE IN BOTH WORLDS Robertson Melbourne 1872 384
    A STRANGE EXPERIENCE AND OTHER STORIES FOR CHRISTMAS Propsting & Cockhead Hobart, Tasmania 1888 372
Holden, J. Railton
    WINGS OF REVOLUTION Hamilton London nd 319
Holden, Richard Cort
    SNOW FURY Dodd, Mead New York 1955 186
Holloway, Emory
    JANICE IN TOMORROW-LAND America Book Co New York 1936 302 juv.
Holly, J. Hunter
    THE DARK PLANET Avalon New York 1962 224
    ENCOUNTER Avalon New York 1959 224
    THE GRAY ALIENS Avalon New York 1963 192
    THE GREEN PLANET Avalon New York 1960 222
Holm, John Cecil
    McGARRITY AND THE PIGEONS Rinehart New York and Toronto 1947 3-239
Hood, Thomas
    VERE VEREKER'S VENGEANCE Hotten London 1865 146
    WHIMS AND ODDITIES Tilt London 1836 425
Hope, Coral
    LISTENING HANDS Macdonald London nd 191
Hope, Edward
    ALICE IN THE DELIGHTED STATES Dial New York 1928 11-303
Hopkins, Livingston
    A COMIC HISTORY OF THE UNITED STATES Cassell New York 1880 384
Hopkins, R. Thurston (Editor)
    ADVENTURES WITH PHANTOMS Quality Press London 1946 5-176
    CAVALCADE OF GHOSTS World's Work Kingswood, Surrey 1956 245
    THE WORLD'S STRANGEST GHOST STORIES World's Work Kingswood, Surrey 1956 2[illegible]
Horler, Syndey
    THE CURSE OF DOONE Hodder & Stoughton London 1928 320
    THE DEVIL COMES TO BOLYBON Marshall London 1951 255
    THE MAN WHO SHOOK THE EARTH Hutchinson London 1933 288
    THE SCREAMING SKULL Hodder & Stoughton London 1930 7-318

Horn, Edward Newman
FASTER, FASTER Coward-McCann New York 1946 215
Horner, Donald W.
THE WORLD'S DOUBLE Simpkin, Marshall, Hamilton, Kent London 1912 243
THEIR WINGED DESTINY (See ibid The World's Double)
Hort, Lt. Col.
THE EMBROIDERED BANNER AND OTHER MARVELS J. & D. Darling London 1850 280
Hostovsky, Egon
THE MIDNIGHT PATIENT Appleton-Century-Crofts New York 1954 278
Houblon, Grahame
THE CRACK IN THE WALL Stockwell London nd 107
Hough, S. B.
EXTINCTION BOMBER Bodley Head London 1956 192
MOMENT OF DECISION Hodder & Stoughton London 1952 190
Houghton, Claude
THE BEAST Quota Press Belfast 1936 15-44
NEIGHBORS Holt New York 1927 310
SIX LIVES AND A BOOK Collins London 1943 255
Household, Geoffrey
TALES OF ADVENTURERS Atlantic-Little, Brown Boston 1952 247
Housman, Laurence
THE BLUE MOON J. Murray London 1904 210
STRANGE ENDS AND DISCOVERIES Cape London 1948 7-189
Howard, Dana
DIANE--SHE CAME FROM VENUS Regency Press London nd (1960) 90
MY FLIGHT TO VENUS Regency Press London nd 92
Howard, Elizabeth Jane and Aickman, Robert
WE ARE FOR THE DARK Cape London 1951 11-285
Howard, George Bronson
SLAVES OF THE LAMP Watt New York 1917 309
Howard, Robert E(rvin)
ALWAYS COMES EVENING Arkham House Sauk City, Wisc. 1957 86 poetry
THE COMING OF CONAN Gnome Press New York 1953 224
CONAN THE BARBARIAN Gnome Press New York 1954 224
CONAN THE CONQUEROR Gnome Press New York 1950 9-255
KING CONAN Gnome Press New York 1953 255
THE SWORD OF CONAN Gnome Press New York 1952 251
Howard, Robert E. and de Camp, L. Sprague
TALES OF CONAN Gnome Press New York 1956 218
Howard, Wendell
THE LAST REFUGE OF A SCOUNDREL AND OTHER STORIES Exposition Press New York 1952 85
Hoyle, Fred
THE BLACK CLOUD Harper New York 1958 260
OSSIAN'S RIDE Harper New York 1959 213
Hoyle, Fred and Geoffrey
FIFTH PLANET Harper New York 1963 217
Hoyle, Fred and Elliot, John
A FOR ANDROMEDA Harper & Row New York 1962 206
Hubbard, L(afayette) Ron(ald)
DEATH'S DEPUTY Fantasy Pub Co Los Angeles 1948 11-167
FINAL BLACKOUT Hadley Providence, R. I. 1948 154
THE KINGSLAYER Fantasy Pub Co Los Angeles 1949 11-208

Hubbard, L. Ron (cont.)
SLAVES OF SLEEP Shasta Chicago 1948 3-207
TRITON Fantasy Pub Co Los Angeles 1949 9-172
TYPEWRITER IN THE SKY & FEAR Gnome Press New York 1951 9-256
Hubbard, T. O'B.
TOMORROW IS A NEW DAY Williams London 1934 3-125
Huddleston, George
THE WHITE FAKIR Ocean London 1932 244
Hughes, Glenn (From a story by John Taine (Eric Temple Bell))
GREEN FIRE. A MELODRAMS OF 1990 French New York 1932 105 play
Hughes, Riley
THE HILLS WERE LIARS Bruce Milwaukee 1955 250
Hull, E(dna) Mayne
PLANETS FOR SALE Fell New York 1954 192
Hull, Richard
THE GHOST IT WAS Putnam New York 1937 245
Hume, Fergus
THE AMETHYST CROSS Cassell New York 1909 304
THE BLUE TALISMAN Clode New York 1928 320
CHRONICLES OF FAIRY LAND: FANTASTIC TALES FOR OLD, ETC. Griffith, Farrar London 1892 344
THE DWARF'S CHAMBER AND OTHER STORIES Ward, Locke, Bowden London 1896 386
THE HARLEQUIN OPAL Rand, McNally Chicago and New York 1893 9-432
THE SOLITARY FARM Dillingham New York 1909 313
THE WHITE FACED PRIEST Warne London and New York nd 7-160
Hunt, Laura Shellabarger
ULTRA, A STORY OF PRE-NATAL INFLUENCE Times-Mirror Press Los Angeles 1923 365
Hunter, Evan
FIND THE FEATHERED SERPENT Winston Philadelphia 1952 206
Hunter, James H.
THE MYSTERY OF MAR SABA Zondervan Grand Rapids, Mich. 1940 414
Hunter, N. C.
THE ASCENSION OF MR. JUDSON Hale London nd 237
Hutchinson, R. C.
THOU HAST A DEVIL Cassell London 1930 5-320
Huxley, Aldous (Leonard)
APE AND ESSENCE Chatto & Windus London 1949 153
THE DEVILS OF LOUDUN Harper New York 1952 327
THE GENIUS AND THE GODDESS Chatto & Windus London 1955 128
ISLAND Harper New York 1962 335
Hyams, Edward S.
THE ASTROLOGER Longmans, Green London and New York 1950 3-244
"998" Pantheon New York 1952 208
NOT IN OUR STARS Longmans, Green London 1949 287
Hyne, C(harles) J. Cutcliffe
A MASTER OF FORTUNE, THE FURTHER ADVENTURES OF CAPT. KETTLE Dillingham New York 1901 317
WISHING SMITH Hale London 1939 282
I. S. (Pseud of Schneider, Isadore)
DR. TRANSIT Boni & Liveright New York 1925 285
Idle, Doreen
YEW TREES FROM THE WINDOW Hodder & Stoughton London 1948 263

Illiowizi, Henry
IN THE PALE Jewish Pub Soc of America Philadelphia 1897 387
THE WEIRD ORIENT Coates Philadelphia 1900 3-360
Ingaleso, Isabella
LINKED LIVES Occult Book Concern New York 1903 232
Ingham, L. H.
THE UNKNOWN DICTATOR Stockwell London nd 287
Ingram, Kenneth
MIDSUMMER SANITY Allan London 1933 296
Iggulden, John
BREAKTHROUGH Chapman & Hall London 1960 240
Ingulphus (Pseud of Gray, A.)
TEDIOUS BRIEF TALES OF GRANTA AND GRANARYE Heffer Cambridge, England 1919 93
Inman, Arthur Crew
OF CASTLE TERROR Brimmer Boston 1923 13-45
Innes, Hammond
WRECKERS MUST BREATHE Collins London 1940 251
Irish, William
THE BLUE RIBBON Hutchinson London 1951 7-208
THE NIGHT I DIED Hutchinson London 1951 7-259
THE PHANTOM LADY Lippincott Philadelphia 1942 291
Irving, Washington
KNICKERBOCKER'S HISTORY OF NEW YORK McKay Philadelphia 1848 414
TALES OF A TRAVELER Brentano New York 1905 457
Irwin, Margaret E(mma Faith) (Pseud of Monsell, Mrs. John Robert)
BLOODSTOCK, AND OTHER STORIES Harcourt, Brace New York 1954 206
Irwin, Will(iam) (Henry)
THE RED BUTTON Bobbs-Merrill Indianapolis 1912 370
Ives, Burl
BURL IVES' TALES OF AMERICA World Cleveland and New York 1954 305
J. J. J.
THE BLUE SHIRTS Simpkin, Marshall, Hamilton, Kent London nd 280
Jackson, Birdsall
PIPE DREAMS AND TWILIGHT TALES Buckles New York 1902 303
Jackson, G. Gibbard
ARCTIC AIR TERROR Low, Marston London nd 250 Juv.
Jackson, Shirley
THE BIRD'S NEST Farrar, Straus & Young New York 1954 276
THE HAUNTING OF HILL HOUSE Viking Press New York 1959 246
THE LOTTERY Farrar, Straus New York 1949 238
WE HAVE ALWAYS LIVED IN THE CASTLE Viking Press New York 1962 224
Jacob, P. W. (Translator)
HINDOO TALES Strahan London 1873 376
Jacobs, Joseph
CELTIC FAIRY TALES Nutt London 1892 267
Jaeger, Cyril K.
THE MAN IN THE TOP HAT Grey Walls Press London 1949 9-264
James I (King of England)
DAEMONOLOGIE & NEWES FROM SCOTLAND Lane Lane London 1924 81, 24
James, Henry
THE GHOSTLY TALES OF HENRY JAMES Rutgers Univ Press New Brunswick, N. J. 1948 766
James, M. H.
BOGIE TALES OF EAST ANGLIA Powsey & Hayes Ipswich, England [illegible]

James, Wentworth
MAGIC MATING Rivers London 1929 256
Jameson, Malcolm
BULLARD OF THE SPACE PATROL World Cleveland and New York 1951 255
Jameson, Storm (Pseud of Chapman, Margaret Storm Jameson)
THE MOMENT OF TRUTH Macmillan New York 1949 179
Janvier, Thomas A.
LEGENDS OF THE CITY OF MEXICO Harper New York and London 1910 165
Jenks, Almet
THE HUNTSMAN AT THE GATE Lippincott Philadelphia 1952 115
Jenks, Anton Shrewsbury
A DEAD PRESIDENT MAKES ANSWER TO THE PRESIDENT'S DAUGHTER Golden Hind Press New York 1928 94
Jenks, Tudor
IMAGINOTIONS Century New York 1894 230
Jerrold, Douglas William
STORY OF A FEATHER Punch Office London 1844 255
Jessopp, Augustus
FRIVOLA, SIMON RYAN, AND OTHER PAPERS Unwin London 1896 296
Johns, Capt. W. E.
THE DEATH RAYS OF ARDILLA Hodder & Stoughton London 1959 187
THE EDGE OF BEYOND Hodder & Stoughton London 1958 191
KINGS OF SPACE Hodder & Stoughton London 1954 192
NOW TO THE STARS Hodder & Stoughton London 1956 189
RETURN TO MARS Hodder & Stoughton London 1955 189
TO OUTER SPACE Hodder & Stoughton London 1957 187
TO WORLDS UNKNOWN Hodder & Stoughton London 1960 157
Johns, Willy
THE FABULOUS JOURNEY OF HIERONYMUS MEEKER Little, Brown Boston 1954 380
Johnson, Henry T.
THE APE MAN Modern London nd no pages
Johnson, Ray W.
ASTERA, THE PLANET THAT COMMITTED SUICIDE Exposition Press New York 1959 27
Johnson, Samuel
RASSELAS, PRINCE OF ABISSINIA Cooke Hartford, Conn. 1803 177
Johnson, Virginia W.
THE CATSKILL FAIRIES Harper New York 1876 163
Johnston, Harold
THE ELECTRIC GUN: A TALE OF LOVE AND SOCIALISM Websdale, Shoesmith Sydney 1911 309
Jokai, Maurus
TALES FROM JOKAI Jarrolds London 1904 275
Jones, Ewart C.
HOW NOW BROWN COW? Home & Van Thal London 1947 7-142
Jones, Guy P. and Constance B.
THERE WAS A LITTLE MAN Random New York 1948 3-245
Jones, Louis C.
SPOOKS OF THE VALLEY Houghton Mifflin Boston 1948 111 Juv.
THINGS THAT GO BUMP IN THE NIGHT Hill & Wang New York 1959 208
Jones, Raymond F.
THE CYBERNETIC BRAINS Avalon New York 1962 219
PLANET OF LIGHT Winston Philadelphia and Toronto 1953 211
RENNAISANCE Gnome Press New York 1951 7-255

Jones, Raymond F. (cont.)
THE SECRET PEOPLE Avalon New York 1956 224
SON OF THE STARS Winston Philadelphia 1952 208
THIS ISLAND EARTH Shasta Chicago 1952 220
THE TOYMAKER Fantasy Pub Co Los Angeles 1951 9-287
THE YEAR WHEN STARDUST FELL Winston Philadelphia 1958 206
Jones, Tupper
THE BUILDING OF THE ALPHA ONE Exposition Press New York 1956 80 verse
Jordan, Mildred
MIRACLE IN BRITTANY Allen London 1953 215
Jorgenson, Ivor
STARHAVEN Avalon New York 1958 220
Judd, Cyril (Pseud of Kornbluth, C. M. and Merrill, Jusith)
GUNNER CADE Simon & Schuster New York 1952 218
OUTPOST MARS Abelard Press New York 1952 258
Jude, Christopher
THE TERROR OF THE SHAPE Low, Marston London nd 250
Juenger, Ernst
9 ON THE MARBLE CLIFFS Lehman London 1947 120
Junor, Charles
DEAD MEN'S TALES Robertson Melbourne 1898 287
Kafka, Franz
IN THE PENAL SETTLEMENT Secker & Warburg London nd 198
SELECTED SHORT STORIES OF FRANZ KAFKA Modern Lib New York 1952 350
Kampf, Harold
WHEN HE SHALL APPEAR Little, Brown Boston 1954 177
Kaner, Hyman
THE SUN QUEEN Kaner Llandudno, Wales 1946 7-204
Karig, Walter
ZOTZ! Rihehart New York 1947 3-268
Karlin, Alma M.
THE DEATH-THORN Allen & Unwin London 1934 346
Karlova, Irina
BROOMSTICK Hurst & Blackett London nd 190
Karp, David
ONE Vanguard New York 1953 311
Kasack, Hermann
THE CITY BEYOND THE RIVER Longmans, Green London and New York 1953 356
Kavan, Anna
SLEEP HAS HIS HOUSE Cassell London 1948 9-190
Kayme, Sargent
ANTING-ANTING STORIES AND OTHER STRANGE TALES OF THE FILIPINOS Small, Maynard Boston 1901 235
Keeler, Harry Stephen
THE FACE OF THE MAN FROM SATURN Dutton New York 1933 254
Keller, Von
TRI-PLANET Warren London 1953 159
Kelleam, Joseph E.
HUNTERS OF SPACE Avalon New York 1961 223
THE LITTLE MEN Avalon New York 1960 226
Keller, David H.
THE ETERNAL CONFLICT Prime Press Philadelphia 1949 191
THE HOMUNCULUS Prime Press Philadelphia 1949 160

Keller, David H. (cont.)
THE LADY DECIDES Prime Press Philadelphia 1950 133
LIFE EVERLASTING Avalon Newark, N. J. 1947 9-382
THE SOLITARY HUNTERS & THE ABYSS New Era Philadelphia 1948 7-265
TALES FROM UNDERWOOD Pellegrini & Cudahy New York 1952 322
Kelley, Francis Clement
PACK RAT Bruce Milwaukee 1942 146
Kellino, Pamela
DEL PALMA Dutton New York 1948 9-254
A LADY POSSESSED (See ibid Del Palma)
Kellogg, John
THE ALLIGATOR LAMP Exposition Press New York 1953 163
Kelly, Howard
DRAGON DOODLES Watts London 1946 80
Kelsey, Franklyn
THE PROWLERS OF THE DEEP Harrap London 1942 240
Kemble, W. F.
PITTED AGAINST ANARCHISTS Abbey Press New York 1899 7-118
Kemp, Robert
THE MALACCA CANE Duckworth London 1954 167
Kennedy, Bart
THE HUMAN COMPASS S. Low & Marston London 1911 315
Kennedy, Douglas
13 STRANGE TALES Lawson & Dunn London 1946 7-96
Keon, Miles Gerald
DION AND THE SIBYLS Benziger New York 1898 475
Keown, Anna Gordon
MR. THEOBALD'S DEVIL Morrow New York 1936 314
Kerby, Susan Alice
MR. KRONION Laurie London 1949 7-223
THE ROARING DOVE Dodd, Mead New York 1948 260
Kerr, Geoffrey
UNDER THE INFLUENCE Lippincott Philadelphia 1954 251
Kerr, Sophie
THE MAN WHO KNEW THE DATE Allen London 1952 264
Kersh, Gerald
THE BRIGHTON MONSTER AND OTHERS Heinemann London 1953 197
THE GREAT WASH Heinemann London 1953 246
THE SECRET MASTERS Ballantine New York 1953 225
Key, Eugene G(eorge)
MARS MOUNTAIN Fantasy Pub Co Everett, Pa. 1936 142
Key, Uel
THE BROKEN FANG AND OTHER EXPERIENCES OF A SPECIALIST IN SPOOKS Hodder & Stoughton London nd 303
King, Basil
THE SPREADING DAWN - STORIES OF THE GREAT TRANSITION Harper New York 1927 318
King, Frank
THE GHOUL Nimmo, Hay & Mitchell London nd 318
GREEN GOLD Nimmo, Hay & Mitchell London 1933 216
King, Godfre Ray
THE MAGIC PRESENCE St. Germain Press Chicago 1935 393
UNVEILED MYSTERIES St. Germain Press Chicago 1934 360

King-Hall, Stephen
POST WAR PIRATE Methuen London 1931 252
Kirk, Laurence
THE GALE OF THE WORLD Cassell London 1948 187
Kirk, Robert
THE SECRET COMMONWEALTH OF ELVES, FAUNS, AND FAIRIES Malsay Stirling, Scotland 1933 128
Kirst, Hans Helmut
THE SEVENTH DAY Doubleday Garden City, N. Y. 1959 424
Kitelle, P. Wayne
VOYAGE INTO THE UNKNOWN Vantage Press New York 1958 132
Kjelgaard, Jim (James Arthur)
FIRE-HUNTER Holiday House New York 1951 217 Juv.
Klimbach, Sophie Mann
THE RING OF THE AGES William-Frederick Press New York 1953 191
Kline, Otis Adelbert
THE OUTLAWS OF MARS Avalon New York 1961 220
PORT OF PERIL Grandon Providence, R. I. 1949 13-249
THE SWORDSMAN OF MARS Avalon New York 1960 218
TAM, SON OF THE TIGER Avalon New York 1962 222
Kneatchbull-Hugessen, E. H.
THE MOUNTAIN SPIRITES KINGDOM Routledge London 1881 372
OTHER STORIES Routledge London 1880 367
TALES AT TEA TIME Macmillan London 1872 357
Kneale, Nigel
TOMATO CAIN AND OTHER STORIES Knopf New York 1950 3-300
Knight, Damon (Editor)
A CENTURY OF SCIENCE FICTION Simon & Schuster New York 1962 352
FAR OUT: 13 SCIENCE FICTION STORIES Simon & Schuster New York 1961 282
Knight, L. A.
THE ASTOUNDING DR. YELL Low London 1950 186
Knights, D. A.
AICHA THE MAURESQUE Quality Press London nd 7-143
Knittel, John
POWER FOR SALE Hutchinson London 1939 5-405
Knowles, Vernon
PITIFUL DUST Lane London 1931 184
Komroff, Manuel (Editor)
TALES OF THE MONKS FROM THE GESTA ROMANORUM Tudor New York 1947 320
Kornbluth, C. M.
CHRISTMAS EVE M. Joseph London 1956 207
A MILE BEYOND THE MOON Doubleday Garden City, N. Y. 1958 239
THE MINDWORM M. Joseph London 1955 256
NOT THIS AUGUST Doubleday Garden City, N. Y. 1955 190
THE SYNDIC Doubleday Garden City, N. Y. 1953 13-223
TAKEOFF Doubleday Garden City, N. Y. 1952 218
Kornbluth, Mary (Editor) (Mrs. C. M.)
SCIENCE FICTION SHOWCASE Doubleday Garden City, N. Y. 1959 264
Kotzebue, Augustus Von
ROLLA; OR, THE VIRGIN OF THE SUN Vennor and Hood London 1801 93
Kreisheimer, H. C.
THE WHOOPING CRANE Pageant Press New York 1955 89

Kreymborg, Alfred
THE FOUR APES AND OTHER FABLES OF OUR DAY Loker Raley New York 1939 230
THE PLANETS: A MODERN ALLEGORY Farrar & Rinehart New York 1938 50
Kroll, Harry Harrison
THE GHOSTS OF SLAVE DRIVERS BEND Bobbs-Merrill Indianapolis 1937 332
Kuebler, Harold W. (Editor)
THE TREASURY OF SCIENCE FICTION CLASSICS Hanover House Garden City, N.Y. 1954 704
Kuttner, Henry
AHEAD OF TIME Ballantine New York 1953 177
FURY Grosset & Dunlap New York 1950 186
Kuttner, Henry and Moore, C(atherine) L.
NO BOUNDARIES Ballantine New York 1955 149
Lagerkvist, Par
THE ETERNAL SMILE, AND OTHER STORIES Random New York 1954 389
Lagerlof, Selma
THE STORY OF COSTA BERLING Gay & Bird, London Little, Brown, Boston 1898 318
Laing, Janet
THE VILLA JANE Century New York 1929 312
Lamb, Harold
A GARDEN TO THE EASTWARD Doubleday Garden City, N. Y. 1947 374
MARCHING SANDS Appleton New York 1920 308
Lampen, Charles Dudley
BARCALI THE MUTINEER: A TALE OF THE GREAT PACIFIC Everett London 1900 312
THE DEAD PRIOR Stock London 1896 221
MIRANGO THE MANEATER: A TALE OF CENTRAL AFRICA Soc Promoting Christian Faith London 1899 248
THE QUEEN OF THE EXTINCT VALCANO Soc for Promoting Christian Faith London 1898 224
O'CALLAGHAN THE SLAVE TRADER Digby, Long London 1901 312
Lampman, Evelyn Sibley
RUSTY'S SPACE SHIP Doubleday Garden City, N. Y. 1957 240 Juv.
"Lancelot Lance"
HORTENSE: A STUDY OF THE FUTURE BY LANCELOT LANCE Sands and McDougall Melbourne 1906 334
Lang, Andrew
THE BOOK OF DREAMS AND GHOSTS Longmans, Green London and New York 1897 301
Lang, Hermann
THE AIR BATTLE, A VISION OF THE FUTURE Penny London 1859 112
Langdon, Norman E.
YOUR STORY, ZALEA Exposition Press New York 1962 131
Langford, George
SENRAC, THE LION MAN Liveright New York 1954 216
Langley, Dorothy
MR. BREMBLE'S BUTTONS Simon & Schuster New York 1947 186
Langley, Kenlis
THE MOUNTAIN OF MYSTERY Nelson London and New York 1929 9-347
Langley, Noel
THE RIFT IN THE LUTE Coward-McCann New York 1953 188
TALES OF MYSTERY AND REVENGE Barker London 1950 189
Langlois, Dora
IN THE SHADOW OF PA-MANKH Low, Marston London 1908 328

La Prade, Ernest
ALICE IN ORCHESTRALIA Doubleday, Doran Garden City, N. Y. 1928 171
Larsen, J. Anker
THE PHILOSOPHER'S STONE Knopf New York 1924 379
Laski, Marghanita
THE VICTORIAN CHAISE LOUNGE Houghton Mifflin Boston 1954 119
La Spina, Greye
INVADERS FROM THE DARK Arkham House Sauk City, Wisc. 1960 168
Lath, J. A.
THE LOST CITY OF THE AZTECS; OR, THE MYSTERY OF THE HIDDEN CRATER Cupples & Leon New York 1934 203 Juv.
Latham, Philip (Pseud of Richardson, R. S.)
FIVE AGAINST VENUS Winston Philadelphia 1952 221
MISSING MEN OF SATURN Winston Philadelphia and Toronto 1953 215
Laver, James
PANIC AMONG PURITANS Farrar & Rinehart New York 1936 296
Lavonda, Marsha
THE MASK OF SATAN Exposition Press New York 1954 389
Law, Winifred
RANGERS OF THE UNIVERSE New Century Sydney 1945 176 Juv.
Lawrence, Margery
THE FLOATING CAFE Jarrolds London nd 303
MASTER OF SHADOWS Hale London 1959 188
THE RENT IN THE VEIL Hale London 1951 391
STRANGE CARAVAN Hale London 1941 304
Lawson, Alfred William
BORN AGAIN Wox, Conrad New York and Philadelphia 1904 5-287
Lawson, J. S.
FABLES; 1950 Exposition Press New York 1950 no pages
Layard, Arthur
THE WONDERFUL ADVENTURES OF SIR JOHN MAUNDEVILLE, KNIGHT Constable Westminster, England 1895 414 Ill.
Layne, Stan
I DOUBTED FLYING SAUCERS Meador Boston 1958 177
Leacock, Stephen
MOONBEAMS FROM THE LARGER LUNACY Lane New York and London 1917 217
Leadbetter, C. W.
THE PERFUME OF EGYPT AND OTHER WEIRD STORIES Theosophical Pub House Adyer, Madras, India 1911 265
Leblanc, Maurice
MAN OF MIRACLES Macauley New York 1931 9-310
Leahy, Martin
DROME Fantasy Pub Co Los Angeles 1952 11-295
Leamy, Edmund
BY THE BARROW RIVER AND OTHER STORIES Sealy, Bryers & Walker Dublin 1907 281
Lee, (Rev.) Frederick (George)
GLIMPSES IN THE TWILIGHT Blackwood Edinburgh and London 1885 456
Lee, Vernon (Pseud of Paget, Violet)
A PHANTOM LOVER. A FANTASTIC STORY Roberts Bros. Boston 1886 134
THE SNAKE LADY, AND OTHER STORIES Grove Press New York 1954 288
Leech, Joseph
GHOSTS AND GLAMOUR Arrowsmith Birstol 1886-1887 187
Lee-Hamilton, Eugene
LORD OF THE DARK RED STAR Scott Pub Co London 1903 7-296

Leeming, John F.
THANKS TO CLAUDIUS Harrap London nd 158
Lees, Robert James
THE CAR OF PHOEBUS Rider 1930 248
THE GATE OF HEAVEN Rider London 1931 253
Le Fanu, J(oseph) Sheridan
THE PURCELL PAPERS Bentley London 1890 3 vol. 336, 273, 289
A STRANGE ADVENTURE IN THE LIFE OF MISS LAURA MILDMAY Home & Van Thal London 1947 108
Lehman, R. C. (Editor)
MR. PUNCH'S PRIZE NOVELS Bradbury, Agnew London 1892 175 Ill.
Leiber, Fritz
CONJURE WIFE Twayne Pub New York 1953 154
GATHER, DARKNESS Pellegrini & Cudahy New York 1950 240
THE GREEN MILLENIUM Abelard Press New York 1953 256
TWO SOUGHT ADVENTURE Gnome Press New York 1957 186
Leiber, Fritz and Blish, James and Pratt, Fletcher
WITCHES THREE Twayne Pub New York 1952 423
Leigh, Edmund
OUR GHOSTS Digby, Long London nd 244
Leight, Walter W.
THE ARCHEOLOGIST AND THE PRINCESS Exposition Press New York 1957 81
Leighton, Clare
SOMETIME--NEVER Macmillan New York 1939 178
Leinster, Murray (Pseud of Jenkins, Will(Iam) F(itzgerald))
CITY ON THE MOON Avalon New York 1957 224
COLONIAL SURVEY Gnome Press New York 1957 185
8 THE FORGOTTEN PLANET Gnome Press New York 1954 177
THE LAST SPACE SHIP Fell New York 1949 9-239
OPERATION: OUTER SPACE Fantasy Press Reading, Pa. 1954 208
OUT OF THIS WORLD Avalon New York 1958 221
SIDEWISE IN TIME Shasta Chicago 1950 211
SPACE PLATFORM Shasta Chicago 1953 222
SPACE TUG Shasta Chicago 1953 223
Leinster, Murray (Editor)
GREAT STORIES OF SCIENCE FICTION Random New York 1951 314
Leo, Bessie
THE ROMANCE OF THE STARS--BEING A SERIES OF ASTROLOGICAL STORIES Fowler London 1914 201
Leonardo da Vinci and Payne, Robert(Editor)
THE DELUGE Twayne Pub New York 1954 99
Leonis, Sheila
MAUT Rider London 1949 96
Le Page, Rand
BEYOND THESE SUNS Warren London 1952 128
BLUE ASP Warren London 1952 128
Le Queux, William
GREAT GOD GOLD Badger Boston 1910 301
THE MYSTERY OF THE GREEN RAY Hodder & Stoughton London 1916 244
STOLEN SOULS Stokes New York and London 1895 305
THE TERROR OF THE AIR Jenkins London nd 312
Lernet-Holenia, Alexander
COUNT LUNA Criterion New York 1956 252

Leroux, Gaston
THE NEW TERROR Macauley New York 1926 256
Leslie, Desmond
THE AMAZING MR. LUTTERWORTH Wingate London 1958 215
ANGELS WEEP Laurie London 1948 9-269
Leslie, Shane
FIFTEEN ODD STORIES Hutchinson London nd 288
SHANE LESLIE'S GHOST BOOK Sheed & Ward New York 1956 160
Lesser, Edward John
INTERRUPT THE MOON Pageant Press New York 1958 188
Lesser, Milton A.
EARTHBOUND Winston Philadelphia 1952 217
SPACEMEN, GO HOME Holt, Rinehart & Winston New York 1961 221
THE STAR SEEKERS Winston Philadelphia 1953 212
Lesser, Milton (Editor)
LOOKING FORWARD Beechhurst New York 1953 400
Lewis, C(live) S(taples)
THE LION' THE WITCH, AND THE WARDROBE Macmillan New York 1950 187 Juv.
THE MAGICIAN'S NEPHEW Macmillan New York 1955 167 Juv.
PRINCE CASPIAN Macmillan New York 1951 186 Juv.
THE SILVER CHAIR Macmillan New York 1953 208 Juv.
THE VOYAGE OF THE DAWN TREADER Macmillan New York 1952 217 Juv.
Lewis, D. B. Wyndham
THE SOUL OF MARSHALL GILLES DA RAIZ Eyre & Spottiswoode London 1952 209
Lewis, Florence Jay
THE CLIMAX Books, Inc. New York 1944 244
Lewis, Maurice
MYSTERIOUS HAPPENINGS Grayson & Grayson London 1936 11-304
Lewis, Oscar
THE LOST YEARS Knopf New York 1951 121
Lewis, Wyndham
THE CHILDERMASS Chatto & Windus London 1928 322
Ley-Piscator, Maria
LOT'S WIFE Bobbs-Merrill Indianapolis 1954 506
Lin Yutang
LOOKING BEYOND Prentice-Hall New York 1955 387
Linklater, Eric
THE CORNERSTONES Macmillan London 1942 83 play
SEALSKIN TROUSERS Hart-Davis London 1947 7-127
A SPELL FOR OLD BONES Macmillan New York 1950 223
THE WIND ON THE MOON Macmillan New York 1944 323
Linton, (Dr.) C. E.
THE EARTHOMOTOR AND OTHER STORIES Statesman Pub Co Salem, Oregon nd (1915) 13-231
Lissendon, George B.
THE SEERESS Cranton London 1927 286
Lister, Stephen
HAIL! BOLONIA Davis London 1948 171
Liston, Edward
THE BOWL OF NIGHT Coward-McCann New York 1948 3-246
Little, William
A VISIT TO TAPOS AND HOW THE SCIENCE OF HEREDITY IS PRACTISED THERE Anderson Ballerat, Australia 1897 138

Livingston, Marjorie
    DELPHIC ECHO Dakers London 1948 5-421
    THE FUTURE OF MR. PURDUE Wright & Brown London nd 7-320
Livingston, Walter
    THE MYSTERY OF BURNLEIGH MANOR Mystery League New York 1930 286
Lock, J. M.
    THE HOPPING HA'PENNY Methuen London 1935 241
Locke, Charles O.
    THE LAST PRINCESS Norton New York 1954 316
Locke, G. E.
    THE PURPLE MIST Page Boston 1924 363
Lockhart, J. G.
    STRANGE TALES OF THE SEVEN SEAS Allan London 1929 210
Lockhart-Ross, H. S.
    HAMTURA. A TALE OF AN UNKNOWN LAND Digby, Long London 1892 288
Lodge, Mrs.
    A SON OF THE GODS Digby, Long London 1898 284
Lofting, Hugh
    DOCTOR DOLITTLE AND THE SECRET LAKE Lippincott Philadelphia 1948 366 Juv
    DOCTOR DOLITTLE'S BIRTHDAY BOOK Stokes New York 1935 216 Juv.
    DOCTOR DOLITTLE'S CARAVAN Stokes New York 1926 342 Juv.
    DOCTOR DOLITTLE'S CIRCUS Stokes New York 1924 379 Juv.
    DOCTOR DOLITTLE'S GARDEN Stokes New York 1927 327 Juv.
    DOCTOR DOLITTLE IN THE MOON Cape London 1929 320 Juv.
    DOCTOR DOLITTLE'S POST OFFICE Stokes New York 1923 359 Juv.
    DOCTOR DOLITTLE'S PUDDLEBY ADVENTURES Lippincott Philadelphia 1952 252 Ju
    DOCTOR DOLITTLE'S RETURN Stokes New York 1933 273 Juv.
    DOCTOR DOLITTLES ZOO Stokes New York 1925 338 Juv.
    THE STORY OF DOCTOR DOLITTLE Stokes New York 1920 180 Juv.
    THE TWILIGHT OF MAGIC Stokes New York 1930 303
    THE VOYAGES OF DOCTOR DOLITTLE Stokes New York 1922 364 Juv.
Lone, Yoti
    AFRICAN FOLK TALES Lunn London 1946 9-240
Long, Charles
    THE INFINITE BRAIN Avalon New York 1957 224
Long, Frank Belknap
    THE HORROR FROM THE HILLS Arkham House Sauk City, Wisc. 1963 110
    JOHN CARSTAIRS, SPACE DETECTIVE Fell New York 1949 7-264
Long, Haniel
    NOTES FOR A NEW MYTHOLOGY The Bookfellows Chicago 1926 167 430 copy edi
Long, Max Freedom
    THE SECRET SCIENCE BEHIND THE MIRACLES Kosmon Los Angeles 1948 402
Long, Paul and Wye, Alan
    THE REMNANTS OF 1927 Long's London 1925 191
Longstreth, Thomas Morris
    TIME FLIGHT Macmillan New York 1954 216 Juv.
Lonsdale, H. M.
    D'ALRA THE BUDDHIST Ward, Lock London nd 317
Lorraine, Paul
    TWO WORLDS Warren London 1952 128
    ZENITH D Warren London 1952 159
Lott, S. Makepeace
    THE JUDGE WILL CALL IT MURDER Rich and Cowan London and New York 1951 209

Loughlin, Richard J. and Popp, Lillian M. (Editors)
JOURNEYS IN SCIENCE FICTION Globe New York 1961 655
Lovecraft, H(oward) P(hillips)
THE CASE OF CHARLES DEXTER WARD Gollancz London 1951 7-160
COLLECTED POEMS Arkham House Sauk City, Wisc. 1963 134 poetry
THE DREAM QUEST OF UNKNOWN KADATH Shroud Pub Buffalo 1955 107 50 copy edition
DREAMS AND FANCIES Arkham House Sauk City, Wisc. 1962 174
THE DUNWICH HORROR AND OTHERS Arkham House Sauk City, Wsic. 1963 431
THE HAUNTER OF THE DARK Gollancz London 1951 5-303
THE SHUTTERED ROOM Arkham House Sauk City, Wisc. 1959 313
SOMETHING ABOUT CATS Arkham House Sauk City, Wisc. 1949 3-305
Lovecraft, H. P. and Derleth, August W.
THE SURVIVOR AND OTHER Arkham House Sauk City, Wisc. 1957 161
Low, (Prof.) A(rchibald) M.
PETER DOWN THE WELL Grayson & Grayson London 1933 192 Juv.
Lowndes, (Mrs.) Belloc
THE LODGER Scribner New York 1913 308
WHAT TIMMY DID Doran New York 1922 212
Lowndes, Robert W.
BELIEVER'S WORLD Avalon New York 1961 224
MYSTERY OF THE THIRD MINE Winston Philadelphia 1953 201
Luban, Milton
THE SPIRIT WAS WILLING Greenberg New York 1951 188
Ludwell, Bernice (Pseud of Stokes, Manning Lee)
HAUNTED SPRING Arcadia House New York 1956 219
Lukens, Adam
ALIEN WORLD Avalon New York 1963 192
CONQUEST OF LIFE Avalon New York 1960 221
THE GLASS CAGE Avalon New York 1962 223
THE SEA PEOPLE Avalon New York 1959 221
SONS OF THE WOLF Avalon New York 1961 224
THE WORLD WITHIN Avalon New York 1962 221
Lull, (Rev.) D.
CELESTIA Reliance New York 1907 238
Lum, Peter
FABULOUS BEASTS Pantheon New York 1951 337
Luna, Kris
STELLA RADIUM DISCHARGE Warren London 1952 128
Lunatic, Nicholas
SATIRIC TALES: CONSISTING OF A VOYAGE TO THE MOON; ALL THE TAILORS; AND THE LAST WITCH OF LONDON Hughes London 1808 212
Lundstrom, Emil Ferdinand
THE LAST FOOL Dorrance Philadelphia 1933 162
Lynch, Bohun
THE MENACE FROM THE MOON Jarrolds London 1925 15-304
Lytle, Andrew (Nelson)
A NAME FOR EVIL Bobbs-Merrill Indianapolis 1947 9-215
A NOVEL, A NOVELLA AND FOUR SHORT STORIES (A Name for Evil and others) McDowell, Obolensky New York 1958 347
Macardle, Dorothy
DARK ENCHANTMENT Doubleday Garden City, N. Y. 1953 314
MacArthur, David S.
THE THUNDERBOLT MEN Lunn London 1947 229

MacCreagh, Gordon
    THE INCA'S RANSOM Chelsea New York 1926 249
    POISONOUS MIST Chelsea New York 1927 250
MacDonald, Donald K. and Roberts, Alaric J.
    YOU DO TAKE IT WITH YOU Vantage Press New York 1953 161
MacDonald, George
    AT THE BACK OF THE NORTH WIND Routledge New York 1882 378 Juv.
MacDonald, Greville
    THE WONDERFUL GOATSKIN Epworth Press London 1944 7-136
MacDonald, John D.
    BALLROOM OF THE SKIES Greenberg New York 1952 206
    WINE OF THE DREAMERS Greenberg New York 1951 219
MacDonald, Robert M.
    THE SECRET OF THE SARGASSO Brentano New York 1909 368 Juv.
MacFarlane, Claire
    WINGED VICTORY Mann Pub Jersey City, N. J. 1954 349
MacGrath, Harold
    THE CARPET FROM BAGHDAD Bobbs-Merrill Indianapolis 1911 390
MacGregor, Ellen
    MISS PICKERELL GOES TO MARS Whittlesey House New York 1951 128 Juv.
MacGregor, Geddes
    FROM A CHRISTIAN GHETTO Longmans New York 1954 152
Machen, Arthur
    DREADS AND DROLLS Knopf New York 1927 220
    THE GREEN ROUND Selwyn & Blount London 1933 218
    TALES OF TERROR AND THE SUPERNATURAL Knopf New York 1948 427
Mackenzie, Compton
    THE LUNATIC REPUBLIC Shatto & Windus London 1959 223
Mackenzie, Nigel
    DAY OF JUDGMENT Wright & Brown London 1956 187
    INVASION FROM SPACE Wright & Brown London 1954 189
    A STORM IS RISING Wright & Brown London 1958 189
    WORLD WITHOUT END Wright & Brown London 1955 159
    THE WRATH TO COME Wright & Brown London 1958 188
MacLaren, Evelyn
    ROCKET RIDER Whitman Chicago 1954 no pages Juv.
MacLeod, Angus
    THE BODY'S GUEST Roy Pub New York 1959 192
MacNaughton, Donald
    THE MOON CHILDREN Vantage Press New York 1954 83 Juv.
MacVicar, Angus
    THE LOST PLANET Burke London 1953 158
    RETURN TO THE LOST PLANET Burke London 1954 158
Madariaga, Salvador de
    HEART OF JADE Creative Age Press New York 1948 540
Maddux, Rachel
    THE GREEN KINGDOM Simon & Schuster New York 1956 561
Madsen, Lenora Kimball
    GREEN-EYE PHANTOMS Exposition Press New York 1954 197 Juv.
Maeterlinck, Maurice
    A MIRACLE OF ST. ANTHONY Boni & Liveright New York 1917 256
Maginn, (Dr.) William
    TEN TALES Partridge London 1933 7-192

Magor, Nancy and Woods, Margaret Murray
LIFE MARCHES ON Skeffington London nd 9-216
Mahoney, Patrick
OUT OF THE SILENCE Storm Pub New York 1948 180
Maine, Charles Eric (Pseud of McIlwain, David)
CRISIS 2000 Hodder & Stoughton London 1956 191
ESCAPEMENT Hodder & Stoughton London 1956 224
HE OWNED THE WORLD Avalon New York 1960 224
HIGH VACUUM Hodder & Stoughton London 1957 192
THE ISOTOPE MAN Lippincott Philadelphia 1957 217
THE MAN WHO COULDN'T SLEEP (See ibid Escapement)
SPACEWAYS SATELLITE Avalon New York 1958 224
TIMELINER Rinehart New York 1955 249
Mair, George B.
THE DAY KRUSCHEV PANICKED Cassell London 1961 172
Malcolm, A. C.
O MEN OF ATHENS Sampson, Low London nd 250
Malcolm, Mary
CHAUCER, THE FLYING SAUCER Exposition Press New York 1954 39
Malcolm-Smith, George
THE GRASS IS ALWAYS GREENER Doubleday Garden City, N. Y. 1947 7-217
PROFESSOR PECKHAM'S ADVENTURE IN A DROP OF WATER Rand, McNally New York and Chicago 1931 144 Juv.
Manifold-Craig, R.
THE WEIRD OF "THE SILKEN THOMAS" Moran Aberdeen 1900 232
Mann, Jack (Pseud of Vivian, E(velyn) Charles)
COULSON GOES SOUTH Wright & Brown London 1935 288
DEAD MAN'S CHEST Godwin New York 1934 292
GEE'S FIRST CASE Wright & Brown London 1936 9-286
THE GLASS TOO MANY Wright & Brown London 1940 284
Mannes, Marya
MESSAGE FROM A STRANGER Viking New York 1948 246
Mannin, Ethel
LUCIFER AND THE CHILD Jarrolds London 1946 238
Mantley, John
THE 27th DAY Dutton New York 1956 248
Manure, Doctor Henry
THE AUTOBIOGRAPHY OF A SCIENTIST Scientific Pub Co Princeton, N. J. 1936 176
Manvell, Roger
THE DREAMERS Simon & Schuster New York 1958 183
Marbo, Camille
THE MAN WHO SURVIVED Harper New York and London 1918 191
Marcel, Philip e Thoby and Pierre
THE PENCIL OF GOD Gollancz London 1951 204
Marchmont, Arthur A.
A DASH FOR A THRONE New Amsterdam Book Co New York 1899 9-352
Margulies, Leo and Friend, Oscar J. (Editors)
FROM OFF THIS WORLD Merlin Press New York 1949 430
THE GIANT ANTHOLOGY OF SCIENCE FICTION Merlin Press New York 1954 591
MY BEST SCIENCE FICTION STORY Merlin Press New York 1949 556
Mark, Ronald and Stover, A. (Editors)
BRAINS FOR JAMES Pirate Press New Orleans 1948 5-47 200 copy edition

Markophrates
LA BRUJO, THE WITCH; OR, A PICTURE OF THE COURT OF ROME Hatchard London 1840 188
Marks, Percy,L.
THE MERGING OF RONALD LETHERIDGE Scott London 1928 156
Marple, J. Clarence and Dennis Albert Nelson
ANONA OF THE MOUND BUILDERS Progressive Wheeling, W. Va. 1920 210
Marryat, Florence (Pseud of Lean, Mrs. Francis)
BLOOD OF THE VAMPIRE Hutchinson London 1897 345
THE DEAD MAN'S MESSAGE Reed New York 1894 5-178
A SOUL ON FIRE Sands London 1898 275
STRANGE TRANSFIGURATION OF HANNAH STUBBS Hutchinson London 1896 330
Mars, Alastair
FIRE IN ANGER Mill & Morrow New York 1957 222
Marsh, Carl
AND WARS SHALL CEASE Broadway Pub Co New York nd (1939) 5-351
Marsh, Richard
BETWEEN THE DARK AND THE DAYLIGHT Digby, Long London 1902 327
BOTH SIDES OF THE VEIL Methuen London 1901 306
THE GODDESS, A DEMON White London 1900 300
Marshall, A. W.
THE GOLDEN HAMMER Marshall London nd 188
Marshall, Edison
DARZEE, GIRL OF INDIA Kinsey New York 1937 280
EARTH GIANT Doubleday Garden City, N. Y. 1960 308
Marshall, Luther
THOMAS BOOBIG Lee & Shepard Boston 1895 349
Marsten, Richard
DANGER: DINOSAURS Winston Philadelphia 1953 210
ROCKET TO LUNA Winston Philadelphia 1953 211
Martin, Clarence W.
UBIQUE, THE SCIENTIFIC BUSHRANGER Bookstall Co Sydney 1910 275
Martin, Eva M.
THE SECRET OF A STAR Theosophical Adyas, Madras, India 1913 139
Martin, Lester
NOAH'S STOWAWAY Author Long Beach, Calif. 1954 152
Martyn, Wyndham
STONES OF ENCHANTMENT Jenkins London nd 253
Marvell, W. Holt
THE PASSIONATE CLOWNS Duckworth London 1927 7-192
Masefield, Lewis
CROSS DOUBLE CROSS Putnam London 1936 11-331
Mason, Van Wyck
TWO TICKETS FOR TANGIER Doubleday Garden City, N. Y. 1955 284
Mason, Gregory
THE GOLDEN ARCHER Twayne Pub New York 1956 296
Mason, J. Edward (Editor)
WITCHES, WARLOCKS AND GHOSTS Oliver and Boys Edinburgh and London nd 118
Masterman, W. S.
CURSE OF THE BECKAVILES Methuen London 1927 230
Matheson, Hugh (Pseud of Mackay, Louis Hugh)
THE BALANCE OF FEAR Gibbs & Phillips London 1961 224
THE THIRD FORCE I. Washburn New York 1960 248

Matheson, Joan
THE CISTERN AND THE FOUNTAIN Scribner New York 1954 256
Matheson, Richard
BORN OF MAN AND WOMAN Chamberlain Press Philadelphia 1954 252
A STIR OF ECHOES Lippincott Philadelphia 1958 220
Mathieson, Una Cooper (Pseud of Gibson, Amanda Melvina Thorley)
A MARRIAGE OF SOULS: A METAPHYSICAL NOVEL "Truth Seeker" Pub Co Perth, Australia 1914 176
Matson, Norman (Haghajim)
ENCHANTED BEGGAR Lippincott Philadelphia 1959 187
Matthews, E. Paul
BEYOND THIS DAY Vantage Press New York 1958 276
Maugham, Robin
THE MAN WITH TWO SHADOWS Harper New York 1959 165
Maugham, W. Somerset
CATALINA Doubleday Garden City, N. Y. 1948 275
Maupassant, Guy de
THE HORLA & OTHER TALES Classic Pub Co London and New York 1928 317
Maxwell, Edward
QUEST FOR PAJARO Heinemann London 1957 116
Mayne, Melinda
THE BEGINNING IS THE END Exposition Press New York 1953 138
McCall, Marie
THE EVENING WOLVES Day New York 1949 279
McCann, Edson
PREFERRED RISK Simon & Schuster New York 1955 248
McClary, Thomas Calvert
THREE THOUSAND YEARS Fantasy Press Reading, Pa. 1954 224
McCloy, Helen
THROUGH A GLASS DARKLY Random New York 1950 238
McCutcheon, George Barr
WEST WIND DRIFT Dodd, Mead New York 1920 368
McGrath, Thomas
THE GATES OF IVORY, THE GATES OF HORN Mainstream Pub New York 1958 128
McInnes, Graham Campbell
LOST ISLAND World Cleveland and New York 1954 254
McIntosh, J. T. (Pseud of Macgregor, James Murdoch)
BORN LEADER Doubleday Garden City, N. Y. 1954 221
THE FITTEST Doubleday Garden City, N. Y. 1955 192
ONE IN THREE HUNDRED Doubleday Garden City, N. Y. 1954 223
WORLD OUT OF MIND Doubleday Garden City, N. Y. 1953 8-222
McIver, G.
NEUROOMIA: A NEW CONTINENT Sonnenschein London 1894 307
McLaren, Jack
THE DEVIL OF THE DEPTHS Allan London 1935 256
McNaughton, Mildred
FOUR GREAT OAKS Creative Age Press New York 1946 327
McWilliams, J. A.
STARMAN Exposition Press New York 1958 143
Mead, Harold
BRIGHT PHOENIX Ballantine New York 1956 184
MARY'S COUNTRY M. Joseph London 1957 288
Mead, Leon
THE BOW-LEGGED GHOST AND OTHER STORIES Warner New York 1899 [illegible]9

Mead, (Edward) Shepherd
THE BIG BALL OF WAX Simon & Schuster New York 1954 246
THE MAGNIFICENT MACINNES Farrar, Straus New York 1949 255
TESSIE, THE HOUND OF CHANNEL ONE Doubleday Garden City, N. Y. 1951 251
Meagher, George E.
TOMORROW'S HORIZON Dorrance Philadelphia 1947 9-136
Meckauer, Walter
THE BOOKS OF THE EMPEROR WU TI Minton, Balch New York 1931 215
Meek, Col. S. P.
THE DRUMS OF TAPAJOS Avalon New York 1961 224
TROYANA Avalon New York 1961 224
Meldrum, David
BUILDERS OF CONTINENTS Exposition Press New York 1957 198
Mendes, Catulle
NO. 56 AND OTHER STORIES Laurie London 1928 11-240
Mandham, Clement A.
A BURIED MYSTERY Digby, Long London 1898 308
Menen, Aubrey
THE FIG TREE Scribner New York 1959 192
THE PREVALENCE OF WITCHES Scribner New York 1948 9-250
RAMAYANA Scribner New York 1954 276
Merak, A. J.
DARK ANDROMEDA Hamilton London 1953 158
Meredith, George
THE RADIUM REBELS Nelson London nd 252 Juv.
Merrill, Judith
SHADOW ON THE HEARTH Doubleday Garden City, N. Y. 1950 277
Merrill, Judith (Editor)
BEYOND HUMAN KEN Random New York 1952 334
BEYOND THE BARRIERS OF SPACE AND TIME Random New York 1954 309
S F: THE YEAR'S GREATEST SCIENCE FICTION AND FANTASY Gnome Press New York 1956 342
S F '957; THE YEAR'S GREATEST SCIENCE FICTION AND FANTASY Gnome Press New York 1957 320
S F '58: THE YEAR'S GREATEST SCIENCE FICTION AND FANTASY Gnome Press New York 1958 380
S F '59: THE YEAR'S GREATEST SCIENCE FICTION AND FANTASY Gnome Press Hicksville, N. Y. 1959 256
THE FIFTH ANNUAL OF THE YEAR'S BEST SCIENCE FICTION Simon & Schuster New York 1960 320
THE SIXTH ANNUAL OF THE YEAR'S BEST SCIENCE FICTION Simon & Schuster New York 1961 318
THE SEVENTH ANNUAL OF THE YEAR'S BEST SCIENCE FICTION Simon & Schuster New York 1962 310
The Eighth ANNUAL OF THE UEAR'S BEST SCIENCE FICTION Simon & Schuster New York 1963 318
Merriman, H. S.
THE PHANTOM FUTURE Copp Clark Toronto 1899 372
Merritt, A(braham) and Bok, Hannes
THE BLACK WHEEL New Collectors Group New York 1947 7-115
Mertins, Gustave F.
A WATCHER OF THE SKIES Crowell New York 1911 376

Merwin, Samuel
THE HOUSE OF MANY WORLDS Doubleday Garden City, N. Y. 1951 216
KILLER TO COME Abelard Press New York 1953 254
THE WHITE WIDOWS Doubleday Garden City, N.Y. 1953 224
Metcalfe, John
ARM'S LENGTH Constable London 1930 349
THE FEASTING DEAD Arkham House Sauk City, Wisc. 1954 123
Meyer, John de
BENJAMIN FRANKLIN CALLS ON THE PRESIDENT Washburn New York 1939 90
Meyrick, Gordon
THE GHOST HUNTERS Crowther London 1947 7-236
McGuire, Sean
BEAST OR MAN Palmer London 1930 7-285
Mian, Mary (Shipman)
THE MERRY MIRACLE Houghton Mifflin Boston 1949 132
Michael, Cecil
ROUND TRIP TO HELL IN A FLYING SAUCER Vantage Press New York 1955 61
Michaud, A. C.
OUR COMING WORLD World Pubn Press Philadelphia 1951 162
Middlemore, (Mrs.) S. G. C.
SPANISH LEGENDARY TALES Chatto & Windus London 1895 302
Miller, Alan
THE KING OF MEN Nash & Grayson London 1931 320
THE PHANTOMS OF A PHYSICIAN Grayson & Grayson London 1934 288
Miller, P. Schuyler
THE TITAN Fantasy Press Reading, Pa. 1952 9-252
Miller, Patrick
THE NATURAL MAN Brentano New York 1924 307
Miller, R. DeWitt
THE LOOS BOARD IN THE FLOOR Vantage Press New York 1951 111
Miller, Thomas
FRED AND THE GORILLAS Routledge London 1870 380 Ill.
Miller, Walter M. Jr.
A CANTICLE FOR LEIBOWITZ Lippincott Philadelphia 1960 320
Milligan, Clarence P.
THE WONDERLAND OF JOHN DEVLIN Christopher Boston 1945 260
Mills, (Lady) Dorothy
THE DARK GODS Duckworth London 1925 284
Mills, G. H. Saxon
INTERRUPTION Heinemann London 1932 333
Mills, J. M. A.
LORDS OF THE EARTH Dakers London nd 9-302
THE TOMB OF THE DARK ONES Occult Pub London nd 285
Mills, Robert P. (Editor)
THE BEST FROM FANTASY AND SCIENCE FICTION: NINTH SERIES ,Doubleday Garden City, N. Y. 1960 264
THE BEST FROM FANTASY AND SCIENCE FICTION: TENTH SERIER Doubleday Garden City, N. Y. 1961 262
THE BEST FROM FANTASY AND SCIENCE FICTION: ELEVENTH SERIES Doubleday Garden City, N. Y. 1962 258
A DECADE OF FANTASY AND SCIENCE FICTION Doubleday Garden City, N. Y. 1960 406
THE WORLDS OF SCIENCE FICTION Dial New York 1963 349

Miles, Samuel (Editor)
THE BEST FROM STARTLING STORIES Holt New York 1953 301
Mitchell, Gladys
THE WORSTED VIPER Joseph London 1943 192
Mitchell, Ronald
DAN OWEN AND THE ANGEL JOE Harper New York and London 1948 3-250
Mitchell, Prof. W(illis)
THE INHABITANTS OF MARS Spofford Malden, Mass. 1895 192
Mitford, Bertram
THE KING'S ASSEGAI Staple Inn Pub London 1926 231
Mittelholzer, Edgar
SHADOWS MOVE AMONG THEM Lippincott Philadelphia 1951 334
THE WEATHER IN MIDDENSHOT Day New York 1952 280
Molesworth, (Mrs.) Mary L.
FAIRIES OF SORTS Macmillan London 1908 249 Juv.
Molner, Ferenc
THE DEVIL Ogilvie Pub New York 1908 189
Moloney, Eileen
THE MERMAID OF ZENNOR AND OTHER CORNISH TALES Ward Leicester, England 1946 108
Moncrief, Augustin-Paradis de
THE ADVENTURES OF ZELOIDE AND AMANZARIFIDINE Dial New York 1929 205
Montague, Joseph
THE CRATER OF KALA Chelsea New York 1925 253
Moore, C(atherine) L.
DOOMSDAY MORNING Doubleday Garden City, N. Y. 1957 216
JUDGMENT NIGHT AND OTHER STORIES Gnome Press New York 1952 344
NORTHWEST OF EARTH Gnome Press New York 1954 212
SHAMBLEAU AND OTHERS Gnome Press New York 1953 224
Moore, George
THE BROOK KERITH Macmillan New York 1916 486
Moore, John Cecil
DANCE AND SKYLARK Macmillan New York 1952 215
Moore, Patrick
THE MASTER OF THE MOON Museum London 1952 223 Juv.
Moord, Ward
BRING THE JUBILEE Farrar, Straus & Young New York 1953 194
Moosdorf, Johanna
FLIGHT TO AFRICA Harcourt, Brace New York 1954 256
Morand, Paul
EAST INDIA AND COMPANY A & C Boni New York 1927 237
Moresby, Lord
A HUNDRED YEARS HENCE; OR, THE MEMOIRS OF CHARLES, LORD MORESBY, WRITTEN BY HIMSELF Longman, Rees Orme, Brown & Green London 1828 210
Morgan, Charles
THE BURNING GLASS St. Martin's Press New York 1954 183 Play
Morley, Felix
GUMPTION ISLAND Caxton Pub Caldwell, Idaho 1956 319
Morley, Lacy Collison
GREEK AND ROMAN GHOST STORIES Blackwell Oxford, England 1912 79
Morrah, Herbert
THE FAITHFUL CITY Methuen London 1922 317

Morris, Gouvenor
THE FOOTPRINT AND OTHER STORIES Scribner New York 1908 336
Morris, Kenneth
BOOK OF THE THREE DRAGONS Longmans, Green New York 1930 206 Juv.
Morris, William
THE ROOTS OF THE MOUNTAINS Reeves & Taylor London 1893 423
Morrish, Furze
BRIDGE OVER DARK GODS Rider London nd 160
Morrison, Arthur
CUNNING MURRELL Doubleday, Page New York 1900 288
THE SHADOWS AROUND US Simpkin, Marshall, Hamilton & Kent London 1891 128
Morrison, Lucile
THE LOST QUEEN OF EGYPT Lippincott Philadelphia 1937 368
Morrison, William
MEL OLIVER AND SPACE ROVER ON MARS Gnome Press New York 1954 191 Juv.
Morrisson, Emeline
THE GLITTERING SERPENT Hale London 1950 352
Morrow, W. C.
LENTALA OF THE SOUTH SEAS--THE ROMANTIC TALE OF A LOST COLONY Stokes New York 1908 278
Morton, Frank
THE ANGEL OF THE EARTHQUAKE Atlas Press Melbourne 1909 217
Morton, Guy (Eugene)
THE BLACK ROBE Minton, Balch New York 1927 3-278
KING OF THE WORLD Hodder & Stoughton London 1927 5-320
Moskowitz, Samuel (Compiler)
EDITOR'S CHOICE IN SCIENCE FICTION McBride New York 1954 300
Mottram, R. H.
VISIT OF THE PRINCESS Hutchinson London nd 7-174
Mudd, William S.
THE OLD BOAT ROCKER Dodd, Mead New York 1935 251
Muddock, J(oyce)E(mmerson) P(reston)
THE DEAD MAN'S SECRET, OR THE VALLEY OF GOLD Chatto & Windus London 1891 310
STORIES, WEIRD AND WONDERFUL Chatto & Windus London 1889 316
Muir, Ward
FURTHER EAST THAN ASIA Simpkin, Marshall London 1919 283
Mulier
SOJOURNERS BY THE WAYSIDE - TRAVELLERS ON THE LONG ROAD Gnostic San Diego, Calif. 1917 203
Mullen, Stanley
KINSMEN OF THE DRAGON Shasta Chicago 1951 336
MOONFOAM & SORCERIES Gorgon Press Denver, Colo. 1948 3-264
Munby, A. N. L.
THE ALABASTER HAND AND OTHER GHOST STORIES Dobson London 1949 192
Mundy, Talbot
GUP BAHADUR Hutchinson London nd 292
COCK O' THE NORTH (See ibid Gup Bahadur)
Munkacsi, Martin
FOOL'S APPRENTICE Staples London 1946 394
Munn, H. Warner
THE WEREWOLF OF PONKERT Grandon Providence, R. I. 1958 138 350 copy edition

Munsell, Frank
CHIPS FOR THE CHIMNEY CORNER Munsell's Steam Press Albany 1871 184
Munster, Countess of
GHOSTLY TALES Hutchinson London 1896 320
Murphy, George Read
BEYOND THE ICE: A NEWLY DISCOVERED REGION ROUND THE NORTH POLE Sampson, Low London 1894 434
Murray, Sir Charles D.
NOUR-ED-DYN, OR THE LIGHT OF FAITH Soc for the Promotion of Christian Knowledge London nd (1884) 128
Murray, D. L.
COME LIKE SHADOWS Hodder & Stoughton London 1955 412
COMMANDER OF THE MISTS Knopf New York 1938 507
Murray, Jacqueline
DAUGHTER OF ATLANTIS Regency Press London nd 166
Myers, Henry
O KING, LIVE FOREVER Crown New York 1953 214
THE UTMOST ISLAND Crown New York 1951 216
Myers, John Myers
SILVERLOCK Dutton New York 1949 11-349
Naish, Reginald T.
THE MIDNIGHT HOUR AND AFTER! Thynne & Jarvis London 1920 225
Narayan, R. K.
GRATEFUL TO LIFE AND DEATH Michigan State College Press East Lansing, Mich. 1953 213
Nathan, Robert
THE COLOR OF EVENING Knopf New York 1960 210
THE INNOCENT EVE Knopf New York 1951 184
JONAH McBride New York 1925 212
MR. WHITTLE AND THE MORNING STAR Knopf New York 1947 3-175
SIR HENRY Knopf New York 1955 187
SON OF AMMITAI (See ibid Jonah)
THERE IS ANOTHER HEAVEN Bobbs-Merrill Indianapolis 1929 7-121
Navarchus
WHEN THE GREAT WAR CAME Hodder & Stoughton London nd 312
THE WORLD'S AWAKENING (See ibid When the Great War Came)
Nearing, Homer Jr.
THE SINISTER RESEARCHES OF C. P. RANSON Doubleday Garden City, N. Y. 1954 217
Negley, Glenn and Patrick, J. Max
THE QUEST FOR UTOPIA Schuman New York 1952 599
Neill, Robert
THE ELEGANT WITCH Doubleday Garden City, N. Y. 1952 11-348
Nembhard, Mabel
FANTASIES Allen London 1896 198
Nemerov, Howard
A COMMODITY OF DREAMS Simon & Schuster New York 1959 245
Nesbitt, E(dith) (Bland, Mrs.)
GRIM TALES Innes London 1893 167
Neville, Derek
BRIGHT MORROW Crowther London 1947 7-157
Nevinson, Henry W.
IN THE DARK BACKWARD Routledge London 1834 272

Newbolt, (Sir) Henry
ALADORE Blackwood Edinburgh and London 1914 362
Newby, P. H.
A JOURNEY TO THE INTERIOR Cape London 1945 7-240
Newman, Bernard
THE FLYING SAUCER Macmillan New York 1950 5-250
SECRET WEAPON Gollancz London 1941 189
SHOOT! Gollancz London 1949 241
Newman, John Henry Cardinal
CALLISTA: A TALE OF THE THIRD CENTURY Longmans, Green London and New York 1890 382
Newton, Bertha
MY LIFE IN TIME Daniel London 1938 236
Niall, Ian (Pseud of McNeillie, John)
THE BOY WHO SAW TOMORROW Heinemann London 1952 259
Nichols, Adelaide
THE HAUNTED CIRCLE AND OTHER OUTDOOR PLAYS Dutton New York 1924 279
Nicholson, John
SPACE SHIP TO VENUS Venture Books Bath, England 1948 233
Nicholson, John Henry
ADVENTURES OF HALEK: AN AUTOBIOGRAPHICAL FRAGMENT Griffith, Farrar London 1882 390
ALMONI: A COMPANION VOLUME TO HALEK Dunlop Brisbane and Sydney 1904 388
Nida, William Lewis
AB THE CAVEMAN A. Flanagan Chicago 1921 166 Juv.
Nielson, Helga
DEEP IN THE SKY Exposition Press New York 1955 161
Nisbet, Hume
STORIES WEIRD AND WONDERFUL White London 1900 127
Nizzi, Guido "Skipper"
THE PARALYZED KINGDOM AND OTHER STORIES Field-Doubleday New York 1947 101
Noel, Sterling
I KILLED STALIN Farrar, Straus & Young New York 1951 3-281
Norday, Michael
DARK MAGIC Vixen Press New York 1954 182
Norman, James
A LITTLE NORTH OF EVERYWHERE Pellegrini & Cudahy New York 1951 7-192
Norris, Frank
NUTRO 29 Rinehart New York 1950 3-307
VANDOVER AND THE BRUTE Doubleday, Page Garden City, N. Y. 1914 354
Norris, Kathleen (Norris, Mrs. Charles Gilman)
THROUGH A GLASS DARKLY Doubleday Garden City, N. Y. 1957 287
North, Andrew (Pseud of Norton, Alice Mary)
SARGASSO OF SPACE Gnome Press New York 1955 185
North, Eric
THE ANT MEN Winston Philadelphia 1955 223
Northcote, Amyas
IN GHOSTLY COMPANY Lane London 1922 287
Norton, Andre (Pseud of Norton, Alice Mary) (See also North, Andrew)
THE BEAST MASTER Harcourt, Brace New York 1959 192
CATSEYE Harcourt, Brace & World New York 1961 193
THE DEFIANT AGENTS Harcourt, Brace & World New York 1962 224
GALACTIC DERELICT World Cleveland 1959 224
JUDGMENT OF JANUS Harcourt, Brace & World New York 1963 220

Norton, Andre (cont.)
KEY OUT OF TIME World Cleveland 1963 224
LORD OF THUNDER Harcourt, Brace & World New York 1962 192
PLAGUE SHIP Gnome Press New York 1956 192 (as Andrew North)
SEA SIEGE Harcourt, Brace New York 1957 216
STAR BORN World Cleveland 1957 212
STAR GATE Harcourt, Brace New York 1958 192
STAR GUARD Harcourt New York 1955 247
STAR MAN'S SON: 2250 A. D. Harcourt, Brace New York 1952 248
STAR RANGERS Harcourt, Brace New York 1953 280
THE STARS ARE OURS World Cleveland 1954 13-237
STORM OVER WARLOCK World Cleveland 1960 251
THE TIME TRADERS World Cleveland 1959 219
Norton, Andre (Editor)
SPACE PIONEERS World Cleveland 1954 7-294
SPACE POLICE World Cleveland 1956 255
SPACE SERVICE World Cleveland 1953 277
Nott, Kathleen
THE DRY DELUGE Hogarth Press London 1947 5-307
Nourse, Alan E(dward)
THE COUNTERFEIT MAN McKay New York 1963 185
RAIDERS FROM THE RINGS McKay New York 1962 211
ROCKET TO LIMBO McKay New York 1957 184
SCAVENGERS IN SPACE McKay New York 1959 180
STAR SURGEON McKay New York 1960 182
TIGER BY THE TAIL McKay New York 1961 184
TROUBLE ON TITAN Winston Philadelphia 1954 221
Nowlan, Philip Francis
ARMAGEDDON 2419 A. D. Avalon New York 1962 224
Noy, John
THE PASS OF THE GREY DOG Hamilton London 1928 311
THE VULTURE Hamilton London nd 285
Noyes, Alfred
BEYOND THE DESERT Stokes New York 1920 85
Nyberg, Bjorn and de Camp, L. Sprague
THE RETURN OF CONAN Gnome Press New York 1957 191
Oboler, Arch
14 RADIO PLAYS Random New York 1940 257
NIGHT OF THE AUK Horizon Press New York 1958 180 Play
O'Brien, Larry Clinton
EARTH WAITS FOR DAWN Vantage Press New York 1956 284
Obruchev, V. A.
PLUTONIA Lawrence & Wishart London 1957 319
O'Connell, Charles C.
THE VANISHING ISLAND Devin-Adair New York 1959 211
O'Donnell, Elliott
THE DEAD RIDERS Rider London 1952 208
THE DEVIL IN THE PULPIT Archer London nd 286
HAUNTED HIGHWAYS AND BYWAYS Nash London 1904 219
HAUNTED PLACES IN ENGLAND Sands London 1919 228
SCOTTISH GHOST STORIES Paul, Trench, Trubner London 1911 293
TREES OF GHOSTLY DREAD Rider London 1958 200
THE UNKNOWN DEPTHS Groening London 1905 315
WEREWOLVES Small, Maynard Boston nd 292

O'Farrell, William
REPEAT PERFORMANCE Allen London 1948 257
Ogden, Antoinette (Translator)
CHRISTMAS STORIES FROM FRENCH AND SPANISH WRITERS McClurg Chicago 1892 265
Ogden, George W.
CUSTODIAN OF GHOSTS Halo London 1951 7-254
Ogilvy, Arthur James
THE APE MAN OF A. J. O. "Daily Post" Hobart, Tasmania 1913 137
O'Harra Family, The
CROHOORE OF THE BILL-HOOK adn THE FETCH Simms & McIntyre London 1848 148
Ohlson, Hereward
THUNDERBOLT OF THE SPACEWAYS Lutterworth London 1954 190
Olander, D. V.
LOVE LIFE OF A FROG Exposition Press New York 1951 85
Olcott, Frances Jenkins
WONDER TALES FROM CHINA SEAS Longmans, Green London 1925 238 Juv.
Oldrey, John
THE DEVIL'S HENCHMEN Methuen London 1926 250
O'Leary, Con
THIS DELICATE CREATURE Constable London 1928 281
Oliver, Chas
MISTS OF DAWN Winston Philadelphia 1952 208
SHADOWS IN THE SUN Ballantine New York 1954 152
ANOTHER KIND Ballantine New York 1955 170
THE WINDS OF TIME Doubleday Garden City, N. Y. 1957 192
Oliver, Jane
MORNING FOR MR. PROTHERO McKay New York 1951 242
Ollier, Charles
FALLACY OF GHOSTS, DREAMS, AND OMENS Ollier London 1848 251
O'Meara, Walter
TALES OF THE TWO BORDERS Bobbs-Merrill Indianapolis 1951 197
O'Neill, Joseph
WIND FROM THE NORTH Cape London 1934 341
O'Neill, Russell
JONATHAN Appleton-Century-Crofts New York 1959 214
Onions, Oliver
GHOSTS IN DAYLIGHT Chapman & Hall London 1924 236
PAINTED FACE AND OTHER GHOST STORIES Heinemann London 1929 294
Oppenheim Mrs. Ansel (Pseud of Emersie, John)
EVELYN: A STORY OF THE WEST AND FAR EAST Broadway New York 1904 385 front.
Oppenheim, E(dwar) Phillips
THE DOUBLE LIFE OF MR. ALFRED BURTON Little, Brown Boston 1913 322
GABRIEL SAMARA Hodder & Stoughton London nd 319
Orb, Clay
THE MAN IN THE MOON IS TALKING Warwick Book Press New York 1946 133
Orcutt, Emma Louise
THE DIVINE SEAL Clark Boston 1909 315
O'Reilly, Rev. A. J.
STRANGE MEMORIES Sadlier New York and Montreal 1881 5-387
O'Reilly, John and Kelly, Walt
THE GLOB Viking New York 1952 63
Orndorff, Frank
KONGO, THE GORILLA MAN Field-Doubleday New York 1945 9-206

O'Rourke, Frank (Pseud of O'Malley, Frank)
THE HEAVENLY WORLD SERIES Barnes New York 1952 192
Orwell, George
1984 Harcourt, Brace New York 1949 3-314
Osborne, David
ALIENS FROM SPACE Avalon New York 1958 223
INVISIBLE BARRIERS Avalon New York 1958 223
Osborne, Duffield
THE LION'S BROOD Doubleday, Page New York 1901 361
Osler, William
PREMATURE ANGEL Dorrance Philadelphia 1954 282
O'Sullivan, J. B.
I DIE POSSESSED Mill-Morrow New York 1953 255
Oudeis
HELL Roxburghe Press Westminster, England nd 125
Ouspensky, P. D.
STRANGE LIFE OF IVAN OSOKIN Holme Press New York and London 1947 5-166
Owen, Anna and Frank
THE BLUE HIGHWAY Abington Press New York 1932 11-140 Juv.
Owen, Frank
THE PORCELAIN MAGICIAN Gnome Press New York 1948 7-256
Owen, Walter
MORE THINGS IN HEAVEN Bakers London 1947 332
Owens, William A.
WALKING ON BORROWED LAND Bobbs-Merrill Indianapolis 1954 304
Padgett, Lewis (Pseud of Kuttner, Henry)
A GNOME THERE WAS Simon & Schuster New York 1950 276
MUTANT Gnome Press New York 1953 210
ROBOTS HAVE NO TAILS Gnome Press New York 1952 224
TOMORROW AND TOMORROW and THE FAIRY CHESSMEN Gnome Press New York 1951 254
Paige, Ethel C. M.
STRANGE EXPERIENCE OF TINA MALONE, THE GIRL WHO HEARD VOICES Waverly Sydney 1922 387
Pain, Barry
SHORT STORIES Harrap London 1928 255
Pakenham, Eve
FANFARONADE Rich & Cowan London 1934 318
Palmer, Cuthbert
THE MAN WITHOUT A NAVEL Dragon Ithaca, N. Y. 1932 70 500 copy edition
Paludan, Muller, Frederick
THE FOUNTAIN OF YOUTH Macmillan London 1867 15-147
Pangborn, Edgar
A MIRROR FOR OBSERVERS Doubleday Garden City, N. Y. 1954 222
WEST OF THE SUN Doubleday Garden City, N. Y. 1953 219
Pape, Richard
AND SO ENDS THE WORLD Elek Books London 1961 222
Pargeter, Edith
BY THIS STRANGE FIRE Reynal & Hitchcock New York 1948 310
Parker, Norton S.
THE STRANGE BEDFELLOWS OF MONTAGUE AMES Hermitage New York 1953 288
Parkman, Sydney
LIFE BEGINS TOMORROW Pellegrini & Cudahy New York 1950 3-302

Parrish, Randall
THE AIR PILOT McClurg Chicago 1913 318
Parsons, Ethel Boyce
DUSK OF DRUIDS Cassell London 1935 317
Patchett, Mrs. Mary Elwyn
FLIGHT TO THE MISTY PLANET Bobbs-Merrill Indianapolis 1956 236 Juv.
SPACE CAPTIVES OF THE GOLDEN MEN Bobbs-Merrill Indianapolis 1953 222 Juv
Paterson, Arthur Elliott
VENUS: ONE WORLD NEARER PARADISE? Traversity Press Penobscot, Maine 1961 132
Patterson, Clonnie V.
VALLEY OF LIGHT Vantage Press New York 1955 269
Payne, Robert
ALEXANDER THE GOD Wyn New York 1954 307
Peacoy, Howard
MAGIC HOURS Toulmin London 1930 9-282
Peacock, Thomas Love
HEADLONG HALL Carey Philadelphia 1816 196
Peake, Mervyn (Laurence)
GORMENGHAST Eyre & Spottiswoode London 1950 454
TITUS ALONE Eyre & Spottiswoode London 1959 223
Pearson, W. T.
THE TEMPLE OF SAEHR Palmer London 1932 132
Peck, Winifred
UNSEEN ARRAY Faber & Faber London 1951 7-247
Peddie, John
THE CRAWFISH WOMAN Wetzel New Orleans 1930 256
Peel, Alfreda Marion
WITCH IN THE MILL Dietz Press Richmond, Va. 1947 118
Pei, Mario (Andrew)
THE SPARROWS OF PARIS Philosophical Lib. New York 1958 121
Pemberton, Max
THE DIAMOND SHIP Cassell London 1912 348
DR. XAVIER Hodder & Stoughton London 1903 302 Ill.
THE PHANTOM ARMY Appleton New York 1898 354
QUEEN OF THE JESTERS Pearson London 1928 5-252
Penfield, Wilder
NO OTHER GODS Little, Brown Boston 1954 340
Penny, F. E.
THE SANYASI Allan London 1936 328
Perry, Stella and Stern, George
LITTLE BRONZE PLAYFELLOWS P. Elder San Francisco 1915 26
Peskett, S. John
BACK TO BAAL Alder London 1932 11-177
Peterkiewicz, Jerzy
THE QUICK AND THE DEAD Macmillan London 1961 247
Peterson, Margaret
MOONFLOWER Hutchinson London nd 252
THE YELLOW PEOPLE; OR, QUEEN OF SHEBA'S TOMB Shaw London 1928 320
Phelps, Gilbert
THE CENTENARIANS Heinemann London 1958 218
Phelps, William Lyon
A DASH AT THE POLE Ball Boston 1909 72

Philbrook, Rose
THE WINGS OF DR. SMIDGE Caxton Caldwell, Idaho 1954 158
Phillips, Alex J.
RABBITS Mariner Press Gravesend, England 1946 6-208
Phillips, Forbes and Hopkins, R. Thurston
WAR AND THE WEIRD Simpkin, Marshall London 1916 182
Phillips, L. M.
THE MIND READER Neely New York and London 1898 312
Phillips, Rog
THE INVOLUNTARY IMMORTALS Avalon New York 1959 223
Phillips, Stephen
CHRIST IN HADES Lane London 1917 97 Ill.
Phillpotts, Eden
ADDRESS UNKNOWN Hutchinson London nd 5-219
BLACK, WHITE AND BRINDLED Macmillan New York 1923 7-344
CHILDREN OF THE MIST Innes London 1898 460
THE FALL OF THE HOUSE OF HERON Hutchinson London nd 5-182
Phineas
THE BLIND MEN AND THE DEVIL Lee & Shepard Boston 1890 7-219
Pick, Robert (Editor)
GERMAN STORIES AND TALES Knopf New York 1954 371
Pierson, Ernest De Lancey
THE BLACK BALL. A FANTASTIC ROMANCE Belford, Clarke Chicago 1889 223
Pilibin, A.
MOUNT KESTREL Gill Dublin 1945 130
Pilkington, Roger
STRINGER'S FOLLY Yates London 1951 256
Pinckney, Josephine
THE GREAT MISCHIEF Viking New York 1948 247
Poe, Edgar Allan and Verne, Jules
THE MYSTERY OF ARTHUR GORDON PYM Assoc Booksellers Westport, Conn. 1961 191
Pohl, Frederick (Julius)
ALTERNATING CURRENTS Ballantine New York 1956 154
Pohl, Frederick (Editor)
ASSIGNMENT IN TOMORROW Hanover House New York 1954 317
SCIENCE FICTION STORIES Columbia Pub New York 1953 130
STAR OF STARS Doubleday Garden City, N. Y. 1960 240
STAR SCIENCE FICTION STORIES Ballantine New York 1953 216
STAR SCIENCE FICTION STORIES, NO. 2 Ballantine New York 1954 195
STAR SHORT NOVELS Ballantine New York 1954 168
Pohl, Frederick and Kornbluth, Cyril M.
GLADIATOR-AT-LAW Ballantine New York 1955 171
SEARCH THE SKY Ballantine New York 1954 165
THE SPACE MERCHANTS Ballantine New York 1953 179
Pohl, Frederick and Williamson, Jack
UNDERSEA CITY Gnome Press Hicksville, N. Y. 1958 188
UNDERSEA FLEET Gnome Press New York 1956 187
UNDER SEA QUEST Gnome Press New York 1954 189
Poor, Katherine Hillwood
THE LODGE IN THE WILDERNESS Hobson New York 1945 238
Pope, (Mrs.) Marion M(anville)
UP THE MATTERHORN IN A BOAT Century New York 1897 199

Potocki, Jan
THE SARAGOSSA MANUSCRIPT Orion Press New York 1960 233
Poulson, Theodore Frederick
THE FLYING WIG Skiff Honolulu 1948 45 500 copy edition
Pourrat, Henri (Editor)
A TREASURY OF FRENCH TALES Houghton Mifflin Boston 1954 240
Powell, "Sandy" H. P.
SECRET BOMBER Wingate London 1958 215
Powys, T(heodore) F.
THE HOUSE WITH THE ECHO Viking New York 1928 234
Praed, (Mrs. Campbell
BY THEIR FRUITS: A NOVEL Cassell London 1908 423
THE OTHER MRS. JACOBS: A MATRIMONIAL COMPLICATION Torg London 1908 378
Pragnell, Festus
THE MACHINE GOD LAUGHS Griffin Pub Co Los Angeles 1949 134
Pratt, Fletcher
ALIEN PLANET Avalon New York 1962 222
DOUBLE IN SPACE Doubleday Garden City, N. Y. 1951 217
DOUBLE JEOPARD Doubleday Garden City, N. Y. 1952 214
INVADERS FROM RIGEL Avalon New York 1960 224
THE UNDYING FIRE Ballantine New York 1953 148
Pratt, Fletcher (Editor)
WORLD OF WONDER Twayne Pub New York 1951 445
Pratt, Fletcher and Piper, H. Beam and Merrill, Judith
THE PETRIFIED PLANET Twayne Pub New York 1952 263
Pratt, Theodore (Pseud of Brace, Timothy)
MR. LIMPET Knopf New York 1942 3-142
Preedy, George R.
THE COURTLY CHARLATAN Jenkins London 1931 11-207
DR. CHAOS AND THE DEVIL SNAR'D Cassell London 1934 204
Prentice, Harry
CAPTURED BY APES Burt New York 1922 5-286
Presland, John
ESCAPE ME--NEVER Appleton New York 1928 247
Prevot, Francis C.
GHOSTIES AND GHOULIES Chelsea London 1923 7-88
Price, Nancy
ACQUAINTED WITH THE NIGHT Ronald Oxford, England nd 11-255
Price, Theodore
GOD IN THE SAND: AN AUSTRALIAN MYSTICAL ROMANCE Stephenson Sydney 1894 288
A Priest
THE OPEN SECRET Arena Pub Co Boston 1893 62
Priestley, J(ohn) B(oynton)
BENIGHTED Heinemann London 1927 265
JENNY VILLIERS Heinemann London 1947 190
THE MAGICIANS Harper New York 1954 251
THE OTHER PLACE, AND OTHER STORIES OF THE SAME SORT Harper New York 1955 265
THE PLAYS OF J. B. PRIESTLEY Heinemann London 1948 477
Prior, Anthony
LONE ELM Skeffington London nd 5-144
Prokopoff, Stephen
THE PROPHET AND THE MIRACLE Vantage Press New York 1955 125

Prokosch, Frederic
STORM AND ECHO Faber & Faber London 1949 9-296
Pryce, Devereux
OUT OF THE AGES Parsons London 1923 320
Pudney, John
SHUFFLEY WANDERERS Lane London 1948 7-224
UNCLE ARTHUR AND OTHER STORIES Longmans, Green London 1939 11-318
Pullar, A. L.
CELESTALIA: A FANTASY, A. D. 1975 Canberra Press Sydney 1933 279
Pym, Herbert
THE MAN WITH THIRTY LIVES Everett London 1909 304
Quiller-Couch, Sir A(rthur) T.
DEAD MAN'S BOOK Cassell London 1887 304
Q'S MYSTERY STORIES Dent London 1937 402
SELECTED STORIES BY Q Dent London 1921 240
Quinn, Roderick Joseph
MOSTYN STAYNE: A NOVEL Robertson Melbourne 1897 334
Quinn, Seabury
ROADS Arkham House Sauk City, Wisc. 1948 5-110
Quiz
MONSTER-LAND Putnam New York 1910 344
Ramuz, C(harles) F.
WHEN THE MOUNTAIN FELL Pantheon New York 1947 9-221
Rand, Ayn
ATLAS SHRUGGED Random New York 1957 1168
Randall, Robert (Pseud of Garrett, Randall and Silverberg, Robert)
THE DAWNING LIGHT Gnome Press New York 1959 191
THE SHROUDED PLANET Gnome Press New York 1957 188
Randolph, Vance
WE ALWAYS LIE TO STRANGERS Columbia Univ Press New York 1951 317
WHO BLOWED UP THE CHURCH HOUSE Columbia Univ Press Neo York 1952 250
Rath, E. J.
THE SIXTH SPEED Cassell London 1910 340
Ray, Rene
THE STRANGE WORLD OF PLANET X Jenkins London 1957 190
WRAXTON MARNE Green London 1946 214
Rayer, F. G.
TOMORROW SOMETIMES COMES Home & Van Thal London 1951 5-256
Raymond, R. W.
THE MAN IN THE MOON & OTHER PEOPLE Ford New York 18753 45
Rayner, A. A.
THE CURRY EXPERIMENT Locker Hanley, Stoke-on-Trent 1947 192
Reador, E. E.
PRIESTESS AND QUEEN Longmans, Green London and New York 1899 308
Reed, Von
DWELLERS IN SPACE Warren London 1953 159
Reeve, Arthur B.
THE GOLD OF THE GODS Harper New York 1915 291
ROMANCE OF ELAINE Hearsts Int Lib New York 1916 352
THE TREASURE TRAIN Harper New York 1917 335
Regnas, C.
THE SAND OF NISON Daniel London 1906 319

Reid, Leslie
    TREVY THE RIVER Dent London 1928 3-299
Reid, C. Lestock
    THE TRAIL OF PHARAOH'S TREASURE Allan London 1935 256
Rember, Winthrop Allen
    EIGHTEEN VISITS TO MARS Vantage Press New York 1956 448
Repp, Ed Earl
    THE RADIUM POOL Fantasy Pub Co Los Angeles 1948 9-188
    THE STELLAR MISSILES Fantasy Pub Co Los Angeles 1949 9-192
Revermort, J. A.
    LUCIUS SCARFIELD Constable London 1908 574
Reynard, Elizabeth
    THE MUTINOUS WIND Houghton Mifflin Boston 1951 210
Reynolds, James
    GALLERY OF GHOSTS Creative Age Press New York 1949 295
Reynolds, Mack
    THE CASE OF THE LITTLE GREEN MEN Phoenix Press New York 1951 224
Reynolds, Philip
    WHEN AND IF Sloane New York 1952 246
    IT HAPPENED LIKE THIS (See ibid When and If)
Rhadamanthus
    THE DEVIL AND ALL No publisher nd 5-135
Rhodes, Kathlyn
    THE WAX IMAGE AND OTHER STORIES Hutchinson London nd 184
Rice, Harry E.
    EVE AND THE EVANGELIST. A ROMANCE OF A. D. 2108 Roxborough Boston 1908 224
Richards, Lysander Salmon
    BREAKING UP; OR, THE BIRTH, DEVELOPMENT AND DEATH OF THE EARTH AND ITS SATELLITE IN STORY Farwell Boston 1896 484
Richard, Guy
    TWO RUBLES TO TIME SQUARE Little, Brown Boston 1956 249
Richards, R. P. J.
    THE BLONDE GODDESS Ken-Pax London nd 9-237
Richardson, Benjamin Ward
    THE SON OF A STAR Longmans, Green London 1889 470
Richardson, Robert S.
    SECOND SATELLITE Whittlesey House New York 1956 191 Juv.
Richer, Clement
    SON OF TI-COYO Knopf New York 1954 256
    TI-COYO AND HIS SHARK: AN IMMORAL FABLE Knopf New York 1951 3-235
Riis, Jacob A.
    HERO TALES OF THE FAR NORTH Macmillan New York 1910 3-328
Riley, James Whitcomb
    ECCENTRIC MR. CLARK New York Book Co New York nd 189
Rinder, Edith W(ingate)
    THE SHADOW OF ARVOR Geddes & Colleagues Edinburgh nd 309
Risse, Heinz
    THE EARTHQUAKE Farrar, Straus & Young New York 1953 254
Rivera, Alejandro Tapia y
    ENARDO AND ROSAEL Philosophical Lib New York 1952 54
Robbins, Clifton
    THE DEVIL'S BEACON Benn London 1933 319

Roberts, Cecil
EIGHT FOR ETERNITY Hodder & Stoughton London 1947 318
Roberts, Charles G. D.
THE FEET OF THE FURTIVE Macmillan New York 1913 384
Roberts, C. B.
THE SECOND MAN Revell New York 1939 7-285
Roberts, Dorothy James
THE ENCHANTED CUP Appleton-Century-Crofts New York 1953 368
LAUNCELOT, MY BROTHER Appleton-Century-Crofts New York 1954 373
Roberts, Leslie
FEATHERS IN THE BED Fortune Press London nd 380
Roberts, R. Ellis
THE OTHER END Palmer London 1923 247
Roberts, Terence
REPORT ON THE STATUS QUO Merlin Press New York 1955 63
Robertson, Frances Forbes
THE DEVIL'S PRONOUN AND OTHER PHANTASIES Reeves & Turner London 1894 122
Robertson, Morgan
THE GRAIN SHIP McClure's & Metropolitan magazines New York nd 242
Robeson, Kenneth (Pseud of Dent, Lester)
THE QUEST OF THE SPIDER Street & Smith New York 1933 252
Robin, C. Ernest
THE CLAIRAUDIENT: A STORY OF PSYCHICAL RESEARCH Angus & Robertson Sydney 1896 347
Robinet, Lee (Pseud)
THE FOREST MAIDEN Browne & Howell Chicago 1914 349
Robinson, Frank M.
THE POWER Lippincott Philadelphia 1956 218
Robinson, Frederick
THE WAR OF THE WORLDS Privately printed Chicago 1914 111
Robinson, Les
THE GIRAFFE'S UNCLE Macquarie Head Press Melbourne 1933 312
Roche, (Mrs.) Regina Maria
THE CHILDREN OF THE ABBEY Rand, McNally New York nd 525
Rochester, George E.
THE BLACK MOLE Popular Lib London nd 7-216
DESPOT OF THE WORLD Hamilton London nd 7-223
THE MOTHEMEN Hutchinson London nd 183
Rock, Wyndam
BLACKATON'S BOY Home & Van Thal London 1948 124
Rockwell, Carey
DANGER IN DEEP SPACE Grosset & Dunlap New York 1953 209 Juv.
THE REVOLT ON VENUS Grosset & Dunlap New York 1954 213 Juv.
STAND BY FOR MARS Grosset & Dunlap New York 1952 210 Juv.
TREACHERY IN OUTER SPACE Grosset & Dunlap New York 1954 210 Juv.
Rodda, Charles
THE HOUSE UPSTAIRS Barrie London 1949 7-146
Rodocanachi, C. P.
FOREVER ULYSSES Viking New York 1938 315
Roe, Ivan
THE SALAMANDER TOUCH Hutchinson London 1952 7-224

Rohmer, Sax (Pseud of Ward, Arthur Sarsfield)
ORCHARD OF TEARS Methuen London 1924 250
SHADOW OF FU-MANCHU Doubleday Garden City, N. Y. 1948 190
SHE WHO SLEEPS Doubleday, Doran Garden City, N. Y. 1928 322
SINS OF SEVERAC BABLON Cassell London 1914 306
SINS OF SUMURU Jenkins London 1950 224
THE SLAVES OF SUMURU Jenkins London 1952 190
VIRGIN IN FLAMES Jenkins London 1953 204
Rolt, L. T. C.
SLEEP NO MORE Constable London 1948 162
Romaines, Jules
TUSSLES WITH TIME Sidgwick & Jackson London 1952 243
Romilly, Eric
BLEEDING FROM THE ROMAN Chapman & Hall London 1949 7-255
Rooke, Daphne
A GROVE OF FEVER TREES Houghton Mifflin Boston 1950 246
"Ropshin" (Pseud of Savinkiv, Boris)
WHAT NEVER HAPPENED Knopf New York 1917 448
Ross, Samuel Albert
THE COMING TERROR: OR, THE AUSTRALIAN REVOLUTION; A ROMANCE OF THE TWENTIETH CENTURY Published by author Sydney 1894 306
Roscoe, Theodore
MURDER ON THE WAY Dodge New York 1935 279
Rose, F(rederick) Horace (Vincent)
BRIDE OF THE KALAHARI Duckworth London 1940 272
Roshwold, Mordecai
LEVEL 7 McGraw-Hill New York 1960 186
A SMALL ARMAGEDDON Heinemann London 1962 211
Roskolenko, Harry
BLACK IS A MAN Padell New York 1954 191
Ross, (Major-General) Charles
WHEN THE DEVIL WAS SICK Murray London 1924 183
Ross, Malcolm
THE MAN WHO LIVED BACKWARDS Farrar, Straus New York 1950 3-461
Rossel, John
DAY AFTER TOMORROW'S WORLD William-Frederick Press New York 1952 31
Rothenberg, Alan Baie
THE MIND READERS Greenberg New York 1956 223
Row, Arthur
RESEARCHES INTO THE UNKNOWN Stockwell London nd 143
Rowe, George
FAIRY BEDMAKER Ward, Lock London 1903 255 Ill.
Rowse, A. L.
WEST COUNTRY STORIES Macmillan London 1945 222
Royde-Smith, Naomi
MADAM JULIA'S TALE Gollancz London 1932 9-288
Roys, Willis E.
FLAME ETERNAL and MAHARAJAH'S SON Osborg New York 1936 403
Ruck, Berta (Pseud of Oliver, Mrs. George)
A WISH A DAY Dodd, Mead New York 1956 283
Rud, Anthony
HOUSE OF THE DAMNED Macauley New York 1934 256
THE ROSE BATH RIDDLE Macauley New York 1934 254

Russell, Addison P.
SUB COOLUM--SKY BUILT HUMAN WORLD Houghton Mifflin Boston 1893 267
Russell, Austin
MR. ARROW Beechhurst Press New York 1947 7-352
Russell, Bertrand (Arthur William)
NIGHTMARES OF EMINENT PERSONS Simon & Schuster New York 1955 177
SATAN IN THE SUBURBS Lane London 1953 138
Russell, Eric Frank
DEEP SPACE Fantasy Press Reading, Pa. 1954 249
DREADFUL SANCTUARY Fantasy Press Reading, Pa. 1951 7-276
MEN, MARTIANS AND MACHINES Roy New York 1956 191
NEXT OF KIN Dobson London 1959 187
SENTINELS FROM SPACE Bouregy & Curl New York 1953 256
THREE TO CONQUER Avalon New York 1956 224
WASP Avalon New York 1957 223
Rutley, C. Bernard
THE CAVE OF WINDS Warne London 1947 256 Juv.
THE EXPLODING RAY Blackie London nd 222
Ryan, Marah Ellis
THE DANCER OF TULUUM McClurg Chicago 1924 310
Ryan, R. R.
ECHO OF A CURSE Jenkins London 1939 1-284
Ryder, Arthur W.
TWENTY-TWO GOBLINS Dent London 1917 220
Ryves, T. E.
BANDERSNATCH Grey Walls Press London 1950 299
S. M. C. (Sister Mary Catherine)
AS THE CLOCK STRUCK TWENTY Ave Maria Press Notre Dame, Ind. 1953 209
Sabini, Ronaldo
MAGNIFICENT HORIZONS Pageant Press New York 1955 168
Sackville, Margaret
ALICIA AND THE TWILIGHT Wells, Gardner, Darton London nd (1928) 92 play
Sackville, Orme
THE JUNGLE GODDESS Modern Pub Co London nd 7-254
St. Clair, Vivian B.
IN A TRANCE: AN HYPNOTIC MYSTERY Crabb & Yelland Melbourne 1892 403
St. John, Arthur
WHY NOT NOW? Daniel London nd 7-333
St. John, Philip (Pseud of del Rey, Lester)
ROCKET JOCKEY Winston Philadelphia 1952 207
ROCKETS TO NOWHERE Winston Philadelphia 1954 223
St. John-Loe, Gladys
THE DOOR OF BEYOND Duckworth London 1926 223
Saint-Laurent, Cecil (Pseud of Laurant-Coby, Jacques)
THE INN OF FIVE LOVERS Prentice-Hall New York 1953 302
Saki (Pseud of Munro, H. H.)
THE CHRONICLES OF CLOVIS BODLEY HEAD London 1912 300
Sale, Richard
LAZARUS #7 Simon & Schuster New York 1942 299
Salmon, Srthur L.
THE FERRY OF SOULS Foulis London 1927 7-94
Sampson, Charles
GHOSTS OF THE BROAD Yachtsman Pub Co London 1931 7-195

Samuel, Joseph
CALL IT A DAY Quality Press London 1945 5-288
Samuel, Maurice
THE DEVIL THAT FAILED Knopf New York 1952 271
Sanborn, R. A.
MR. MUDGE CUTS ACROSS; A FANTASY ON FRIENDSHIP Sutton House Los Angeles 1937 263
Sandoz, Maurice
THE HOUSE WITHOUT WINDOWS Campion London 1950 101 Ill.
Sansom, William
SOMETHING TERRIBLE, SOMETHING LOVELY Hogarth Press London 1948 232
SOUTH Harcourt, Brace New York 1950 198
Santesson, Hans Stefan (Editor)
THE FANTASTIC UNIVERSE OMNIBUS Prentice-Hall Englewood Cliffs, N. J. 1960 270
Sapte, W. (Jr.)
HOSTS OF GHOSTS Family Reader Office London nd 130
"Sarban"
THE DOLL MAKER AND OTHER TALES OF THE UNCANNY Davies London 1954 189
RINGSTONES Davies London 1951 7-283
THE SOUND OF HIS HORN Davies London 1952 154
Sartre, Jean Paul
THE CHIPS ARE DOWN Rider London 1951 7-187
Saunders, Louise
MAGIC LANTERNS Scribner New York 1923 179
Saunders, Paul
BRING OUT YOUR DEAD Humphries Boston 1935 232
Saurat, Denis
DEATH & THE DREAMER Westhouse London 1946 7-150
Saurat, Denis (Editor)
ANGELS AND BEASTS Westhouse London 1947 285
Savage, Richard
WHEN THE MOON DIED Ward, Lock London 1955 189
Savidge, E. van Pedroe
THE FLYING SUBMARINE Stockwell London nd 255
Savill, Mervyn (Editor)
SNAPDRAGON Assoc Booksellers Westport, Conn. 1956 235
Schachner, Nat(han)
SPACE LAWYER Gnome Press New York 1953 222
Schaeffer, Jack
THE CANYON Houghton Mifflin Boston 1953 132
"Schire" (Pseud of Gardner, E. D.)
HIGH MAGIC'S AID Houghton London 1949 352
Schmitz, James H.
AGENT OF VEGA Gnome Press Hicksville, N. Y. 1960 191
A TALE OF TWO CLOCKS Dodd, Mead New York 1962 206
Schoonover, Lawrence L.
CENTRAL PASSAGE Sloane New York 1962 246
Schramm, Wilbur
WINDWAGON SMITH & OTHER YARNS Harcourt, Brace New York 1948 342
Scoffern, David
A HOLIDAY IN HADES Rialto Press London 1907 104

Scott, Edward
THE MARVELLOUS EXPERIENCE OF JOHN RYDAL Brown, Langham London 1904 312
Scott, Eleanor
RANDALL'S ROUND Benn London 1929 255
Scott, Jeremy (Editor)
AT CLOSE OF EVE Jarrolds London nd 224
THE UNCERTAIN ELEMENT Jarrolds London nd 273
Scott, R. T. M.
THE NAMELESS ONES Dutton New York 1947 254
Scrymsour, Ella
THE BRIDGE OF DESTANCES Allan London 1924 276
"Sea-Lion"
THE INVISIBLE SHIPS Hutchinson London nd 208
PHANTOM FLEET Collins London 1946 192
THIS CREEPING EVIL Hutchinson London 1950 9-176
Segal, Lesley Keen
MANY ENCHANTMENTS Davies London 1936 287
Sellings, Arthur
TIME TRANSFER Joseph London 1956 240
Sernicoli, Davide
THE LAND WHICH LOVETH SILENCE Low, Marston London nd 216
Seton, Anya (Pseud of Chase, A. S.)
DRAGONWYCK Houghton Mifflin Boston 1943 316
Severn, David
THE FUTURE TOOK US Bodley Head London 1957 175 Juv.
Shafer, Robert
THE CONQUERED PLACE Putnam New York 1954 313
Shane, Sir Leslie
SHANE LESLIE'S GHOST BOOK Sheed & Ward New York 1957 172
Shanks, Edward
THE DARK GREEN CIRCLE Bobbs-Merrill Indianapolis 1936 320
Shannon, Frank
ONCE AROUND THE PARK Morrow New York 1952 186
Sharp, Robert
HORROR CASTLE Gray London 1936 256
Shaver, Richard
I REMEMBER LEMURIA Venture Books Evanston, Ill, 1949 215
Shaw, Brian
LOST WORLD Warren London 1953 159
Shaw, George Bernard
MAN AND SUPERMAN Constable London 1903 244 Play
Shaw, Stanley
THE LOCUST HORDE Hodder & Stoughton London 1934 319
Shay, Frank
HERE'S AUDACITY. AMERICA'S LEGENDARY HEROES Macauley New York 1930 256
Sheckley, Robert
CITIZEN IN SPACE Ballantine New York 1955 200
IMMORTALITY DELIVERED Avalon New York 1958 221
UNTOUCHED BY HUMAN HANDS Ballantine New York 1954 169
Sheehan, Perley Poore
THE ABYSS OF WONDERS Polaris Press Reading, Pa. 1953 190
THE WHISPERING CHORUS Benn London 1928 7-288

Sheldon, Ray
ATOMS IN ACTION Hamilton London 1953 159
HOUSE OF ENTROPY Hamilton London 1953 160
THE METAL EATER Hamilton London 1954 159
Shelton, F. W.
CRYSTALLINE; OR, THE HEIRESS OF FALL DOWN CASTLE Scribner New York 1854 11-202 Ill.
Sheppard, Alfred Tresidder
HERE COMES AN OLD SAILOR Hodder & Stoughton London 1927 5-415
Sheridan, (Mrs.)
THE HISTORY OF NOURJAHAD Mathews & Marrot London 1927 120
Sherlock, Philip M.
ANANSI, THE SPIDER MAN Crowell New York 1954 112 Juv.
Sherry, Oliver
MANDRAKE Jarrolds London 1929 9-287
Shiel, M(atthew) P(hipps)
THE BEST SHORT STORIES OF M. P. SHIEL Gollancz London 1948 310
THE LOST VIOL Clode New York 1905 309
Shiras, Wilmar (Mrs.)
CHILDREN OF THE ATOM Gnome Press New York 1953 216
Shorthouse, J. Henry
JOHN INGLESANT Macmillan London 1882 2 vol. 730
Shumway, Harry Irving
THE WONDERFUL VOYAGES OF CAP'N PENNY Little, Brown Boston 1929 275
Shute, Nevil (Pseud. of Norway, Nevil S.)
IN THE WET Heinemann London 1953 354
ON THE BEACH Morrow New York 1957 320
Sibold, Rosalind
CYNTHIA Greenwich New York 1957 32
Silve, Claude
EASTWARD IN EDEN Creative Age Press New York 1945 271
Silver, R. Norman
WARDERS OF THE DEEP Ward, Lock London 1903 397
Silverberg, Robert
COLLISION COURSE Avalon New York 1961 224
HUNTERS FROM SPACE Avalon New York 1961 222
LOST RACE OF MARS Winston Philadelphia 1960 120 Juv.
REVOLT ON ALPHA C Crowell New York 1955 148 Juv.
STARMAN'S QUEST Gnome Press Hicksville, N. Y. 1959 185
Simak, Clifford D.
CITY Gnome Press New York 1952 224
COSMIC ENGINEERS Gnome Press New York 1950 224
RING AROUND THE SUN Simon & Schuster New York 1953 242
STRANGERS IN THE UNIVERSE Simon & Schuster New York 1956 371
TIME AND AGAIN Simon & Schuster New York 1951 235
TIME IS THE SIMPLEST THING Doubleday Garden City, N. Y. 1961 263
WAY STATION Doubleday Garden City, N. Y. 1963 210
THE WORLDS OF CLIFFORD SIMAK Simon & Schuster New York 1960 378
Simpkins, J. M.
A LITTLE CONTAB WITH SOCRATES Meador Boston 1946 7-128
Simpson, Helen de Guery (Pseud of Browne, Mrs. J. Denis)
BOOMERANG Heinemann London 1932 514

(Sinbad) (Pseud of Dingle, Aylward Edward)
THE AGE OLD KINGDOM Hutchinson London nd 176
Sinclair, Andrew
THE PROJECT Faber & Faber London 1960 190
Sinclair, May
TALES TOLD BY SIMPSON Macmillan New York 1930 3-297
Sinclair, Upton
I, GOVERNOR OF CALIFORNIA AND HOW I ENDED POVERTY Epic League Los Angeles nd (1934) 64 wraps
WE, PEOPLE OF AMERICA AND HOW WE ENDED POVERTY Epic League Pasadena, Calif nd 64 wraps
Sinderby, Donald
MOTHER-IN-LAW INDIA Marriot London nd 312
Singer, Isaac Bashevis
GIMPEL THE FOOL Noonday Press New York 1957 205
Siodmak, Curt
RIDERS TO THE STARS Ballantine New York 1954 166
SKYPORT Crown New York 1959 223
Sitwell, Osbert
DEATH OF A GOD AND OTHER STORIES Macmillan London 1949 247
MAN WHO LOST HIMSELF Duckworth London 1929 288
Sizemore, Julius C. and Wilkie G.
THE SEA PEOPLE Exposition Press New York 1957 263
Slater, Henry J.
SHIP OF DESTINY Crowell New York 1952 7-200
THE SMASHED WORLD Jarrolds London 1952 221
Slaughter, Frank G(ill)
EPEDEMIC! Doubleday Garden City, N. Y. 1961 286
Sloath, Frederick
THE SEVENTH VIAL Jenkins London 1920 3-312
Sleigh, Bernard
THE GATES OF HORN Aldine House London 1926 244
WITCHCRAFT Oriole Berkeley Heights, N. J. 1934 89 106 copy edition
Sloane, William (Editor)
SPACE, SPACE, SPACE Watts New York 1953 288
STORIES FOR TOMORROW Funk & Wagnalls New York 1954 640
Slobodkin, Louis
THE SPACE SHIP UNDER THE APPLE TREE Macmillan New York 1952 114 Juv.
Slocombe, George
ESCAPE INTO THE PAST Harrap London 1943 335
Slosson, Annie Trumbull
SEVEN DREAMERS Harper New York and London 1899 281
Smedley, Constance
TALES FROM TIMBUKTU Dent London 1935 179 Ill.
Smile, R. Elton
THE MANATITLANS; OR, A RECORD OF RECENT SCIENTIFIC EXPLORATIONS IN THE ANDEAN LA PLATA, S. A. Riverside Cambridge, England 1877 478
Smith, Barbara Dale
SARISKA BENORI McCubbin Melbourne 1922 322
Smith, Clark Ashton
THE ABOMINATIONS OF YONDO Arkham House Sauk City, Wisc. 1960 227
THE DARK CHATEAU AND OTHER POEMS Arkham House Sauk City, Wisc. 1951 68
GENIUS LOCI Arkham House Sauk City, Wisc. 1948 3-228
NERO, AND OTHER POEMS Futile Press Lakeport, La. 1937 24
SPELLS AND PHILTRES

Smith, Edward Elmer
CHILDREN OF THE LENS Fantasy Press Reading, Pa. 1954 293
FIRST LENSMAN Fantasy Press Reading, Pa. 1950 306
GALACTIC PATROL Fantasy Press Reading, Pa. 1950 273
GRAY LENSMAN Fantasy Press Reading, Pa. 1951 306
SECOND STAGE LENSMAN Fantasy Press Reading, Pa. 1953 307
THE SKYLARK OF VALERON Fantasy Press Reading, Pa. 1949 252
SKYLARK THREE Fantasy Press Reading, Pa. 1948 247
TRIPLANETARY Fantasy Press Reading, Pa. 1948 287
THE VORTEX BLASTER Gnome Press Hicksville, N. Y. 1960 191
Smith, Eleanor
THE MAN IN GREY Hutchinson London nd (1941) 256
Smith, Evelyn E.
THE PERFECT PLANET Avalon New York 1962 221
Smith, George O(liver)
FIRE IN THE HEAVENS Avalon New York 1958 224
HELLFLOWER Abelard Press New York 1953 264
HIGHWAYS IN HIDING Gnome Press New York 1956 223
LOST IN SPACE Avalon New York 1959 224
NOMAD Prime Press Philadelphia 1950 286
PATH OF UNREASON Gnome Press Hicksville, N. Y. 1959 185
PATTERN FOR CONQUEST Gnome Press New York 1949 9-252
TROUBLED STAR Avalon New York 1957 220
Smith, H(arry) Allen
THE AGE OF THE TAIL Little, Brown Boston 1955 167
Smith, James
ORIGINAL STORY: A TALE OF A WORLD Maryborough Advertiser Melbourne 1875 122
Smith, J. Moyr
THE PRINCE OF ARGOLIS Holt New York 1878 126 Ill.
Smith, Joe
DAGMAR OF GREEN HILLS Pageant Press New York 1957 124
Smith, Surrey
THE VILLAGE THAT WANDERED Boardman London 1960 223
Smith, William Augustus
HIS PSEUDOIC MAJESTY Liberty Pub Co New York 1903 7-397
Smith, W. Oakes
THE SALAMANDER, A TALE FOR CHRISTMAS FOUND AMONG THE PAPERS OF THE LATE ERNEST HELFENSTEIN Putnam New York 1848 19-249
Smithson, Annie M. P.
THE WHITE OWL Talbot Dublin and Cork 1937 300
Snell, Edmund
THE PURPLE SHADOW Unwin London 1927 7-288
Sohl, Jerry
THE ALTERED EGO Rinehart New York 1954 248
COSTIGAN'S NEEDLE Rinehart New York 1953 9-223
THE HAPLOIDS Rinehart New York 1952 248
THE ODIOUS ONES Rinehart New York 1959 245
POINT ULTIMATE Rinehart New York 1955 244
THE TRANSCENDENT MAN Rinehart New York 1953 244
Sonne, Hans Christian
ENTERPRISE ISLAND Business Bourse New York 1948 115
Sorenson, Villy
TIGER IN THE KITCHEN Abelard-Schuman New York 1957 215

Soutar, Andrew
KHARDUNI. A MYSTERY OF THE SECRET SERVICE Macauley New York 1934 256
THE PERVERTED VILLAGE Hutchinson London nd 476
Southall, Ivan
SIMON BLACK IN SPACE Angus & Robertson Sydney and London 1952 223
Southon, Arthur E.
A YELLOW NAPOLEON Revell New York and Chicago 1928 9-253
Southworth, Mrs. EDEN
THE SPECTRE LOVER Peterson Philadelphia 1875 416
Sowden, Louis
THE MAN WHO WAS EMPEROR Hale London 1946 240
TOMORROW'S COMET Hale London 1951 302
Spanner, E(dward) F.
THE SEA GHOULS Low London nd 250
Spaull, George T.
WHERE THE STARS ARE BORN Kerr-Cros Pub Co London nd 202 Juv.
Spectorsky, A. C.
MAN INTO BEAST Doubleday Garden City, N. Y. 1947 368
"Spectre Stricken"
GHOSTLY VISITORS Allen and The Psychological Press London 1882 128
Spencer, D. A. and Randerson, W.
NORTH SEA MONSTER Houghton & Scott-Snell London 1934 246
Spivey, Thomas Sawyer
SEVEN SONS OF BALLYHACK Cosmopolitan Press New York 1911 317
Spotswood, Christopher
VOYAGE OF WILL ROGERS TO THE SOUTH POLE Examiner's Office Launceston, Australia 1888 372
Spurrell, H. G. F.
OUT OF THE PAST Greening London 1903 300
Squires, Marjorie
THE WITCHBOWL Hurst & Blackett London nd 223
Stables, W(illiam) Gordon
FRANK HARDINGE Frowde, Hodder & Stoughton London 1908 352 Ill.
IN THE GREAT WHITE LAND Blackie London and Glasgow 1903 11-288
Stacpoole, H(enry) de Vere
GOBLIN MARKET Doran New York 1927 308
THE ISLAND OF LOST WOMEN Sears New York 1930 287
THE VENGEANCE OF MYNHEER VAN LIK & OTHER STORIES Hutchinson London 1934 286
Stallard, (Mrs.) Arthur
THE UTTERMOST Murray London 1926 382
Stamm, Russell
INVISIBLE SCARLET O'NEILL Whitman Racine, Wisc. 1943 238 Juv.
Staniland, Meaburn
BACK TO THE FUTURE Vane London 1947 7-264
Stanley, Alfred M.
TOMORROW'S YESTERDAY Dorrance Philadelphia 1949 7-174
Stanley, Dorothy
MISS PIM'S CAMOUFLAGE Hutchinson London 1918 256
Stanton, Coralie and Hosken, Heath
THE OLDEST LAND Faber & Faber London 1926 276
Stapledon, (William) Olaf
A MAN DIVIDED Methuen London 1950 187
TO THE END OF TIME Funk & Wagnalls New York 1953 790 (reprints Last and First Men, The Star Maker, Odd John, Sirius, The Fl

Staughton, Simon
PRINCE LUCIFER. A BIOGRAPHY OF THE DEVIL Eynesbury London 1950 270
Stead, Robert J. C.
THE COPPER DISC Crime Club New York 1931 312
Stead, William T.
IF CHRIST CAME TO CHICAGO Laird & Lee Chicago 1894 472
Steele, Wilbur Daniel
THE BEST STORIES OF WILBUR DANIEL STEELE Doubleday Garden City, N. Y. 1946 469
Steen, Marguerite
THE UNQUIET SPIRIT Doubleday Garden City, N. Y. 1956 253
Steiger, Andrew Jacob
THE MOON MAN Philosophical Lib New York 1961 318
Steinbeck, John
THE SHORT REIGN OF PIPPIN IV Viking New York 1957 188
Stephens, James
HERE ARE LADIES Macmillan New York 1913 5-345
Sterling, George
A WINE OF WIZARDRY AND OTHER POEMS Robertson San Francisco 1909 137
Sterling, John
THE ONYX RING Whittemore, Niles, Hall Boston 1856 263
Stern, David
FRANCIS GOES TO WASHINGTON Farrar, Straus New York 1948 3-243
Stern, G. B.
A DUCK TO WATER Macmillan New York 1950 117
JOHNNY FORSAKEN Macmillan New York 1954 236
Stern, J. David
EIDOLON Messner New York 1952 246
Sterne, Julian
THE SECRET OF THE ZODIAC Boswell London 1933 7-320
Stevens, E. S.
THE EARTHEN DRUM Mills & Boon London nd 3-204
THE VEIL, A ROMANCE OF TUNISIA Mills & Boon London 1909 407
Stevens, Francis (Pseud of Bennett, Gertrude)
THE HEADS OF CERBERUS Polaris Press Reading, Pa. 1952 191
Stevenson, Robert Louis
TALES OF TUSITALA. A SELECTION OF THE BEST SHORT STORIES Art & Educational London, Glasgow 1946 445
Stewart, Donald Ogden
A PARODY OUTLINE OF HISTORY Doran New York 1921 230
Stewart, George R.
EARTH ABIDES Gollancz London 1949 334
Stewart, Will (Pseud of Williamson, Jack)
SEETEE SHIP Gnome Press New York 1951 255
SEETEE SHOCK Simon & Schuster New York 1950 238
Stilgebauer, Edward
THE SHIP OF DEATH Brentano New York 1918 3-232
Stimson, F(rederic) J(essup)
IN THE THREE ZONES Scribner New York 1893 204
Stine, W(ilbur) M(orris)
AMOS MEAKIN'S GHOST Acorn Philadelphia 1924 327
Stinetorf, Louise A.
BEYOND THE HUNGRY COUNTRY Lippincott Philadelphia 1954 352

Stock, E. Elliot
THE RING OF UG, AND OTHER WEIRD TALES Ouseley London nd 172
Stocking, Charles F.
CARMEN ARIZA Maestro Chicago 1927 649
Stoddard, Charles
NORTH OF THE STARS Dodge New York 1937 256
Stoddard, William O.
ULRIC THE JARL...THE STORY OF A PENITENT THIEF Eaton and Maine New York 1899 342 Ill.
Stoker, Bram (i. e. Abraham)
LADY ATHLYNE Reynolds New York 1908 333
Stoker, M. B.
THE GILDED LIZARD Macdonald London 1946 7-208
Stone, Weldon
DEVIL TAKE A WHITTLER Rinehart New York 1948 3-252
Stone, William S.
THE SHIP OF FLAME Knopf New York 1945 5-k65
Stonier, G. W.
THE MEMOIRS OF A GHOST Grey Walls Press London 1947 3-109
Stormont, Lan
TAN MING Exposition Press New York 1955 471
Strong, L(eonard) A. G.
THE LAST ENEMY Knopf New York 1936 375
Strunsky, Simeon
SINBAD AND HIS FRIENDS Holt New York 1921 261
TWO CAME TO TOWN Dutton New York 1947 9-219
Stuart, W. J.
FORBIDDEN PLANET Farrar, Straus & Cudahy New York 1955 191
Sturgeon, Theodore (Pseud of Waldo, Edward Hamilton)
CAVIAR Ballantine New York 1955 16 7
THE DREAMING JEWELS Greenberg New York 1950 217
E PLURIBUS UNICORN Abelard Press New York 1953 271
MORE THAN HUMAN Farrar, Straus & Young New York 1953 233
A TOUCH OF STRANGE Doubleday Garden City, N. Y. 1958 262
A WAY HOME Funk & Wagnalls New York 1955 344
WITHOUT SORCERY Prime Press Philadelphia 1948 13-355
THUNDER AND ROSES (See ibid A Way Home)
Sturm, Justin
INDEX TO SYBIL Dorrance Philadelphia 1951 293
Suddaby, Donald
THE DEATH OF METAL Oxford Univ Press London 1952 192 Ill.
MASTERLESS SWORDS Laurie London 1947 251
PRISONERS OF SATURN Bodley Head London 1957 190
THE STAR RAIDERS Oxford Univ Press London 1950 232 Ill.
Sullivan, Alan
THE PASSING OF OUL-I-BUT AND OTHER STORIES Dent, London Dutton, New York 1913 302
"Summer Spring"
BACKWARDS AND FORWARDS Glaisher London 1894 286
Supervielle, Jules
ALONG THE ROAD TO BETHLEHEM Dutton New York 1933 65 Ill.
Sutphen, (William Gilbert) Van Tassel
IN JEOPARDY Harper New York 1922 300

Sutter, A. Oliver
THE SUPER-WOMAN Stockwell London nd 235
Sutton, Lee
VENUS BOY Lothrop New York 1955 182 Juv.
Swain, Dwight V.
CRY CHAOS Hamilton London nd 136
Swan, Thor
FURFOOZE Privately Published , Murray & Gee Hollywood 1939 170
Sydmort, Theodore
THE SACRED FIRE: A SUBJECT FROM THE RECORDS OF FATHER DENNISS Walls London 1926 184
Sykes, Claude W.
THE NINE POINTED STAR Hamilton London nd 7-249
Sylva, Carmen (Pseud of Queen Elizabeth of Roumania)
PILGRIM SORROW. A CYCLE OF TALES Holt New York 1884 262
Sylvester, John
MASTER OF THE WORLD Ward, Lock London 1949 224 Juv.
Syrett, Netta
THE HOUSE THAT WAS Rich & Cowan London nd 254
Szilard, Leo
THE VOICE OF THE DOLPHINS Simon & Schuster New York 1961 122
Tabori, Paul
SOLO Low, Marston London 1949 232
Tagore, Rabrindranath
THE HUNGRY STONES AND OTHER STORIES Macmillan New York 1916 271
Taine, John (Pseud of Bell, Eric Temple)
THE COSMIC GEOIDS Fantasy Pub Co Los Angeles 1949 9-179
THE CRYSTAL HORDE Fantasy Press Reading, Pa. 1952 9-284
G. O. G. 666 Fantasy Press Reading, Pa. 1954 251
SEEDS OF LIFE Fantasy Press Reading, Pa. 1951 9-255
THE SINGER Gorham Press Boston 1916 166
Talbot, Hake
RIM OF THE PIT Simon & Schuster New York 1944 187
Talbot, Marjorie
GHOSTS INCORPORATED Pageant Press New York 1957 218
Tallant, Robert
ANGEL IN THE WARDROBE Doubleday Garden City, N. Y. 1948 271
MRS. CANDY AND SATURDAY NIGHT Doubleday Garden City, N. Y. 1947 269
MRS. CANDY STRIKES IT RICH Doubleday Garden City, N. Y. 1954 253
Tandrup, Harold
JONAH AND THE VOICE Davies London 1937 336
Tane, Arthur
DICK-DOCK'S ADVENTURES Pageant Press New York 1955 80
Taney, Ahmet Raif
MYSTERIES OF THE COSMOS Exposition Press New York 1959 56
Tarcov, Oscar
BRAVO MY MONSTER Regnery Chicago 1953 133
Tate, Sylvia
NEVER BY CHANCE Harper New York 1947 282
Tatham, H. F. W.
THE FOOTPRINTS IN THE SNOW, AND OTHER TALES Macmillan London 1910 187
Taylor, Alfred Joseph
THE HAUNTED GRANGE Daily Post Hobart, Tasmania 191- 117

Taylor, Joseph
APPARITIONS: OR, THE MYSTERY OF GHOSTS, HOBGOBLINS, AND HAUNTED HOUSES
Lackington, Allen London 1814 222
Taylor, Malcolm
P. X. Houghton Mifflin Cambridge, Mass 1943 231
Taylor, Marie E.
THE MYSTERIOUS FIVE Christopher Boston 1930 147
Taylor, M. Imlay
THE HOUSE OF THE WIZARD McClurg Chicago 1900 340
Teague, Robert L.
THE CLIMATE OF CANDOR Pageant Press New York 1962 198
Temple, William F.
THE FOUR SIDED TRIANGLE Long London 1949 5-240
Tenn, William (Editor) (Pseud of Klass, Philip)
CHILDREN OF WONDER Simon & Schuster New York 1953 336
THE HUMAN ANGLE Ballantine New York 1956 152
OF ALL POSSIBLE WORLDS Ballantine New York 1955 159
Tennyson, Alfred
THE DEVIL AND THE LADY Macmillan New York 1930 58 Play 500 copy edition
Terrot, Charles
THE ANGEL WHO PAWNED HER HARP Dutton New York 1954 254
Thatcher, A. and Hogarth, C. J.
THE TRANSFORMATION OF UNCLE PARKER Allan London nd 203 Juv.
Thiuson, Ismar
THE DIOTHAS: OR, A FAR LOOK AHEAD Putnam New York 1883 308
Thomas, Eugene
THE DANCING DEAD Sears New York 1933 297
Thomas, Lowell (Jackson)
TALL STORIES Funk & Wagnalls New York and London 1931 245
Thompson, Ames (Editor)
STRANGE ADVENTURE STORIES FOR BOYS Cupples & Leon New York 1935 4 vol. in
Thompson, Francis
ABRAHAM'S WIFE Vanguard New York 1953 191
Thompson, Ruth Plumly
THE GIANT HORSE OF OZ Reilly & lee Chicago and New York 1928 17-283 Juv.
Thomson, H. Douglas and amsay, C. Clark (Editors)
THE HOLIDAY BOOK Odhams Press London 1934 1024
Thorndyke, Russell
THE MASTER OF THE MACABRE Rich & Cowan London 1946 7-192
Thorne, Guy
HARDER THAN STEEL Laurie London nd 217
Thurber, James
THE THIRTEEN CLOCKS Simon & Schuster New York 1950 344
Tilton, Dwight
ON SATAN'S MOUNT Clark Boston 1903 459
Timbs, John
SUPERNATURAL STORIES Warne London and New York nd (c. 1885) 465
Timperley, Rosemary
CHILD IN THE DARK Crowell New York 1956 256
Todd, Ruthven
SPACE CAT Scribner New York 1952 72 Juv.
SPACE CAT AND THE KITTENS Scribner New York 1958 94 Juv.
SPACE CAT VISITS VENUS Scribner New York 1955 87 Juv.

Tolkien, J(ohn) R(onald) R(euel)
FARMER GILES OF HAM Houghton Mifflin Boston 1950 79 Ill.
THE FELLOWSHIP OF THE RING Houghton Mifflin Boston 1954 423
THE RETURN OF THE KING Houghton Mifflin Boston 1956 416
THE TWO TOWERS Houghton Mifflin Boston 1955 352
Tombleson, J. B.
UNDER THE LABEL J. Heritage London 1934 7-288
Tomlinson, H. M.
OLD JUNK Milrose London 1918 228
Tonks, Angela
MIND OUT OF TIME Knopf New York 1959 266
Topelius, Z.
THE SURGEON'S STORIES--SECOND CYCLE, TIMES OF BATTLE AND REST Jansen, McClurg Chicago 1883 393
THE SURGEON'S STORIES--FIFTH CYCLE, TIMES OF LINNAEUS Jansen, McClurg Chicago 1884 394
THE SURGEON'S STORIES--SIXTH CYCLE, TIMES OF ALCHEMY Jansen, McClurg Chicago 1884 331
Torge, Miguel (Pseud of Rocha, Adolfo)
FARRAUSCO THE BLACKBIRD, AND OTHER STORIES FROM THE PORTUGESE Golden Griffin Books New York 1951 93
Toye, Nina
THE SHADOW OF FEAR Heinemann London 1921 243
Tracy, Louis
THE GLEAVE MYSTERY Clode New York 1926 318
Train, Arthur and Wood, Robert W.
THE MOON MAKER Krueger Hamburg, N. Y. 1958 84
Trantner, Nigel
ISLAND TWILIGHT Ward, Lock London 1947 191
Trevelan, G. E.
TRANCE BY APPOINTMENT Harrap London 1939 268
Trevena, John
FURZE THE CRUEL Rivers London 1907 391
Trevor, Elleston
THE IMMORTAL ERROR Swan London 1946 189
Troubetzkoy, Princess Paul
JONLYS THE WITCH Methuen London 1935 314
Trowbridge, John
THE ELECTRICAL BOY; OR, THE CAREER OF GREATMAN AND GREATTHINGS Roberts Boston 1891 390 Juv.
Trowbridge, John
THE RESOLUTE MR. PANSY Roberts Boston 1897 206 Juv.
True, John Preston
THE IRON STAR Little, Brown Boston 1899 146
Tsiolkovskii, Konstantine
BEYOND THE PLANET EARTH Pergamon Press New York 1960 190
Tubb, E(dward) C(harles)
ALIEN DUST Avalon New York 1957 223
Tucker, Prentiss
IN THE LAND OF THE LIVING DEAD Rosicrucian Fellowship Oceanside, Calif. 1921 168
Tucker, Wilson
THE CITY IN THE SEA Rinehart New York 1951 250

Tucker, Wilson (cont.)
THE LINCOLN HUNTERS Rinehart New York 1958 211
THE LONG LOUD SILENCE Rinehart New York 1952 217
THE SCIENCE FICTION SUBTREASURY Rinehart New York 1954 252
TIME BOMB Rinehart New York 1955 256
THE TIME MASTERS Rinehart New York 1953 249
WILD TALENT Rinehart New York 1954 250
Tugel, Ludwig
THE VISITANT Secker London 1931 351
Turgeniev, Ivan S.
DREAM TALES Heinemann London 1897 323
Turner, James
MY LIFE WITH BORLEY RECTORY Lane London 1950 9-272
Turner, Edgar
THE SUBMARINE GIRL Paul London 1909 336
Turney, Catherine
THE OTHER ONE Holt New York 1952 248
Tutuola, Amos
MY LIFE IN THE BUSH OF GHOSTS Grove Press New York 1955 174
THE PALM-WINE DRINKARD Grove Press New York 1953 130
Twain, Mark (Pseud of Clemens, Samuel L.)
REPORT FROM PARADISE Harper New York 1952 118
Tweed, Adelaide M.
THE EARTH ADVENTURES OF OLLIBOLLY THE MOON MAN Exposition Press New York 1952 86 Juv.
Tweedale, Violet
GHOSTS I HAVE SEEN Jenkins London nd 313
THE GREEN LADY Jenkins London 1921 312
Umbstaetter, H. D.
THE RED HOT DOLLAR AND OTHER STORIES FROM THE BLACK CAT Page Boston 1911 239
Untermeyer, Sonia
THE FAT OF THE CAT AND OTHER STORIES Harcourt, Brace New York 1925 283 Ill.
Upton, Smyth
THE LAST OF THE VAMPIRES Whereat Weston-Super-Mare, England 1845 76
Upward, Allen
THE YELLOW HAND Digby, Long London 1904 320
Urn, Althea
FIVE MILES FROM CANDIA Holt New York 1959 188
Usher, Wilfrid
THE GREAT HOLD-UP MYSTERY World Synd Cleveland and New York 1929 288
Vale, Rena M.
THE RED COURT Nelson Pub Co Chicago 1952 148
Valentiner, Brigitta
DREAMS AND TALES Greenwich New York 1958 159
Vance, Jack (Pseud of Kuttner, Henry)
BIG PLANET Avalon New York 1957 223
THE LANGUAGES OF PAO Avalon New York 1958 223
TO LIVE FOREVER Ballantine New York 1956 185
VANDALS OF THE VOID Winston Philadelphia 1953 222
Vandel, Jean Gaston
ENEMY BEYOND PLUTO Hector Kelly London 1954 192
Van der Elst, Violet
THE TORTURE CHAMBER AND OTHER STORIES Doge Press London 1937 237

Van Doren, Mark
MORTAL SUMMER Prairie Press Iowa City, Iowa 1954 65
NOBODY SAY A WORD Holt New York 1953 284
van Eeden, Frederik
THE QUEST Luce Boston 1907 519
Van Lhin, Erik
BATTLE ON MERCURY Winston Philadelphia 1953 207
POLICE YOUR PLANET Avalon New York 1956 224
Van Petten, Albert Archer
THE GREAT MAN'S LIFE: 1925 to 2000 A. C. Utopian Pub New York 1959 319
Van Stack, Henry
FLAMES OF DARKNESS Vantage Press New York 1954 443
van Vogt, A(lfred) E(lton)
AWAY AND BEYOND Pellegrini & Cudahy New York 1952 309
DESTINATION: UNIVERSE Pellegrini & Cudahy New York 1952 310
EMPIRE OF THE ATOM Shasta Chicago 1956 192
THE HOUSE THAT STOOD STILL Greenberg New York 1950 3-210
MASTERS OF TIME Fantasy Press Reading, Pa. 1950 11-227
THE MIND CAGE Simon & Schuster New York 1957 220
THE MIXED MEN Gnome Press New York 1952 223
THE VOYAGE OF THE SPACE BEAGLE Simon & Schuster New York 1950 256
THE WAR AGAINST THE RULL Simon & Schuster New York 1959 244
THE WEAPON SHOPS OF ISHER Greenberg New York 1951 3-231
THE WORLD OF A Simon & Schuster New York 1948 246
THE BEAST Doubleday Garden City, N. Y. 1963 207
van Vogt, A. E. and Hull, E. Mayne
OUT OF THE UNKNOWN Fantasy Pub Co Los Angeles 1948 2-141
Vare, Danielle
THE DOGE'S RING Methuen London 1949 212
Vasseur, John
TYPHON'S BEARD Doran New York 1927 9-261
Vaughan, Hilda
IRON AND GOLD Macmillan New York 1948 234
Vaughan, T. H.
THE EATER OF HEARTS S. Marshall London nd 344
Venning, Hugh
THE END Dismond & Stapleton Buffalo, N. Y. 1948 7-303
Vercors (Pseud of Bruller, Jean)
YOU SHALL KNOW THEM Little, Brown Boston 1953 249
BORDERLINE (See ibid You Shall Know Them)
Verne, Jules
ADVENTURES IN SOUTHERN AFRICA Hutchinson London nd 206
UNDERGROUND CITY, OR, THE CHILD OF THE CAVERN Porter & Coates Philadelphia 1873 246
Verner, Gerald (Editor)
"COME NOT, LUCIFER" Westhouse London 1945 267
PRINCE OF DARKNESS Westhouse London 1946 250
Vernon, Roger Lee
ROBOT HUNT Avalon New York 1959 224
Verrill, A(lpheus) Hyatt
THE BRIDGE OF LIGHT Fantasy Press Reading, Pa. 1950 248
Verron, Robert
THE POINT OF NO RETURN Wright & Brown London 1955 190

Very, Pierre
IN WHAT STRANGE LAND? Wingate London 1949 9-215
Vetch, Thomas
THE AMBER CITY Biggs & Dibenham London nd (c. 1888) 291
Vidal, Gore
MESSIAH Dutton New York 1954 254
Vilmorin, Louise de
THE RETURN OF ERICA Hamilton London 1949 5-112
Vincent, Joyce
THE CELESTIAL HAND; A SENSATIONAL STORY McCartie Sydney 1903 137
Vinton, Arthur Dudley
LOOKING FURTHER BACKWARD No publisher Albany, N. Y. 1890 236
Vivian, E(velyn) Charles
LADY OF THE TERRACES Hodder & Stoughton London 1925 9-219
STAR DUST Hutchinson London 1925 287
Voltaire, Francois Marie
THE PRINCESS OF BABYLON Bladon London 1768 348
THE WHITE BULL Murray London 1774 387
Vonnegut, Kurt Jr.
PLAYER PIANO Scribner New York 1952 295
THE SIRENS OF TITAN Houghton Mifflin Boston 1961 319
Voss, Richard
AMATA Neale Washington 1901 5-116
Voss-Bark, C.
SEALED ENTRANCE Chapman & Hall London 1947 5-224
Waer, Jack
17 AND BLACK Viking New York 1954 241
Wakefield, H(erbert) Russell
STRAYERS FROM SHEOL Arkham House Sauk City, Wisc. 1961 186
Walker, Danton (Editor)
SPOOKS DELUXE Watts New York 1956 188
Walker, Jerry
A DATE WITH DESTINY Cosmos New York 1949 288
MISSION ACCOMPLISHED Cosmos New York 1947 11-246
Wall, Mervyn
THE RETURN OF FURSEY Pilot Press London 1948 234
Wallace, F. L.
ADDRESS: CENTAURI Gnome Press New York 1955 220
Wallerstein, James
THE DEMON'S MIRROR Bellamy New York 1951 11-341
Wallis, George C.
THE CALL OF PETER GASKELL World's Work Kingswood, Surrey 1948 130
Wallop, Douglass
THE YEAR THE YANKEES LOST THE PENNANT Norton New York 1954 250
WHAT HAS FOUR WHEELS AND FLIES? Norton New York 1958 192
Walpole, Hugh
FOUR FANTASTIC TALES Macmillan London 1932 923
THE SILVER THORN Doubleday, Doran Garden City, N. Y. 1928 333
Walsh, Goodwin
VOICE OF THE MURDERER Putnam New York 1926 309
Walsh, James Morgan
THE HAND OF DOOM Hamilton London 1927 288

Walsh, Maurice
SON OF A TINKER Lippincott Philadelphia 1952 245
SONS OF THE SWORDMAKER Stokes New York 1939 297
Walsh, William Emmet
THE DOOM OF CONAIRE MOR Carrier New York and London 1929 340
Walter, William Grey
THE CURVE OF THE SNOWFLAKE Norton New York 1956 282
Walters, Hugh
BLAST-OFF AT 0300 Criterion New York 1958 187 Juv.
Walton, Bryce
SONS OF THE OCEAN DEEPS Winston Philadelphia 1952 216
Wanderer
WHIMS Gilbert & Rivington London 1889 305 Ill.
Wandrei, Donald
THE WEB OF EASTER ISLAND Arkham House Sauk City, Wisc. 1948 3-191
Ward, Lynd (Kendall)
GOD'S MAN Cape and Smith New York 1929 144
MADMAN'S DRUM Cape and Smith New York 1930 128
Warman, Eric
A MATTER OF LIFE AND DEATH World Film Pub London 1946 7-124
Warner, Anne W.
THE PANTHER, A TALE OF TEMPTATION Small, Maynard Boston 1908 91 Ill.
Warner, Sylvia Townsend
SUMMER WILL SHOW Viking New York 1936 421
Warren, B. C.
ARSAKETH - A TALE OF THE LURAY CAVERNS Lovell New York 1893 273
Warren, J. Russell
THIS INWARD HORROR Dutton New York 1948 256
THIS MORTAL COIL (See ibid This Inward Horror)
Warshawsky, Samuel Jesse
THE WOMAN OF DESTINY Messner New York 1936 256
Warwick, Anne (Pseud of Cranston, Mrs. Ruth)
THE SHREIKING HANDS AND OTHER MIXED SHORTS Gandy London nd 183
Water, Silas
THE MAN WITH ABSOLUTE MOTION Rich & Cowan London 195? 206
Watson, E. L. Grant
MOONLIGHT IN UR Douglas London 1932 286
Watson, Frederick
CREDULITY ISLAND Jenkins London 1916 243
Watson, Golbert
THE AMAZING GUEST Cassell London 1925 329
Watson, H. B. Marriot
THE BIG FISH Little, Brown Boston 1912 319
MARSHUNA Longmans, Green London 1888 298
Watts-Dunton, Theodore
AYLWIN Dodd, Mead New York 1899 460
Waugh, Evelyn
LOVE AMONG THE RUINS Chapman & Hall London 1953 52
Webb, Ripley (Major)
FULL CYCLE Rider London nd 176
Webster, Elizabeth Charlotte
CEREMONY OF INNOCENCE Harcourt, Brace New York 1949 248

Webster, F. A. M.
THE BLACK SHADOW Moffat, Yard New York 1923 342
STAR LADY Hutchinson London nd 288
THE CURSE OF THE LION United Press Ltd London 1922 11-282
THE LAND OF FORGOTTEN WOMEN Skeffington London 1950 256
LORD OF THE LEOPARDS Hutchinson London nd 256
LOST CITY OF LIGHT Warne London 1934 288 Ill.
THE MAN WHO KNEW Allan London 1935 256
MUBENDI GIRL Hutchinson London nd 304
Webster, Henry Mitchell
THE QUARTZ EYE Bobbs-Merrill Indianapolis 1928 321
Weinbaum Stanley G(rauman)
THE BLACK FLAME Fantasy Press Reading, Pa. 1948 9-240
THE DARK OTHER Fantasy Pub Co Los Angeles 1950 9-256
A MARTIAN ODYSSEY Fantasy Press Reading, Pa. 1949 289
THE RED PERI Fantasy Press Reading, Pa. 1952 9-270
Welborne, M. W.
SOME FANTASIES OF FATE Digby, Long London 1899 3-280
A Well Known Author
THE MASTER SINNER Long London 1901 182
Wellard, James H(oward)
NIGHT IN BABYLON St. Martin's Press New York 1953 302
Wellman, Manly Wade
THE DARK DESTROYERS Avalon New York 1959 224
GIANTS FROM ETERNITY Avalon New York 1959 223
ISLAND IN THE SKY Avalon New York 1961 223
TWICE IN TIME Avalon New York 1957 222
Wellman, Paul (Iselin)
THE FIERY FLOWER Doubleday Garden City, N. Y. 1959 285
Wells, Basil
DOORWAYS TO SPACE Fantasy Pub Co Los Angeles 1951 11-206
PLANETS OF ADVENTURE Fantasy Pub Co Los Angeles 1949 11-280
Wells, George
THE WEIRD IDOL OF PENANG TOWERS Macdonald London 1928 274
West, Anthony
ANOTHER KIND Houghton Mifflin Boston 1952 351
THE VINTAGE Houghton Mifflin Boston 1950 310
West, Wallace
THE BIRD OF TIME Gnome Press Hicksville, N. Y. 1959 256
LORDS OF ATLANTIS Avalon New York 1960 220
THE MEMORY BANK Avalon New York 1961 222
OUTPOSTS IN SPACE Avalon New York 1962 220
Westerman, John F. C.
THE LOOTED GOLD Ward, Lock London 1932 256 Ill. Juv.
THE STOLEN MONOPLANE Oxford Univ Press London 1936 255 Juv.
Westerman, Percy F.
THE FLYING SUBMARINE Dean London nd 248
THE WAR OF THE WIRELESS WAVES Oxford Univ Press London 1926 287 Ill. Juv
Weston, George
QUEEN OF THE WORLD Dodd, Mead New York 1923 259
Weston, Jessie L. (Translator)
FOUR LAIS OF MARIE DE FRANCE David Nutt London 1910 5-101
Whatley, Joseph L.
PURGATORY OF THE CONQUERED Greenwich New York 1957 112

Wheatley, Dennis
THE HAUNTING OF TOBY JUG Hutchinson London 1948 292
THE MAN WHO MISSED THE WAR Hutchinson London 1945 288
THE SATANIST Hutchinson London 1960 448
THE KA OF GIFFORD HOLARY Hutchinson London 1958 384
THE STAR OF ILL OMEN Hutchinson London 1952 320
TO THE DEVIL: A DAUGHTER Hutchinson London 1953 384
UNCHARTED SEAS Hutchinson London nd 190
THE BLACK MAGIC OMNIBUS (Reprints of The Devil Rides Out, Strange Conflict, To the Devil: A Daughter)
Wheeler, Francis
UNHOLY ALLIANCE Skeffington London 1951 240
Wherry, Edith
THE LAMP STILL BURNS Vantage Press New York 1955 355
White, Edward Lucas
ANDIVIUS HEDULIS Dutton New York 1921 597
White, F(red) M(errick)
THE CARDINAL MOTH Ward, Lock London 1905 291
THE FIVE KNOTS Little, Brown Boston 1908 340
THE SLAVE OF SILENCE Little, Brown Boston 1906 318
White, T(erence H(anbury)
EARTH STOPPED Collins London 1934 252
GONE TO GROUND Collins London 1935 267
THE MASTER Putnam New York 1957 256
THE ONCE AND FUTURE KING (Reprints of Sword in the Stone, The Ill-Made Knight, The Witch in the Wood)
Whitehead, A. E.
DEALINGS WITH THE DEAD Redway London 1898 220
Whiteside, Edward
A WARNING FROM MARS Interplanetary Pub New York 1948 9-79
Wibberly, Leonard
McGILLICUDDY McGOTHAM Little, Brown Boston 1956 111
THE MOUSE THAT ROARED Little, Brown Boston 1955 279
MRS. SEARWOOD'S SECRET WEAPON Little, Brown Boston 1954 294
TAKE ME TO YOUR PRESIDENT Putnam New York 1957 186
Wicker, Tom
THE DEVIL MUST Harper New York 1957 280
Widney, Stanley A.
ELEVATOR TO THE MOON Follett New York 1955 128 Juv.
Wilcox, F. M.
LIVING ON William-Frederick Press New York 1952 52
Wilde, Oscar
NOVELS & TALES Nichols New York 1915 372
Wildig, Laura
PANDORA'S SHOCKS Hurst & Blackett London 1927 288
Wilding, Philip
SHADOW OVER THE EARTH Philosophical Lib New York 1956 160
SPACEFLIGHT VENUS Hennel Locke London 1954 190
Wiley, Ray H.
ON THE TRAIL OF 1960 Exposition Press New York 1950 156
Wilkins, (Rev.) John
THE MATHEMATICAL AND PHILOSOPHICAL WORKS OF JOHN WILKINS Whittingham London 1802 2 vol. 261, 260

Wilkins (Freeman), Mary E.
A HUMBLE ROMANCE & OTHER STORIES Harper New York 1887 436
THE POT OF GOLD AND OTHER STORIES Lothrop Boston 1892 324 Ill.

Wilkins, Vaughan
CITY OF FROZEN FIRE Cape London 1950 381
FANFARE FOR A WITCH Macmillan New York 1954 270
VALLEY BEYOND TIME St. Martin's Press New York 1955 304

Williams, Alfred Rowberry
DREAMS FROM THE PAST Stockwell London nd 191

Williams, Francis
IT HAPPENED TOMORROW Abelard Press New York 1952 217
THE RICHARDSON STORY Heinemann London 1951 209

Williams, Geoffrey
THE MAGICIANS OF CHARNO Murray London 1913 304 Ill. Juv.

Williams, Islwyn
DANGEROUS WATERS Gryphon London 1952 224
NEWBURY IN ORM Gryphon London 1952 191

Williams, Jay
THE WITCHES Random New York 1957 339

Williams, Robert Moore
WALK UP THE SKY Avalon New York 1962 224

Williams, Speedy
JOURNEY THROUGH SPACE Exposition Press New York 1958 108

Williamson, Jack
THE COMETEERS Fantasy Press Reading, Pa. 1951 310
DARKER THAN YOU THINK Fantasy Press Reading, Pa. 1948 310
DRAGON'S ISLAND Simon & Schuster New York 1951 246
THE HUMANOIDS Simon & Schuster New York 1949 239
THE LEGION OF TIME Fantasy Press Reading, Pa. 1952 9-242

Williamson, Jack and Gunn, James E(dward)
STAR BRIDGE Gnome Press New York 1955 221

Williamson, Thames (Ross)
THE MAN WHO CANNOT DIE Small, Maynard Boston 1926 406
UNDER THE LINDEN TREE Doubleday, Doran Garden City, N. Y. 1935 290

Wilson,
WILSON'S TALES OF THE BORDERS Croome London nd (c. 1905) 224

Wilson, Angus (Editor)
A. D. 2500 Heinemann London 1955 241

Wilson, Henry Lovejoy
OF LUNAR KINGDOMS Caxton Caldwell, Idaho 1937 120

Wilson, Richard
THE GIRLS FROM PLANET 5 Ballantine New York 1955 184

Winch, E.
THE MOUNTAIN OF GOLD Hurst & Blackett London nd 288

Wingfield-Stratford, Barbara
THE AMAZING EPILOGUE; OR, THE FURTHER DAY AND NIGHT SCENES OF JERRY HAWTHORN Lovatt, Dickson London 1933 342

Winslow, Horatio and Quirk, Leslie
INTO THIN AIR Gollancz London 1928 288

Winslow, Thyra Samter (Pseud of Hyde (Mrs.) Nelson Waldorf)
THE SEX WITHOUT SENTIMENT Abelard-Schuman New York 1954 312

Winsor, Kathleen
THE LOVERS Appleton-Century-Crofts New York 1952 362

Winterbotham, R. R.
JOYCE OF THE SECRET SQUADRON Whitman Racine, Wisc. 1942 11-251 Juv.
Winterbotham, Russ
THE MEN FROM ARCTURUS Avalon New York 1963 192
THE SPACE EGG Avalon New York 1958 224
Winwar, Frances (Pseud of Grebanier, Mrs. B. D. N.)
THE SAINT AND THE DEVIL Harper New York 1948 331
Wittels, Fritz
THE JEWELER OF BAGDAD Cape London 1927 192
Wolfe, Bernard
LIMBO Random New York 1952 438
Wolff, Carl Felix
THE PALE MOUNTAINS Minton, Balch New York 1927 204 Juv.
Wollheim, Donald A.
THE SECRET OF SATURN'S RINGS Winston Philadelphia 1954 218
THE SECRET OF THE MARTIAN MOONS Winston Philadelphia 1955 217
SECRET OF THE NINTH PLANET Winston Philadelphia 1959 203
Wollheim, Donald A. (Editor)
EVERY BOY'S BOOK OF SCIENCE FICTION Fell New York 1951 254 Juv.
FLIGHT INTO SPACE Fell New York 1950 251
PRIZE SCIENCE FICTION McBride New York 1953 230
TERROR IN THE MODERN VEIN Hanover House Garden City, N. Y. 1955 315
Woodforde, Christopher
A PAD IN THE STRAW Dent London 1952 235
Woodiwiss, John C.
SMUGGLER'S RIDE Quality Press London 1946 9-246
Woods, Margaret L.
THE INVADER Chapman & Dodd London nd 252
Worts, George F.
PETER THE BRAZEN Lippincott Philadelphia 1919 379
Wray, Roger
THE DWELLER IN THE HALF-LIGHT Odhams Press London nd 320
Wright, Kenneth
MYSTERIOUS PLANET Winston Philadelphia 1953 209
Wright, R. H.
THE OUTER DARKNESS Greening London 1906 312
Wright, S(ydney) Fowler
THE BELL STREET MURDERS Macauley New York 1931 256
SPIDER'S WAR Abelard Press New York 1954 256
THE THRONE OF SATURN Arkham House Sauk City, Wisc. 1950 3-186
Wright, Thomas
THE BLUE FIREDRAKE Simpkin, Marshall, Hamilton, Kent London 1892 293
Wu Cheng-En
MONKEY Allen & Unwin London 1942 9-305
Wyatt, Horace
MALICE IN KULTURLAND Car Illust. London 1914 80
Wyckoff, Nicholas
THE BRAINTREE MISSION Macmillan New York 1957 191
Wylie, Philip
THE ANSWER Rinehart New York 1955 63
THE DISAPPEARANCE Rinehart New York 1951 405
FINLEY WREN Knopf New York 1934 192
TOMORROW Rinehart New York 1954 372

Wylwynne, Kythe
THE DREAM-WOMAN Unwin London 1901 343
Wyman, Justus E(dwi) and Surendorf, Charles
Mister Pimney Ackerman New York 1945 20 Ill.
Wyndham, John (Pseud of Harris, John Beynon)
THE DAY OF THE TRIFFIDS Joseph London 1951 7-302
THE MIDWICH CUCKOOS Ballantine New York 1957 247
THE KRAKEN WAKES (See ibid Out of the Deeps)
OUT OF THE DEEPS Ballantine New York 1953 182
RE-BIRTH Ballantino New York 1955 185
THE SEEDS OF TIME Joseph London 1957 272
Wynne, Madeline Yale
AN ANCESTRAL INVASION AND OTHER STORIES Country Life Press Garden City, N. Y. 1920 3-164
Yefremov, I. (See also Efremov, I.)
STORIES Foreign Languages Pub House Moscow 1954 7-260
Yorke, Jacqueline
BRIDES OF THE DEVIL Comyne London nd 192
Yorke, Preston
SPACE-TIME TASK FORCE Kelly London 1953 192
Youd, Christopher
THE WINTER SWAN Dobson London 1949 7-268
Young, Briant Sayre
THE FOUNDATION Maribeck Press Los Angeles 1934 363 100 copy edition
Young, Ella
CELTIC WONDER TALES RETOLD BY ELLA YOUNG Maunsel Dublin 1910 201
Young, Francis Brett
SEA HORSES Knopf New York 1925 321
Younghusband, (Sir) Francis
THE COMING COUNTRY Murray London 1928 309
Yulee, Wickliffe
OVERSHADOWED Rider London 1920 384
Zagat, Arthur Leo
SEVEN OUT OF TIME Fantasy Press Reading, Pa. 1949 240
Zangwill, Israel
THE KING OF SCHNORRERS Shoe String Press Hambden, Conn 1953 189
THE PREMIER AND THE PAINTER, A FANTASY Heinemann London 1888 502
Zanuck, Darryl F(rancis) and de Haas, Arline
NOAH'S ARK Grosset & Dunlap New York 1928 276
Zarem, Lewis
THE GREEN MAN FROM SPACE Dutton New York 1955 160 Juv.
Zuber, Stanley
THE GOLDEN PROMISE Pageant Press New York 1955 127
Biggle, Lloyd
ALL THE COLORS OF DARKNESS Doubleday Garden City, N. Y. 1963 210
Burgess, Anthony
THE WANTING SEED Norton New York 1963 285
Cross, John Keir (Editor)
BEST HORROR STORIES Faber & Faber London 1958 280

AB THE CAVEMAN	Nida, William Lewis
THE ABANDONED	Gallico, Paul
THE ABOMINABLE TWILIGHT	Campbell, Reginald
THE ABOMINATIONS OF YONDO	Smith, Clark Ashton
ABRAHAM'S WIFE	Thompson, Francis
THE ABYSS OF WONDERS	Sheehan, Perley Poore
ACCOUNT OF A RACE OF HUMAN BEINGS WITH TAILS	Anonymous
ACQUAINTED WITH THE NIGHT	Price, Nancy
ACROSS THE SEA OF STARS	Clarke, Arthur C.
ACROSS TIME	Grinnell, David
A. D. 2018	Gibson, Rev. Edmund H.
A. D. 2500	Wilson, Angus
ADDRESS: CENTAURI	Wallace, F. L.
ADDRESS UNKNOWN	Phillpotts, Eden
ADOLF IN BLUNDERLAND	Dyrenforth, James and Kester Max
THE ADVENTURE OF THE BLUE ROOM	Fowler, Sydney
ADVENTURES IN SOUTHERN AFRICA	Verne, Jules
ADVENTURES IN TOMORROW	Crossen, Kendall Foster
ADVENTURES OF HALEK	Nicholson, John Henry
THE ADVENTURES OF HATIM TAI	Forbes, Duncan
THE ADVENTURES OF JOHN JOHNS	Carrel, Frederic
THE ADVENTURES OF SEVEN FOUR FOOTED FORESTERS	Greenwood, James
THE ADVENTURES OF ZELOIDE AND AMANZARIFDINE	Moncrief, Augustin-Paradis de
ADVENTURES WITH PHANTOMS	Hopkins, R. Thurston
Advise AND CONSENT	Drury, Allen
A FOR ANDROMEDA	Hoyle, Fred and Elliot, John
AFRICAN FOLK TALES	Lone, Yoti
AFRICAN GENESIS	Frobenius, Leo and Fox, Douglas C.
THE AFTER DEATH	Brandon, Henry
AFTER THE RAIN	Bowen, John
AFTER THE VERDICT	Hichens, Robert S.
AFTER 12,000 YEARS	Coblentz, Stanton A.
AGAINST THE FALL OF NIGHT	Clarke, Arthur C.
THE AGE OF THE TAIL	Smith, H. Allen
THE AGE OLD KINGDOM	(Sinbad)
AGENT OF VEGA	Schmitz, James H.
AHEAD OF TIME	Kuttner, Henry
AICHA THE MAURESQUE	Knights, D. A.
THE AIR BATTLE, A VISION OF THE FUTURE	Lang, Hermann
THE AIR KILLER	Corbett, James
THE AIR KING'S TREASURE	Graham-White, Claude and Harper, Harry
THE AIR PILOT	Parrish, Randall
THE AIRMEN OF SHEBA'S TEMPLE	Dempster, Guy
THE ALABASTER HAND	Munby, A. N. L.
ALADORE	Newbolt, Henry
ALAS, BABYLON	Frank, Pat
ALAS! THAT GREAT CITY	Ashton, Francis
ALEXANDER THE GOD	Payne, Robert
ALFRED HITCHCOCK PRESENTS: STORIES THEY WOULDN'T LET ME DO ON T V	Hitchcock, Alfred

ALICE IN ORCHESTRALIA	La Prade, Ernest
ALICE IN THE DELIGHTED STATES	Hope, Edward
ALICIA AND THE TWILIGHT	Sackville, Margaret
ALIEN DUST	Rubb, E. C.
ALIEN MINDS	Evans, E. E.
ALIEN PLANET	Pratt, Fletcher
ALIEN WORLD	Lukens, Adam
ALIENS FROM SPACE	Osborne, David
ALL ABOUT H. HATTERR	Desani, G. V.
ALL ABOUT THE FUTURE	Greenberg, Martin
ALL MEN ARE MORTAL	de Beauvoir, Simone
ALL THE COLORS OF DARKNESS	Biggle, Lloyd
THE ALLIGATOR LAMP	Kellogg, John
ALLISTO--A ROMANCE	Emersie, John
ALMONI: A COMPANION VOLUME TO HALEK	Nicholson, John Henry
ALONG THE ROAD TO BETHLEHEM	Supervielle, Jules
ALPHA AND OMEGA	Bell, Neil
THE ALTERED EGO	Sohl, Jerry
ALTERNATING CURRENTS	Pohl, Frederick
ALWAYS COMES EVENING	Howard, Robert E.
AMATA	Voss, Richard
AMATEUR GHOST STORIES	Fry, H. R.
THE AMAZING EPILOGUE	Wingfield-Stratford, Barbara
THE AMAZING GUEST	Watson, Gilbert
THE AMAZING MR. LUTTERWORTH	Leslie, Desmond
THE AMAZON STRIKES AGAIN	Fearn, John Russell
THE AMAZON'S DIAMOND QUEST	Fearn, John Russell
THE AMBER CITY	Vetch, Thomas
THE AMERICAN FAUST	Paulton, Edward
THE AMETHYST CROSS	Hume, Fergus
AMONG THE FREAKS	Alden, W. L.
AMOROUS GHOST	Bessand-Massenet, Pierre
AMOS MEAKIN'S GHOST	Stine, W. M.
THE AMPHIBIOUS VOYAGE	Gillmore, Parker
AN ANCESTRAL INVASION	Wynne, Madeline Yale
ANANSI, THE SPIDER MAN	Sherlock, Philip M.
AND SO ENDS THE WORLD	Pape, Richard
AND SO FOREVER	Dunn, Gertrude
....AND SOME WERE HUMAN	del Rey, Lester
AND THEN YOU CAME	Bridge, Ann
AND THUS HE CAME	Brady, Cyrus Townsend
AND WARS SHALL CEASE	Marsh, Carl
ANDIVIUS HEDULIS	White, Edward Lucas
ANGEL IN THE WARDROBE	Tallant, Robert
THE ANGEL OF THE EARTHQUAKE	Morton, Frank
THE ANGEL WHO PAWNED HER HARP	Terrot, Charles
ANGELS AND BEASTS	Saurat, Denis
ANGELS AND SPACESHIPS	Brown, Fredric
ANGELS WEEP	Leslie, Desmond
ANGILIN: A VENITE KING	Hallen, A. L.
ANNO DOMINI 2000	Coury, Phil
ANONA OF THE MOUND BUILDERS	Marple, J. Clarence and Dennis, Albert N.

ANOTHER KIND	Oliver, Chad
ANOTHER KIND	West, Anthony
ANOTHER SPACE, ANOTHER TIME	Campbell, H. J.
THE ANSWER	Wylie, Philip
THE ANT MEN	North, Eric
THE ANTHEM SPRINTERS	Bradbury, Ray
ANTING-ANTING STORIES	Kayme, Sargent
ANTRO: THE LIFE GIVER	Deegan, John Jo.
APE AND ESSENCE	Huxley, Aldous
THE APE MAN	Johnson, Henry T.
THE APE MAN OF A. J. O.	Ogilvy, Arthur James
APPARITIONS	Taylor, Joseph
THE ARCHEOLOGIST AND THE PRINCESS	Leight, Walter W.
ARCTIC AIR TERROR	Jackson, G. Gibbard
ARK OF VENUS	Clason, Clyde B.
THE ARM OF MRS. EGAN	Harvey, William Fryer
ARMAGEDDON 2419 A. D.	Nowlan, Philip Francis
ARMED WITH MADNESS	Butts, Mary
ARM'S LENGTH	Metcalfe, John
AROUND THE FIRE: STORIES OF BEGINNINGS	Burr, Hanford M.
THE ARRIVAL OF MASTER JINKS	Chappell, Connery
AS IT WAS IN THE BEGINNING	Deamer, Dulcie
AS THE CLOCK STRUCK TWENTY	S. M. C.
Arsareth - A TALE OF THE LURAY CAVERNS	Warren, B. C.
THE ASCENSION OF MR. JUDSON	Hunter, N. C.
ASSIGNMENT IN ETERNITY	Heinlein, Robert A.
ASSIGNMENT IN TOMORROW	Pohl, Frederik
ASTERA, THE PLANET THAT COMMITTED SUICIDE	Johnson, Ray W.
THE ASTOUNDING DR. YELL	Knight, L. A.
THE ASTOUNDING SCIENCE FICTION ANTHOLOGY	Campbell, John W.
ASTRO BUBBLES	Field, Marlo
THE ASTROLOGER	Hyams, Edward S.
AT CLOSE OF EVE	Scott, Jeremy
AT THE BACK OF THE NORTH WIND	MacDonald, George
AT THE QUEEN'S MERCY	Blodgett, Mabel Fuller
ATLAS SHRUGGED	Rand, Ayn
ATOM AT SPITHEAD	Divine, David
ATOMIC VALLEY	Duff, Douglas V.
ATOMS IN ACTION	Sheldon, Roy
ATTA	Bellamy, Francis Rufus
ATTACK FROM ATLANTIS	del Rey, Lester
THE ATTACK ON THE FARM	Arnold, Andrew W.
AUCTIONING OF MARY ANGEL	Dawson, Conningsby
AURIFONDA; OR, ADVENTURES IN THE GOLD REGIONS	Anonymous
AURILLY, THE VIRGIN ISLE	Garrett, Charles W.
THE AUTOBIOGRAPHY OF A SCIENTIST	Manure, Doctor Henry
AWAY AND BEYOND	van Vogt, A. E.
AYLWIN	Watts-Dunton, Theodore
AZTIRC	Crawford, Merwin Richard
BACK TO NATURE	Alexander, R. W.
BACK TO BAAL	Peskett, S. John
BACK TO THE FUTURE	Staniland, Meaburn

BACKWARDS AND FORWARDS	"Summer Spring"
THE BALANCE OF FEAR	Matheson, Hugh
THE BALL OF THE VEGETABLES	Eytinge, Margaret
BALLROOM OF THE SKIES	MacDonald, John D.
BANDERSNATCH	Ryves, T. E.
BANTAN AND THE ISLAND GODDESS	Gardner, Maurice B.
BANTAN DEFIANT	Gardner, Maurice B.
BANTAN FEARLESS	Gardner, Maurice B.
BANTAN--GODLIKE ISLANDER	Gardner, Maurice B.
BANTAN INCREDIBLE	Gardner, Maurice B.
BANTAN PRIMEVAL	Gardner, Maurice B.
BANTAN VALIANT	Gardner, Maurice B.
BANTAN'S ISLAND PERIL	Gardner, Maurice B.
BARCALI THE MUTINEER	Lampen, Charles Dudley
BASIL NETHERBY	Benson, A. C.
BATTLE FOR THE STARS	Hamilton, Edmond
BATTLE ON MERCURY	Van Lhin, Erik
BEACHHEADS IN SPACE	Derleth, August W.
THE BEAR KING	Greenwood, James
THE BEAST	Houghton, Claude
THE BEAST	van Vogt, A. E.
THE BEAST MASTER	Norton, Andre
BEAST OR MAN	M'Guire, Sean
THE BEAUTIFUL BEQUEST	Hatch, Eric
BEETLE'S CAREER	Fraser, Ronald
THE BEGINNING IS THE END	Mayne, Melinda
BELIEVER'S WORLD	Lowndes, Robert
THE BELL STREET MURDERS	Wright, S. Fowler
THE BELOVED OF SENNACHERIB	De Loucanton, Baroness Alexandra
BELSHAZAR	David William Stearns
BEN BEOR	Bien, H. M.
BENIGHTED	Priestley, J. B.
BENJAMIN FRANKLIN CALLS ON THE PRESIDENT	Mayer, John de
BEST AMERICAN SHORT STORIES OF 1943	Foley, Martha
BEST BLACK MAGIC STORIES	Cross, John Keir
THE BEST FROM FANTASY AND SCIENCE FICTION	Boucher, Anthony and McComas, J. Franc
THE BEST FROM F & S F: SECOND SERIES	Boucher, Anthony and McComas, J. Franci
THE BEST FROM F & S F: THIRD SERIES	Boucher, Anthony and McComas, J. Franci
THE BEST FROM F & S F: FOURTH SERIES	Boucher, Anthony
THE BEST FROM F & S F: FIFTH SERIES	Boucher, Anthony
THE BEST FROM F & S F: SIXTH SERIES	Boucher, Anthony
THE BEST FROM F & S F: SEVENTH SERIES	Boucher, Anthony
THE BEST FROM F & S F: EIGHTH SERIES	Boucher, Anthony
THE BEST FROM F & S F: NINTH SERIES	Mills, Robert P.
THE BEST FROM F & S F: TENTH SERIES	Mills, Robert P.
THE BEST FROM F & S F: ELEVENTH SERIES	Mills, Robert P.
THE BEST FROM STARTLING STORIES	Mines, Samuel
BEST HORROR STORIES	Cross, John Keir
BEST S F. SCIENCE FICTION STORIES	Crispin, Edmund
BEST S F TWO	Crispin, Edmund
BEST S F THREE	Crispin, Edmund
THE BEST SCIENCE FICTION STORIES: 1949	Bleiler, Everett F. and Dikty, Theodore

THE BEST SCIENCE FICTION STORIES: 1950	Bleiler, Everett F. and Dikty, Theodore
THE BEST SCIENCE FICTION STORIES: 1951	Bleiler and Dikty
THE BEST SCIENCE FICTION STORIES: 1952	Bleiler and Dikty
THE BEST SCIENCE FICTION STORIES: 1953	Bleiler and Dikty
THE BEST SCIENCE FICTION STORIES: 1954	Bleiler and Dikty
THE BEST S F STORIES AND NOVELS: 1955	Dikty, Theodore E.
THE BEST S F STORIES AND NOVELS: 9th SERIES	Dikty, T. E.
THE BEST SHORT STORIES OF M P SHIEL	Shiel, M. P.
THE BEST STORIES OF W D STEELE	Steele, Wilbur Daniel
BETWEEN PLANETS	Heinlein, Robert A.
BETWEEN THE DARK AND THE DAYLIGHT	Marsh, Richard
BEYOND DEATH'S CURTAIN	Harper, Constance Ward
BEYOND EDEN	Duncan, David
BEYOND HUMAN KEN	Merrill, Judith A.
BEYOND INFINITY	Carr, Robert Spencer
BEYOND THE BARRIERS OF SPACE AND TIME	Merrill, Judith
BEYOND THE DESERT	Noyes, Alfred
BEYOND THE FOURTH DOOR	Deegan, Jon J.
BEYOND THE HUNGRY COUNTRY	Stinetorf, Louise A.
BEYOND THE ICE	Murphy, George Read
BEYOND THE PLANET EARTH	Tsiolkovskii, Konstantine
BEYOND THE SEAS	Stamper, W. J.
BEYOND THE SUNRISE	Anonymous
BEYOND THE VISIBLE	Campbell, J. H.
BEYOND THESE SUNS	Le Page, Rand
BEYOND THIRTY and THE MAN-EATER	Burroughs, Edgar Rice
BEYOND THIS DAY	Matthews, E. Paul
BEYOND THIS HORIZON	Heinlein, Robert A.
BEYOND TIME AND SPACE	Derleth, August W.
THE BIG BALL OF WAX	Mead, Shepherd
THE BIG BOOK OF SCIENCE FICTION	Conklin, Groff
THE BIG EYE	Ehrlich, Max
THE BIG FISH	Watson, H. B. Marriot
IG PLANET	Vance, Jack
IO-MUTON	Elliott, Lee
HE BIRD OF TIME	West, Wallace
HE BIRD'S NEST	Jackson, Shirley
HE BISHOP OF HELL	Bowen, Marjorie
BIT OF ATLANTIS	Erskine, Douglas
HE BLACK BALL	Pierson, Ernest de Lancey
HE BLACK CLOUD	Hoyle, Fred
HE BLACK FLAME	Weinbaum, Stanley G.
HE BLACK FOX	Heard, Gerald
LACK IS A MAN	Roskolenko, Harry
HE BLACK MOLE	Rochester, George E.
E BLACK MOUNTAIN	Hillgarth, Alan
E BLACK ROBE	Morton, Guy
E BLACK SHADOW	Webster, F. A. M.
E BLACK STAR PASSES	Campbell, John W.
ACK TREASURE	Brown, Vinson
E BLACK WHEEL	Merritt, A. and Bok, Hannes
ACK, WHITE AND BRINDLED	Phillpotts, Eden

BLACKATON'S BOY	Rock, Wyndan
BLAST-OFF AT 0300	Walters, Hugh
BLEEDING FROM THE ROMAN	Romilly, Eric
BLESSING UNBOUNDED	Blamires, Harry
THE BLIND MEN AND THE DEVIL	Phineas
THE BLIND SPOT	Hall, Austin and Flint, Homer Eon
THE BLONDE GODDESS	Richards, R. P. J.
BLOOD	Ewers, Hanns Heinz
THE BLOOD OF A POET	Cocteau, Jean
BLOOD OF THE VAMPIRE	Marryat, Florence
THE BLOOD RUSHED TO MY POCKETS	Foa, George
BLOODSTOCK, AND OTHER STORIES	Irwin, Margaret E.
BLUE ASP	Le Page, and
THE BLUE BARBARIANS	Coblentz, Stanton A.
BLUE CORDON	Carter, Dee
THE BLUE FIREDRAKE	Wright, Thomas
THE BLUE HIGHWAY	Owen, Anna and Frank
THE BLUE MOON	Housman, Laurence
THE BLUE RIBBON	Irish, William
THE BLUE SHIRTS	J. J. J.
THE BLUE TALISMAN	Hume, Fergus
BODYGUARD, AND FOUR OTHER SHORT NOVELS	Gold, H. L.
THE BODY'S GUEST	MacLeod, Angus
BOGIE TALES OF EAST ANGLIA	James, M. H.
THE BOOK OF DREAMS AND GHOSTS	Lang, Andrew
THE BOOK OF JOANNA	Borodin, George
A BOOK OF MODERN GHOSTS	Asquith, Cynthia
THE BOOK OF THE GOLDEN KEY	Amos, Ruse and Hayter, Flora
BOOK OF THE THREE DRAGONS	Morris, Kenneth
THE BOOK OF WERE-WOLVES	Baring-Gould, S.
THE BOOKS OF THE EMPEROR WU TI	Meckauer, Walter
BOOMERANG	Simpson, Helen de Guery
BORDERLINE	Crawshay-Williams, Eliot
BORN AGAIN	Lawson, Alfred William
BORN IN CAPTIVITY	Berry, Bryan
BORN LEADER	McIntosh, J. T.
BORN OF MAN AND WOMAN	Matheson, ichard
BOTH SIDES OF THE VEIL	Marsh, Richard
THE BOW-LEGGED GHOST AND OTHER STORIES	Mead, Leon
THE BOWL OF NIGHT	Liston, Edward
THE BOY WHO SAW TOMORROW	Niall, Ian
THE BRAIN	Harrison, Michael
BRAIN ULTIMATE	Campbbll, H. J.
BRAINS FOR JANES	Mark, Ronald and Stover, A.
THE BRAINTREE MISSION	Wyckoff, Nicholas
BRAVO, MY MONSTER	Tarcov, Oscar
BREAKING UP; OR, THE BIRTH AND DEATH OF THE EARTH	Richards, Lysander Salmon
BREAKTHROUGH	Iggulden, John
BRIDE OF THE KALAHARI	Rose, F. Horace
BRIDES OF THE DEVIL	Yorke, Jacqueline
THE BRIDGE OF DISTANCES	Scrymsour, Ella
THE BRIDGE OF LIGHT	Verrill, A. Hyatt

RIDGE OVER DARK GODS	Morrish, Furze
RIDGE TO YESTERDAY	Arch, E. L.
RIEF CANDLES	Coles, Manning
RIGHT MORROW	Neville, Derek
HE BRIGHT PHOENIX	Mead, Harold
HE BRIGHTON MONSTER	Kersh, Gerald
RIMSTONE IN THE GARDEN	Cadell, Elizabeth
RING OUT YOUR DEAD	Saunders, Paul
RING THE JUBILEE	Moore, Ward
HE BROKEN FANG	Key, Uel
HE BROKEN MEN	Gielgud, Val
HE BROKEN SWORD	Anderson, Poul
HE BROOK KERITH	Moore, George
ROOMSTICK	Karlova, Irina
BROTHER OF THE SHADOW	Colmore, George
UDDHA'S RETURN	Gazdanov, Gaito
UILDERS OF CONTINENTS	Meldrum, David
HE BUILDING OF THE ALPHA ONE	Jones, Tupper
HE BUILDING OF THELEMA	Ashbee, C. R.
ULLARD OF THE SPACE PATROL	Jameson, Malcolm
ULO AND LELE	Bretnall, George H.
HE BUMP ON BRANNIGAN'S HEAD	Connolly, Myles
BURIED MYSTERY	Mandham, Clement A.
URL IVES' TALES OF AMERICA	Ives, Burl
HE BURNING GLASS	Morgan, Charles
THE BARROW RIVER	Leamy, Edmund
THE WATERS OF BABYLON	de Koven, (Mrs.) Reginald
THEIR FRUITS	Praed, Campbell
THIS STRANGE FIRE	Pargeter, Edith
ALL IT A DAY	Samuel, Joseph
HE CALL OF PETER GASKELL	Wallis, George C.
ALLISTA: A TALE OF THE THIRD CENTURY	Newman, John Henry Cardinal
MBODIAN QUEST	Casey, Robert J.
NDLELIGHT ATTIC	Hallack, Cecily E.
E CANDLE VIRGINS	Baillie-Saunders, Margaret
CANTICLE FOR LEIBOWITZ	Miller, Walter M. Jr.
E CANYON	Schaeffer, Jack
E CAPEBERRY BUSH	Guinn, Jack
E CAPTIVE GODDESS	Bull, Lois
PTURED BY APES	Prentice, Harry
E CAR OF PHOEBUS	Lees, Robert James
E CARDINAL MOTH	White, F. M.
RMEN, ARIZA	Stocking, Charles F.
E CARNELIAN CUBE	de Camp, L. Sprague and Pratt, Fletcher
E CARPET FROM BAGDAD	MacGrath, Harold
E CASE OF CHARLES DEXTER WARD	Lovecraft, H. P.
E CASE OF THE LITTLE GREEN MEN	Reynolds, Mack
E CASE OF THE WEIRD SISTERS	Armstrong, Charlotte
E CASTLE OF INCHVALLY	Anonymous
STLE OF IRON	de Camp, L. Sprague and Pratt, Fletcher
E CATAFALQUE	Goldston, Robert C.
ALINA	Maugham, W. Somerset

CATSEYE	Norton, Andre
THE CATSKILL FAIRIES	Johnson, Virginia W.
CAVALCADE OF GHOSTS	Hopkins, R. Thurston
THE CAVE AND THE ROCK	Faure, Raoul Cohen
THE CAVE OF A THOUSAND COLUMNS	Gratton-Smith, T. E.
THE CAVE OF WINDS	Rutley, C. Bernard
THE CAVES OF STEEL	Asimov, Isaac
CAVIAR	Sturgeon, Theodore
CELESTIA	Lull, (Ref.) D.
THE CELESTIAL HAND	Vincent, Joyce
CELTIC FAIRY TALES	Jacobs, Joseph
CELTIC WONDER TALES	Young, Ella
THE CENTENARIANS	Phelps, Gilbert
CENTRAL PASSAGE	Schoonover, Lawrence L.
CEREMONY OF INNOCENCE	Webster, Elizabeth Charlotte
CELESTALIA: A FANTASY A. D. 1975	Pullar, A. L.
A CENTURY OF SCIENCE FICTION	Knight, Damon
CHAIN REACTION	Hodder-Williams, Christopher
CHAMPAGNE CHARLIE	Franklin, Jay
CHANCES AND CHANGES; OR, LIFE AS IT IS	Anonymous
A CHANGE OF MIND	Glaskin, Gerald M.
CHAUCER, THE FLYING SAUCER	Malcolm, Mary
CHEATING THE DEVIL	Burbridge, Juanita Cassil
CHILD IN THE DARK	Timperley, Rosemary
THE CHILDERMASS	Lewis, Wyndham
CHILDHOOD'S END	Clarke, Arthur C.
THE CHILDREN OF THE ABBEY	Roche, Regina Maria
CHILDREN OF THE ATOM	Shiras, Wilmar
CHILDREN OF THE LENS	Smith, Edward Elmer
CHILDREN OF THE MIST	Phillpotts, Eden
CHILDREN OF THE VOID	Dexter, William
CHILDREN OF WONDER	Tenn, William
CHILDREN, RACEHORSES AND GHOSTS	Cooper, Edward H.
CHINESE PUZZLE	Godden, Rumer
THE CHIPS ARE DOWN	Sartre, Jean Paul
CHIPS FOR THE CHIMNEY CORNER	Munsell, Frank
CHRIST IN HADES	Phillips, Stephen
CHRISTMAS EVE	Kornbluth, C. M.
CHRISTMAS EVE WITH THE SPIRITS	Anonymous
CHRISTMAS GIFT AND OTHER STORIES	Gordon, Edward
CHRISTMAS STORIES FROM FRENCH AND SPANISH WRITERS	Ogden, Antoinette
THE CHRONICLES OF CLOVIS	Saki
CHRONICLES OF FAIRY LAND	Hume, Fergus
CHRONICLES OF KANUL THE KUTE	Black, Frank Burn
CHRYSAL: OR, THE ADVENTURES OF A GUINEA	An Adept
CINDERELLA'S DAUGHTER	Erskine, John
THE CISTERN AND THE FOUNTAIN	Matheson, Jean
CITIZEN IN SPACE	Sheckley, Robert
CITIZEN OF THE GALAXY	Heinlein, Robert A.
CITY	Simak, Clifford D.
THE CITY AND THE STARS	Clarke, Arthur C.
THE CITY AT WORLD'S END	Hamilton, Edmond

THE CITY BEYOND THE RIVER	Kasack, Hermann
THE CITY IN THE SEA	Tucker, Wilson
THE CITY OF NO ESCAPE	Bridges, T. C.
CITY OF FROZEN FIRE	Wilkins, Vaughan
THE CITY OF THE SORCEROR	Gilson, Major Charles
CITY ON THE MOON	Leinster, Murray
THE CLAIRAUDIENT	Robin, C. Ernest
THE CLAIRVOYANTS	Farjeon, Benjamin Leopold
A CLASH OF CYMBALS	Blish, James
THE CLIMATE OF CANDOR	Teague, Robert L.
THE CLIMAX	Lewis, Florence Jay
THE CLOAK AESIR	Campbell, John W.
CLOVIS	Fessier, Michael
COLD EYES	Dwyer, James Francis
COLD WAR IN HELL	Blamires, Harry
COLLECTED POEMS	Lovecraft, H. P.
HE COLLECTED TALES OF A E COPPARD	Coppard, A. E.
HE COLLECTED TALES OF WALTER DE LA MARE	de la Mare, Walter
HE COLLECTED WRITINGS OF AMBROSE BIERCE	Bierce, Ambrose
COLLISION COURSE	Silverberg, Robert
OLONEL TO PRINCESS	Germaine, Victor Wallace
OLONIAL SURVEY	Leinster, Murray
HE COLOR OF EVENING	Nathan, Robert
OLYMBIA	"Clotilda"
OME AND GO	Coles, Manning
OME LIKE SHADOWS	Murray, D. L.
COME NOT, LUCIFER"	Verner, Gerald
HE COMETEERS	Williamson, Jack
COMIC HISTORY OF THE UNITED STATES	Hopkins, Livingston
OMING ATTRACTIONS	Greenberg, Martin
HE COMING COUNTRY	Younghusband, Francis
HE COMING OF CONAN	Howard, Robert E.
HE COMING TERROR	Ross, Samuel Albert
OMMANDER OF THE MISTS	Murray, D. L.
COMMODITY OF DREAMS	Nemerov, Howard
ONAN THE BARBARIAN	Howard, Robert E.
ONAN THE CONQUEROR	Howard, Robert E.
NCLUDING	Green, Henry
NFERENCE AT COLD COMFORT FARM	Gibbons, Stella
E CONJUROR	Barcynska, Countess
CONJUROR OF PHANTOMS	Harding, John William
E CONQUERED PLACE	Shafer, Robert
E CONQUEST OF DON PEDRO	Fergusson, Harvey
NQUEST OF EARTH	Banister, Manly
NQUEST OF LIFE	Lukens, Adam
E CONTEMPORARY MOUSE	Barnard, Patricia
E CONTINENT MAKERS	de Camp, L. Sprague
E CONTINENTAL CLASSICS --VOL. 14	Anonymous anthology
E CONTINENTAL CLASSICS--VOL. 15	Anonymous anthology
E COPPER DISC	Stead, Robert J. C.
E CORNERSTONES	Linklater, Eric
RRIDORS OF TIME	Deegan, Jon J.

COSMIC ENGINEERS	Simak, Clifford D.
THE COSMIC GEOIDS	Taine, John
COSTIGAN'S NEEDLE	Sohl, Jerry
COULSON GOES SOUTH	Mann, Jack
COUNT LUNA	Lernet-Holenia, Alexander
THE COUNTERFEIT MAN	Nourse, Alan E.
COURT INTRIGUES NEW ATLANTIS	Author of "Secret Memoirs"
THE COURTLY CHARLATAN	Proody, George R.
THE COURTS OF THE MORNING	Buchan, John
THE CRACK IN THE WALL	Houblon, Grahame
THE CRATER OF KALA	Montague, Joseph
THE CRAWFISH WOMAN	Peddie, John
CREDULITY ISLAND	Watson, Frederick
CRISIS 2000	Maine, Charles Eric
CROHOORE OF THE BILL HOOK	O'Hara Family, The
CROSS DOUBLE CROSS	Masefield, Lewis
CRUSOE WARBURTON	Germaine, Victor Wallace
CRY CHAOS	Swain, Dwight V.
CRYSTAL CLEAR	Cadell, Elizabeth
THE CRYSTAL HORDE	Taine, John
CRYSTALLINE; OR, THE HEIRESS OF FALL DOWN CASTLE	Shelton, F. W.
CUNNING MURRELL	Morrison, Arthur
THE CURRENTS OF SPACE	Asimov, Isaac
THE CURRY EXPERIMENT	Rayner, A. A.
THE CURSE OF DOONE	Horler, Sydney
THE CURSE OF INTELLECT	Anonymous
THE CURSE OF THE LION	Webster, F. A. M.
CURSE OF THE RECKAVILES	Masterman, W. S.
THE CURSE OF YIG	Bishop, Zealia
THE CURVE OF THE SNOWFLAKE	Walter, William Grey
CUSTODIANS OF GHOSTS	Ogden, George W.
THE CYBERNETIC BRAINS	Jones, Raymond F.
CYNTHIA	Sibold, Rosalind
DAEMONOLOGIE & NEWES FROM SCOTLAND	James I
DAGMAR OF GREEN HILLS	Smith, Joe
D'ALRA THE BUDDHIST	Lonsdale, H. M.
THE DAMS CAN BREAK	Christian, Emeline Fate
DAN OWEN AND THE ANGEL JOE	Mitchell, Ronald
DANCE AND SKYLARK	Moore, John Cecil
DANCE OF DEATH	Charlot, Jean
THE DANCE OF DEATH	Holbein, Hans
THE DANCER OF TULUUM	Ryan, Marah Ellis
THE DANCING DEAD	Thomas, Eugene
DANDELION WINE	Bradbury, Ray
DANGER: DINOSAURS	Marston, Richard
DANGER IN DEEP SPACE	Rockwell, Carey
DANGEROUS WATER	Williams, Islwyn
DARK ANDROMEDA	Merak, A. J.
DARK ATLANTIS	Craigie, David
THE DARK CHATEAU	Smith, Clark Ashton
THE DARK DESTROYERS	Wellman, Manly Wade
DARK DOMINION	Duncan, David

DARK DOMINION	Hauser, Marianne
DARK ENCHANTMENT	Macardle, Dorothy
THE DARK FANTASTIC	Echard, Margaret
THE DARK FRONTIER	Ambler, Eric
THE DARK GATEWAY	Burke, Jonathan
THE DARK GODS	Mills, Dorothy
THE DARK GREEN CIRCLE	Shanks, Edward
DARK MAGIC	Norday, Michael
DARK MIND, DARK HEART	Derleth, August
THE DARK OTHER	Weinbaum, Stanley G.
THE DARK PLANET	Holly, J. Hunter
DARK SANCTUARY	Gregory, H. B.
THE DARK STAR	Costa, March
THE DARK STRANGER	Charques, Dorothy
DARKER THAN YOU THINK	Williamson, Jack
DARZEE, GIRL OF INDIA	Marshall, Edison
A DASH AT THE POLE	Phelps, William Lyon
A DATE WITH DESTINY	Walker, Jerry
DAUGHTER OF ATLANTIS	Murray, Jacqueline
DAUGHTER OF THE SUN	Gregory, Jackson
DAVID STARR: SPACE RANGER	French, Paul
THE DAWNING LIGHT	Randall, Robert
DAY AFTER TOMORROW'S WORLD	Rossel, John
DAY AND NIGHT STORIES	Sullivan, T. S.
THE DAY IT RAINED FOREVER	Bradbury, Ray
THE DAY KRUSCHEV PANICKED	Mair, George B.
DAY OF JUDGMENT	Mackenzie, Nigel
DAY OF THE GIANTS	del Rey, Lester
THE DAY OF THE TRIFFIDS	Wyndham, John
DEAD MAN'S CHEST	Mann, Jack
DEAD MAN'S DIARY	Anonymous
THE DEAD MAN'S MESSAGE	Marryat, Florence
DEAD MAN'S ROCK	Quiller-Couch, A. T.
THE DEAD MAN'S SECRET	Muddock, J. E. P.
DEAD MEN'S TALES	Junor, Charles
A DEAD PRESIDENT MAKES ANSWER TO THE PRESIDENT'S DAUGHTER	Jenks, Anton S.
HE DEAD PRIOR	Lampen, Charles Dudley
HE DEAD RIDERS	O'Donnell, Elliott
EALINGS WITH THE DEAD	Whitehead, A. E.
EALS WITH THE DEVIL	Davenport, Basil
EAR GUEST AND GHOST	Dee, Sylvia
EATH & THE DREAMER	Saurat, Denis
HE DEATH BELL	Marshall, Edison
EATH BY APPARITION	Campbell, Reginald
EATH OF A GOD AND OTHER STORIES	Sitwell, Osbert
EATH OF A WORLD	Farjeon, J. Jefferson
HE DEATH OF METAL	Suddaby, Donald
HE DEATH RAYS OF ARDILLA	Johns, Capt. W. E.
HE DEATH-THORN	Karlin, Alma M.
EATH'S DEPUTY	Hubbard, L. Ron
DECADE OF FANTASY AND SCIENCE FICTION	Mills, Robert P.
EEP FREEZE	Butler, Joan

DEEP IN THE SKY	Nielson, Helga
THE DEEP RANGE	Clarke, Arthur C.
DEEP SPACE	Russell, Eric Frank
THE DEFIANT AGENTS	Norton, Andre
DEFY THE FOUL FIEND	Collier, John
DELIVER US FROM EVIL	Abdullah, Achmed
DEL PALMA	Kellino, Pamela
DELPHIC ECHO	Livingston, Marjorie
THE DELUGE	Leonardo da Vinci and Payne, Robert
THE DEMETRIAN	Harding, Ellison
DEMI-GODS	Biggs, John (jr.)
DEMOCRACY	Desmond, Shaw
THE DEMOLISHED MAN	Bester, Alfred
THE DEMON'S MIRROR	Wallerstein, James
THE DEPARTMENT OF QUEER COMPLAINTS	Dickson, Carter
DESPOT OF THE WORLD	Rochester, George E.
DESTINATION HELL--STANDING ROOM ONLY	Day, Millard F.
DESTINATION; UNIVERSE	van Vogt, A. E.
DESTINY'S ORBIT	Grinnell, David
THE DESTROYERS	Carter, John F. Jr.
THE DEVIL	Molnar, Ferenc
THE DEVIL AND ALL	Rhadamanthus
THE DEVIL AND THE LADY	Tennyson, Alfred
THE DEVIL AND X Y Z	Browne, Barum
DEVIL-BROTHER	Baron, Walter
DEVIL BY THE TAIL	Fumento, Rocco
THE DEVIL COMES TO BOLYBON	Horler, Sydney
THE DEVIL HAS THE BEST TUNES	Fletcher, H. L. V.
THE DEVIL IN THE CHEESE	Cushing, Tom
THE DEVIL IN THE PULPIT	O'Donnell, Elliott
THE DEVIL IN VELVET	Carr, John Dickson
THE DEVIL IN WOODFORD WELLS	Hobson, Harold
THE DEVIL MUST	Wicker, Tom
THE DEVIL OF THE DEPTHS	McLaren, Jack
DEVIL TAKE A WHITTLER	Stone, Weldon
THE DEVIL THAT FAILED	Samuel, Maurice
THE DEVIL'S ADVOCATE	Caldwell, Taylor
THE DEVIL'S BEACON	Robbins, Clifton
THE DEVIL'S CASE	Buchanan, Robert
THE DEVIL'S DIARY	Elshemus, Louis M.
THE DEVIL'S HENCHMEN	Oldrey, John
THE DEVIL'S HUNTING GROUNDS	Blamires, Harry
THE DEVILS OF LOUDUN	Huxley, Aldous
THE DEVIL'S PRONOUN	Robertson, Frances Forbes
DEVIL'S RECKONING	Burton, Miles
THE DEVIL'S SPAWN	Birking, Charles Lloyd
THE DEVIL'S SPOON	Du Bois, Theodora
DEVLIN THE BARBER	Farjeon, Benjamin Leopold
THE DIABOLIQUES	D'Aurevilly, Jules Barbey
THE DIAMOND SHIP	Pemberton, Max
DIANE—SHE CAME FROM VENUS	Howard, Dana
DICK-DOCK'S ADVENTURES	Tano, Arthur

DIMENSION OF HORROR	Bounds, S. J.
DION AND THE SIBYLS	Keon, Miles Gerald
THE DIOTHAS; OR, A FAR LOOK AHEAD	Thiusen, Lamar
DIRGE FOR A DEAD WITCH	Duke, Winifred
THE DISAPPEARANCE	Wylie, Philip
DIVIDE AND RULE	de Camp, L. Sprague
THE DIVINE SEAL	Orcutt, Emma Louise
DR. CHAOS AND THE DEVIL SHAR'D	Freedy, George R.
DOCTOR DOLITTLE AND THE SECRET LAKE	Lofting, Hugh
DOCTOR DOLITTLE IN THE MOON	Lofting, Hugh
DOCTOR DOLITTLE'S BIRTHDAY BOOK	Lofting, Hugh
DOCTOR DOLITTLE'S CARAVAN	Lofting, Hugh
DOCTOR DOLITTLE'S CIRCUS	Lofting, Hugh
DOCTOR DOLITTLE'S GARDEN	Lofting, Hugh
DOCTOR DOLITTLE'S POST OFFICE	Lofting, Hugh
DOCTOR DOLITTLE'S PUDDLEBY ADVENTURES	Lofting, Hugh
DOCTOR DOLITTLE'S RETURN	Lofting, Hugh
DOCTOR DOLITTLE'S ZOO	Lofting, Hugh
THE DOCTOR TO THE DEAD	Bennett, John
DR. MOREL	Bramson, Karen
DOCTOR NO	Fleming, Ian
DR. TRANSIT	I. S.
DR. XAVIER	Pemberton, Max
DOCTOR ZIL'S EXPERIMENT	Goodchild, George
THE DOCTOR'S SECRET	Dorn, Dorothy Louise
DOG IN THE SKY	Corwin, Norman
A DOG'S HEAD	Dutourd, Jean
THE DOGE'S RING	Vare, Danielle
THE DOLL MAKER AND OTHER TALES OF THE UNCANNY	Sarban
DOMNEI	Cabell, James Branch
DON CAMILLO'S DILEMMA	Guareschi, Giovanni
DONALDSON	Alington, Adrian
DON'T BREAK THE SEAL	Burrage, A. M.
DON'T INHALE IT	Balint, Emery
THE DOOM OF CONAIRE MOR	Walsh, William Emmet
THE DOOMINGTON WANDERER	Golding, Louis
DOOMSDAY MORNING	Moore, C. L.
DOOMSDAY VILLAGE	Colvin, Ian
THE DOOR INTO SUMMER	Heinlein, Robert A.
THE DOOR OF BEYOND	St. John-Loe, Gladys
THE DOOR OF DEATH	Esteven, John
DOORWAYS TO SPACE	Wells, Basil
DOROTHY AND WIZARD IN OZ	Baum, L. Frank
THE DOUBLE AXE	Haggard, Audrey
DOUBLE IN SPACE	Pratt, Fletcher
DOUBLE JEOPARDY	Pratt, Fletcher
THE DOUBLE LIFE OF MR. ALFRED BURTON	Oppenheim, E. Phillips
DOUBLE STAR	Heinlein, Robert A.
DOWN TO EARTH	Capon, Paul
THE DOWNS SO FREE	Baker, Frank
THE DOWRY	Gould, Maggy
DRAGON DOODLES	Kelly, Howard
THE DRAGON IN THE SEA	Herbert, Frank

DRAGON RUN	Dawson, Carley
DRAGON'S ISLAND	Williamson, Jack
DRAGONWYCK	Seton, Anya
THE DREADFUL DRAGON OF HAY HILL	Beerbohm, Max
DREADFUL SANCTUARY	Russell, Eric Frank
DREADS AND DROLLS	Machen, Arthur
DREAM IN THE STONE	Faralla, Dana
THE DREAM OF RAVAN	Anonymous
THE DREAM OF UBERTUS	Ferrar, William M.
DREAM QUEST OF UNKNOWN KADATH	Lovecraft, H. P.
DREAM TALES	Turgeniev, Ivan S.
DREAM WARNINGS AND MYSTERIES	Anonymous anthology
THE DREAM-WOMAN	Wylwynne, Kythe
THE DREAMERS	Manvell, Roger
THE DREAMING JEWELS	Sturgeon, Theodore
DREAMLAND AND GHOSTLAND	Doyle, A. Conan
DREAMS AND FANCIES	Lovecraft, H. P.
DREAMS AND TALES	Valentiner, Brigitta
DREAMS FROM THE PAST	Williams, Alfred Newberry
THE DRIFTING DIAMOND	Colcord, Lincoln
DRONE	Leahy, Martin
THE DRUMS OF DAMBALLA	Bedford-Jones, H.
THE DRUMS OF TAPAJOS	Meek, Col S. P.
THE DRY DELUGE	Nott, Kathleen
THE DUCK HUNT	Claus, Hugo
A DUCK TO WATER	Stern, G. B.
DUMB SPIRIT	Hedges, Doris
THE DUNWICH HORROR	Lovecraft, H. P.
THE DUPLICATED MAN	Blish, James and Lowndes, Robert W.
DUSK OF DRUIDS	Parsons, Ethel Boyce
THE DWARF'S CHAMBER	Hume, Fergus
THE DWELLER IN THE HALF-LIGHT	Wray, Roger
THE EAGLE'S SHADOW	Cabell, James Branch
EARTH ABIDES	Stewart, George R.
THE EARTH ADVENTURES OF OLLIBOLLY	Tweed, Adelaide M.
EARTH GIANT	Marshall, Edison
EARTH IS ROOM ENOUGH	Asimov, Isaac
EARTH STOPPED	White, T. H.
EARTH WAITS FOR DAWN	O'Brien, Larry Clinton
EARTHBOUND	Lesser, Milton A.
THE EARTHEN DRUM	Stevens, E. S.
EARTHLIGHT	Clarke, Arthue C.
EARTHMAN, COME HOME	Blish, James
EARTHMAN'S BURDEN	Anderson, Poul and Dickson, Gordon
THE EARTHOMOTOR AND OTHER STORIES	Linton, C. E.
THE EARTHQUAKE	Risse, Heinz
EAST INDIA AND COMPANY	Morand, Paul
EASTWARD IN EDEN	Silve, Claude
THE EATER OF HEARTS	Vaughan, T. H.
ECCENTRIC MR. CLARK	Riley, James Whitcomb
ECHO OF A CURSE	Ryan, R. R.
THE ECHOING WORLDS	Burke, Jonathan

THE EDGE OF BEYOND	Johns, Capt. W. E.
EDGE OF TIME	Grinnell, David
EDITOR'S CHOICE IN SCIENCE FICTION	Moskowitz, Samuel
EIDOLON	Stern, J. D.
EIGHT FOR ETERNITY	Roberts, Cecil
EIGHT KEYS TO EDEN	Clifton, Mark
EIGHTEEN VISITS TO MARS	Rember, Winthrop Allen
THE EIGHTH ANNUAL YEAR'S BEST SCIENCE FICTION	Merrill, Judith
EL DORADO	Cromie, Robert
THE ELECTRIC GUN	Johnston, Harold
THE ELECTRICAL BOY	Trowbridge, John
THE ELEGANT WITCH	Neill, Robert
ELEVATOR TO THE MOON	Widney, Stanley A.
ELIXIR OF LIFE	Balzac, Honore de
THE ELIZABETH GOUDGE READER	Goudge, Elizabeth
AN ELPHIN LAND	Geach, Edwina Catherine
THE EMBROIDERED BANNER AND OTHER MARVELS	Hort, Lt. Col.
THE EMERALD CITY OF OZ	Baum, L. Frank
THE EMIGRANTS: OR, THE ISLE OF ESMERALDA	Author of, "The Island of Atlantis"
AN EMPEROR IN THE DOCK	De Veer, W.
THE EMPEROR OF HALLELUJAH ISLAND	Goodchild, George
EMPIRE OF CHAOS	Bulmer, H. K.
EMPIRE OF THE ATOM	van Vogt, A. E.
EMPTY VICTORY	Godwin, George
ENARDO AND ROSAEL	Rivera, Alejandro Tapia y
THE ENCHANTED	Coatsworth, E. J.
ENCHANTED BEGGAR	Matson, Norman
THE ENCHANTED CUP	Roberts, Dorothy James
THE ENCHANTED FLIVVER	Brayley, Berton
THE ENCHANTED ISLAND OF YEW	Baum, L. Frank
THE ENCHANTED WOOD	Graham, Janet Pollock
ENCOUNTER	Holly, J. Hunter
THE END	Venning, Hugh
THE END OF ETERNITY	Asimov, Isaac
ENEMY BEYOND PLUTO	Vastell, Jean Gaston
THE ENEMY STARS	Anderson, Poul
ENTERPRISE! ISLAND	Sonne, Hans Christian
ENTERPRISE 2115	Grey, Charles
EPEDEMIC!	Slaughter, Frank G.
EQUITANIA, OR THE LAND OF EQUITY	Henry, Dr. W. O.
ERNESTINE TAKES OVER	Brooks, Walter R.
ESCAPE INTO THE PAST	Slocombe, George
ESCAPE ME--NEVER	Presland, John
ESCAPEMENT	Maine, Charles Eric
THE ETERNAL CONFLICT	Keller, David H.
THE ETERNAL ECHO	Cradock, Phyllis
THE ETERNAL SMILE	Lagerkvist, Par
EVE AND THE EVANGELIST	Rice, Harry E.
EVELYN: A STORY OF THE WEST AND FAR EAST	Oppenheim, Mrs. Ansel
THE EVENING WOLVES	McCall, Marie
EVENINGS AT WOODLAWN	Ellet, Mrs.
EVERY BOY'S BOOK OF OUTER SPACE STORIES	Dikty, T. E.

EVERY BOY'S BOOK OF SCIENCE FICTION	Wollheim, Donald A.
EVIDENCE BEFORE GABRIEL	Frost, Conrad
THE EXILES OF TIME	Bond, Nelson F.
THE EXORCISM	Blackstock, Charity
EXPEDITION TO EARTH	Clarke, Arthur C.
THE EXPLODING RAY	Rutley, C. Bernard
EXPLORATIONS IN THE SIT-TREE DESERT	Gould, F. C.
EXTINCTION BOMBER	Hough, S. B.
FABLES - 1950	Lawson, J. S.
FABULOUS BEASTS	Lum, Peter
THE FABULOUS JOURNEY OF HIERONYMUS MEEKER	Johns, Willy
THE FABULOUS WINK	Bennett, Kem
THE FACE OF THE MAN FROM SATURN	Keeler, Harry Stephen
FACIAL JUSTICE	Hartley, L. P.
FAIRIES OF SORTS	Molesworth, Mary L.
FAIRY BEDMAKER	Rowe, George
FAIRY TALES FROM THE LAND OF THE WATTLE	Earnest, Olga D. A.
THE FAITHFUL CITY	Morrah, Herbert
THE FALL. A TALE OF EDEN	Searel, George
FALL OF A DICTATOR	Gask, Arthur
A FALL OF MOONDUST	Clarke, Arthur C.
THE FALL OF THE HOUSE OF HERON	Phillpotts, Eden
FALLACY OF GHOSTS, DREAMS AND OMENS	Ollier, Charles
THE FALLEN SKY	Crowcroft, Peter
THE FAMILY WITCH	Cox, A. B.
FANCIES AND GOODNIGHTS	Collier, John
FANFARE FOR A WITCH	Wilkins, Vaughan
FANFARONADE	Pakenham, Evo
THE FANTASTIC HISTORY OF THE CELEBRATED PIERROT	Assollant, Alfred
FANTASTIC TALES OF THE RHINELAND	Erckmann, Emile and Chatrian, Alexandre
THE FANTASTIC UNIVERSE OMNIBUS	Santesson, Hans Stefan
FANTASIES	Nembhard, Mabel
FAR AND AWAY	Boucher, Anthony
FAR BOUNDARIES	Derleth, August W.
FAR OUT	Knight, Damon
FARAWAY HILLS ARE GREEN	Dranker, Charles
FARMER GILES OF HAM	Tolkien, J. R. R.
FARMER IN THE SKY	Heinlein, Robert A.
FARRAUSCO THE BLACKBIRD	Torga, Miguel
FASTER, FASTER	Bair, Patrick
FASTER, FASTER	Horn, Edward Newman
THE FAT OF THE CAT	Untermeyer, Sonia
FEAR IS THE SAME	Dickson, Carter
THE FEASTING DEAD	Metcalfe, John
FEATHERS IN THE BED	Roberts, Leslie
FEET OF CLAY; A FANTASY	Arne, Aaron
THE FEET OF THE FURTIVE	Roberts, Charles G. D.
THE FELLOWSHIP OF THE RING	Tolkien, J. R. R.
THE FERRY OF SOULS	Salmon, Arthur L.
FEW WERE LEFT	Rein, Harold
THE FIERY FLOWER	Wellman, Paul
FIFTEEN ODD STORIES	Leslie, Shane

THE FIFTH ANNUAL YEAR'S BEST SCIENCE FICTION	Merrill, Judith
THE FIFTH GALAXY READER	Gold, H. L.
THE FIFTH MIRACLE	Cowen, William Joyce
FIFTH PLANET	Hoyle, Fred and Geoffrey
FIFTY ADVENTURES INTO THE UNKNOWN	Anonymous anthology
FIFTY STRANGEST STORIES EVER TOLD	Anonymous anthology
FIFTY YEARS HENCE	Grimshaw, Robert
THE FIG TREE	Menon, Aubrey
FIGHTING AGAINST MILLIONS	Carter, Nick
FINAL BLACKOUT	Hubbard, L. Ron
FIND THE FEATHERED SERPENT	Hunter, Evan
A FINE AND PRIVATE PLACE	Beagle, Peter S.
FINISHED	Haggard, H. Rider
FINNLEY WREN	Wylie, Philip
FIRE AND SLEET AND CANDLELIGHT	Derleth, August W.
FIRE AND WATER	Delcarol, Marwin
FIRE, BURN	Carr, John Dickson
FIRE IN ANGER	Mars, Alastair
FIRE IN THE HEAVENS	Smith, George O.
A FIRE OF DRIFTWOOD	Broster, D. K.
FIRE-HUNTER	Kjelgaard, Jim
FIRES BURN BLUE	Caldecott, Sir Andrew
FIRST LENSMAN	Smith, Edward Elmer
THE FITTEST	McIntosh, J. T.
FIVE AGAINST VENUS	Latham, Phillip
FIVE GALAXY SHORT NOVELS	Gold, H. L.
THE FIVE KNOTS	White, Fred M.
FIVE MILES FROM CANDIA	Urn, Althea
FIVE SCIENCE FICTION NOVELS	Greenberg, Martin
FIVE WINDS	Bowen, Marjorie
FLAME ETERNAL & MAHARAJAH'S SON	Roys, Willis E.
FLAMES OF DARKNESS	Van Stack, Henry
THE FLAMING SWORD	Anonymous
FLIGHT INTO SPACE	Wollheim, Donald A.
FLIGHT INTO YESTERDAY	Harness, Charles L.
FLIGHT TO AFRICA	Moosdorf, Johanna
FLIGHT TO THE MISTY PLANET	Patchett, Mrs. Mary Elwyn
THE FLOATING CAFE	Lawrence, Margery
THE FLYING BUCCANEER	Binns, Jack
THE FLYING SAUCER	Newman, Bernard
THE FLYING SUBMARINE	Savidge, E. van Pedroe
THE FLYING SUBMARINE	Westerman, Percy F.
FLYING TO AMY-RAN FASTNESS	Craine, E. J.
THE FLYING WIG	Poulson, Theodore Frederic
FOLK TALES OF THE NORTH COUNTRY	Grice, Frederick
FOLK TALES OF YORKSHIRE	Gee, H. L.
FOOL'S APPRENTICE	Munkacsi, Martin
THE FOOTPRINT AND OTHER STORIES	Morris, Gouvenor
THE FOOTPRINTS IN THE SNOW	Tatham, H. F. W.
FORBIDDEN AREA	Frank, Pat
FORBIDDEN MARCHES	De Fontmell, E. V.
FORBIDDEN PLANET	Stuart, W. J.

THE FOREST LAUGH	Heyse, Paul J. Von
THE FOREST LOVERS	Hewlett, Maurice
THE FOREST MAIDEN	Robinet, Lee
THE FOREST SHIP	Hoelriegel, Arnold
FOREVER ULYSSES	Rodocanachi, C. P.
THE FORGOTTEN PLANET	Leinster, Murray
THE FORGOTTEN STAR	Greene, Joseph
FOUNDATION	Asimov, Isaac
THE FOUNDATION	Young, Briant Sayre
FOUNDATION AND EMPIRE	Asimov, Isaac
THE FOUNTAIN OF YOUTH	Colum, Padraic
THE FOUNTAIN OF YOUTH	Paludan-Muller, Frederick
THE FOUR APES AND OTHER FABLES OF OUR DAY	Kreymborg, Alfred
FOUR FANTASTIC TALES	Walpole, Hugh
FOUR GREAT OAKS	McNaughton, Mildred
FOUR LAIS OF MARIE DE FRANCE	Weston, Jessie L.
THE FOUR SIDED TRIANGLE	Temple, William F.
14 RADIO PLAYS	Oboler, Arch
THE FOURTH BOOK OF JORKENS	Dunsany, Lord
THE FOURTH GALAXY READER	Gold, H. L.
THE FOURTH SEAL	Groom, Pelham
FRANCIS GOES TO WASHINGTON	Stern, David
FRANK HARDINGE	Stables, W. Gordon
FRED AND THE GORILLAS	Miller, Thomas
FREDDY AND THE BASEBALL TEAM FROM MARS	Brooks, Walter R.
FREDDY AND THE MEN FROM MARS	Brooks, Walter R.
FREDDY AND THE SPACE SHIP	Brooks, Walter R.
FRIVOLA, SIMON RYAN AND OTHER PAPERS	Jessopp, Augustus
FROM A CHRISTIAN GHETTO	MacGregor, Geddes
FROM OFF THIS WORLD	Margulies, Leo and Friend, Oscar J.
FROM THE OCEAN, FROM THE STARS	Clarke, Arthur C.
FROM THE SOULD OF THE TI-TREE	Geach, Edwina Catherine
FROM THE WORLD'S END	Green, Roger Lancelyn
FROM UNKNOWN WORLDS	Campbell, John W.
FROM WHAT FAR STAR?	Berry, Bryan
THE FROZEN DEATH	Graham, Winifred
FULL CIRCLE	Ariss, Bruce
FULL CIRCLE	Cecil, Henry
FULL CYCLE	Webb, Ripley
FULFILMENT AT NOON	Fraser, Helen
FURFOOZE	Swan, Thor
FURTHER EAST THAN ASIA	Muir, Ward
FURY	Kuttner, Henry
FURZE THE CRUEL	Trevena, John
FUTURE IMPERFECT	Chetwynd, Bridgett
THE FUTURE OF MR. PURDUE	Livingston, Marjorie
FUTURE TENSE	Crossen, Kendall Foster
THE FUTURE TOOK US	Severn David
GABRIEL AND THE CREATURES	Heard, Gerald
GABRIEL SAMARA	Oppenheim, E. Phillips
GADGET CITY	Evans, I. O.
GALACTIC DERELICT	Norton, Andre
GALACTIC INTRIGUE	Bulmer, H. K

GALACTIC PATROL	Smith, Edward Elmer
THE GALAXY READER OF SCIENCE FICTION	Gold, H. L.
THE GALE OF THE WORLD	Kirk, Laurence
GALLANTRY	Cabell, James Branch
GALLERY OF GHOSTS	Reynolds, James
GAMBLES WITH DESTINY	Griffith, George
THE GARDEN OF VISION	Beck, L. Adams
A GARDEN TO THE EASTWARD	Lamb, Harold
THE GATE OF HEAVEN	Lees, Robert James
THE GATES OF HORN	Sleigh, Bernard
THE GATES OF IVORY, THE GATES OF HORN	McGrath, Thomas
THE GATEWAY TO REMEMBRANCE	Cradock, Phyllis
GATHER, DARKNESS	Leiber, Fritz
GEE'S FIRST CASE	Mann, Jack
THE GENESIS OF NAM	Goodrich, Charles
THE GENIUS AND THE GODDESS	Huxley, Aldous
GENIUS LOCI	Smith, Clark Ashton
GENUS HOMO	de Camp, L. Sprague and Miller, P. S.
GERMAN STORIES AND TALES	Pick, Robert
GERMAN TALES OF TERROR	Anonymous anthology
THE GERRARD STREET MYSTERY	Dent, John Charles
THE GHOST HUNTERS	Meyrick, Gordon
THE GHOST IT WAS	Hull, Richard
THE GHOST OF GORDON GREGORY	Groom, Arthur
GHOST STORIES	Anonymous
GHOST STORIES	Beer, Alec
GHOST STORIES AND OTHER QUEER TALES	Anonymous anthology
GHOST STORIES AND PRESENTIMENTS	Anonymous anthology
GHOST STORIES OF OLD NEW ORLEANS	de Lavigne, Jeanne
GHOSTIES AND GHOULIES	Prevot, Francis C.
GHOSTLY TALES	Munster, Countess of
THE GHOSTLY TALES OF HENRY JAMES	James, Henry
GHOSTLY TALES TO BE TOLD	Davenport, Basil
GHOSTLY VISITORS	"Spectre Stricken"
GHOSTS AND GLAMOUR	Leech, Joseph
GHOSTS I HAVE SEEN	Tweedale, Violet
GHOSTS IN DAYLIGHT	Onions, Oliver
GHOSTS INCORPORATED	Talbot, Marjorie
GHOSTS OF SIN-CHANG	Garvais, Albert
THE GHOSTS OF SLAVE DRIVERS BEND	Kroll, Harry Harrison
GHOSTS OF THE BROAD	Sampson, Charles
THE GHOUL	King, Frank
THE GIANT ANTHOLOGY OF SCIENCE FICTION	Margulies, Leo and Friend, Oscar J.
THE GIANT HORSE OF OZ	Thompson, Ruth Plumly
GIANTS FROM ETERNITY	Wellman, Manly Wade
THE GIFT	Beresford, J. D. and Tyson, Esme Wynne
GILDA OF OZ	Baum, L. Frank
THE GILDED LIZARD	Stoker, M. B.
GIMPEL THE FOOL	Singer, Isaac Bashevis
THE GIRAFFE'S UNCLE	Robinson, Les
THE GIRLS FROM PLANET 5	Wilson, Richard
GISELE THE OUTLAW	Desent, George W.

GLADIATOR-AT-LAW	Pohl, Frederik and Kornbluth, C. M.
THE GLASS CAGE	Lukens, Adam
THE GLASS TOO MANY	Mann, Jack
THE GLEAVE MYSTERY	Tracy, Louis
GLIMPSES IN THE TWILIGHT	Lee, Rev. Frederick
THE GLITTERING SERPENT	Morrisson, Emmeline
THE GLOB	O'Reilly, John and Kelly, Walt
GLORY ROAD	Heinlein, Robert A.
THE GLORY THAT WAS	de Camp, L. Sprague
A GNOME THERE WAS	Padgett, Lewis
THE GO-BETWEEN	Hartley, L. P.
GOBLIN MARKET	Stacpoole, H. de Vere
GOD IN THE SAND	Price, Theodore
THE GOD ON THE MOUNTAIN	Furnell, John
THE GODDESS. A DEMON	Marsh, Richard
A GODDESS ARRIVES	Gardner, G. B.
A GODDESS FROM THE SEA	Beddoes, W. T. H.
A GODDESS NAMED GOLD	Bhattacharya, Bhabani
GOD'S MAN	Ward, Lynd
G. O. G. 666	Taine, John
GOING WEST	Bramwell, James
THE GOLD OF OPHIR	Gwinn, D. Howard
THE GOLD OF THE GODS	Reeve, Arthur B.
THE GOLD WORSHIPPERS	Author of "Whitefriars"
THE GOLDEN AMAZON RETURNS	Fearn, John Russell
THE GOLDEN AMAZON'S TRIUMPH	Fearn, John Russell
THE GOLDEN APE	Chase, Adam
THE GOLDEN APPLES OF THE SUN	Bradbury, Ray
THE GOLDEN ARCHER	Mason, Gregory
THE GOLDEN ARGOSY	Cartmell, Cleve and Grayson, Charles
GOLDEN GODDESS	Edon, Rob
THE GOLDEN HAMMER	Marshall, A. W.
THE GOLDEN HORIZON	Connolly, Cyril
THE GOLDEN LAKE	Dawe, W. Carleton
THE GOLDEN PHOENIX	Carlton, Mary Shaffer
THE GOLDEN PROMISE	Zuber, Stanley
THE GOLDEN ROPE	Brodie-Innes, J. W.
THE GOLDEN SNAKE	Campbell, Donald
GONE TO GROUND	White, T. H.
GOOD-BYE WHITE MAN	Bouie, Frederic Vernon
THE GOOSE ON THE GRAVE	Hawkes, John
THE GORGEOUS GHOUL	Babcock, Dwight W.
GORMENGHAST	Peake, Merwyn
THE GRAIN SHIP	Robertson, Morgan
THE GRASS IS ALWAYS GREENER	Malcolm-Smith, George
GRATEFUL TO LIFE AND DEATH	Narayan, R. K.
THE GRAY ALIENS	Holly, J. Hunter
GRAY LENSMAN	Smith, Edward Elmer
THE GRAY MAN	Crockett, S. R.
THE GREAT AWAKENING	Draper, Blance A.
GREAT GHOST STORIES	Dawson, William and Dawson, Coningsby
GREAT GOD GOLD	Le Queux, William

THE GREAT HOLD-UP MYSTERY	Usher, Wilfred
THE GREAT IDEA	Hazlitt, Henry
THE GREAT IMAGE	Beresford, Leslie
THE GREAT MAN'S LIFE: 1925 to 2000 A.C.	Van Petten, Albert Archer
THE GREAT MISCHIEF	Pinckney, Josephine
THE GREAT ONES	Deegan, Jon J.
THE GREAT PERIL	Hawker, Caleb
GREAT STORIES OF SCIENCE FICTION	Leinster, Murray.
THE GREAT WASH	Kersh, Gerald
GREEK AND ROMAN GHOST STORIES	Morley, Lacy Collison
THE GREEN ENIGMA	Caven, Stewart
GREEN-EYE PHANTOMS	Madsen, Lenora Kimball
GREEN FIRE. A MELODRAMA OF 1990	Hughes, Glenn
GREEN GOLD	King, Frank
THE GREEN HILLS OF EARTH	Heinlein, Robert A.
THE GREEN KINGDOM	Maddux, Rachel
THE GREEN LADY	Tweedale, Violet
THE GREEN MAN FROM SPACE	Zarem, Lewis
THE GREEN MARE	Ayme, Marcel
THE GREEN MILLENIUM	Leiber, Fritz
THE GREEN MOUSTACHE	Dawson, Warrington
THE GREEN ODYSSEY	Farmer, Philip
THE GREEN PLANET	Holly, J. Hunter
THE GREEN ROUND	Machen, Arthur
GRIM TALES	Nesbit, E.
THE GRIM THIRTEEN	Green, Frederick
A GROVE OF FEVER TREES	Rooke, Daphne
GRUGAN'S GOD	Andrews, Frank Emerson
THE GUARDIAN DEMONS	Dawson, Warrington
GUMPTION ISLAND	Morley, Felix
GUNNER CADE	Judd, Cyril
GUP BAHADUR	Mundy, Talbot
HACKENFELLER'S APE	Brophy, Brigid
HAIL! COLONIA	Lister, Stephen
THE HALF-GOD	Dorrington, Albert
HALF MAGIC	Eager, Edward
THE HALF-PINT JINNI	Dolbier, Maurice
HALLOWMAS ABBEY	Graham, Winifred
HAMTURA. A TALE OF AN UNKNOWN LAND	Lockhart-Ross, H. S.
THE HAND OF DOOM	Walsh, James Morgan
THE HANDS OF NARA	Child, Washburn
HANGOVER SQUARE	Hamilton, Patrick
THE HAPLOIDS	Sohl, Jerry
THE HAPPY HIGHWAYMAN	Charteris, Leslie
HAPPY RETURNS	Coles, Manning
HARBOTTLE, A MODERN PILGRIM'S PROGRESS	Hargrave, John
HARDER THAN STEEL	Thorne, Guy
THE HARLEQUIN OPAL	Hume, Fergus
THE HARLOT KILLER	Barnard, Allan
THE HAUNTED CIRCLE AND OTHER OUTDOOR PLAYS	Nichols, Adelaide
THE HAUNTED GRANGE	Taylor, Alfred Joseph
HAUNTED HIGHWAYS AND BYWAYS	O'Donnell, Elliott

THE HAUNTED MAN	Gaunt, Jeffrey
HAUNTED PLACES IN ENGLAND 8	O'Donnell, Elliott
HAUNTED SPRING	Ludwell, Bernice
THE HAUNTED STARS	Hamilton, Edmond
THE HAUNTER OF THE DARK	Lovecraft, H. P.
THE HAUNTING OF HILL HOUSE	Jackson, Shorley
THE HAUNTING OF TOBY JUG	Wheatley, Denis
HAVE SPACE SUIT—WILL TRAVEL	Heinlein, Robert A.
HE OWNED THE WORLD	Maine, Charles Eric
HE WHO RIDES A TIGER	Bhattacharya, Bhabani
HEADLONG HALL	Peacock Thomas Love
THE HEADS OF CERBERUS	Stevens, Francis
HEART OF JADE	Madariaga, Salvador de
HEAVEN TAKES A HAND	Crawshay-Williams, Eliot
THE HEAVENLY WORLD SERIES	O'Rourke, Frank
THE HEIGHTS	Bryant, Marguerite
HEIRS OF MERLIN	Atkey, Philip
HELL	Oudeis
HELLFLOWER	Smith, George O.
HERE ARE LADIES	Stephens, James
HERE COMES AN OLD SAILOR	Sheppard, Alfred Tresidder
HERE TODAY	Coates, John
HERE'S AUDACITY	Shay, Frank
HERO TALES OF THE FAR NORTH	Riis, Jacob A.
HERO'S WALK	Crane, Robert
THE HIDDEN CITY	Bridges, T. C.
HIDDEN FACES	Dali, Salvador
HIDDEN SARIA	Halford, John
THE HIDDEN UNIVERSE	Farley, Ralph Milne
HIDDEN WORLD	Coblentz, Stanton A.
THE HIGH CRUSADE	Anderson, Poul
HIGH MAGIC'S AID	"Schire"
HIGH SNOW	"Ganpat"
HIGH VACUUM	Maine, Charles Eric
HIGH WATER AT CATFISH BEND	Burman, Ben Lucien
HIGHWAYS IN HIDING	Smith, George O.
THE HILLS WERE LIARS	Hughes, Riley
HINCHBRIDGE HAUNTED	Cupples, George
HINDOO TALES	Jacob, P. W.
HIS PSEUDOIC MAJESTY	Smith, William Augustus
THE HISTORY OF BENJAMIN KENNICOTT	Anonymous
THE HISTORY OF NOURJAHAD	Sheridan, Mrs.
THE HOCUS ROOT	Foster, L. B.
HOLE IN HEAVEN	Fawcett, F. Dubrez
HOLIDAY	Deamer, Dulcie
THE HOLIDAY BOOK	Thomson, H. Douglas and Ramsay, C. Clark
A HOLIDAY IN HADES	Scoffern, David
HOME FIRES BURNING	Henriques, Robert D. Q.
THE HOMUNCULUS	Keller, David H.
HONEY FOR THE GHOST	Golding, Louis
THE HOPPING HA'PENNY	Lock, J. M.
THE HORLA & OTHER TALES	Maupassant, Guy de
A HORNBOOK FOR WITCHES	Drake, Leah Bodine

HORROR CASTLE	Sharp, Robert
THE HORROR FROM THE HILLS	Long, Frank Belknap
THE HORROR OF ABBOTT'S GRANGE	Cowles, Frederick I.
HORRORS OF SMILING MANOR	Gardner, Maurice B.
HORTENSE; A STUDY OF THE FUTURE	"Lancelot Lance"
HOSTS OF GHOSTS	Sapte, W.
HOTEL COSMOS	Burke, Jonathan
THE HOUSE OF DREAMS	Dawson, William J.
HOUSE OF ENTROPY	Sheldon, Roy
THE HOUSE OF LIVING DEATH	Blore, Trevor
THE HOUSE OF MANY WORLDS	Merwin, Samuel
HOUSE OF THE DAMNED	Rud, Anthony
THE HOUSE OF THE SPHINX	Evans, Henry Ridgeley
THE HOUSE OF THE WIZARD	Taylor, M. Imlay
THE HOUSE THAT STOOD STILL	van Vogt, A. E.
THE HOUSE THAT WAS	Syrett, Netta
THE HOUSE UPSTAIRS	Rodda, Charles
THE HOUSE WITH THE ECHO	Powys, T. F.
THE HOUSE WITHOUT WINDOWS	Sandoz, Maurice
HOW NOW BROWN COW	Jones, Ewart C.
THE HUMAN ANGLE	Tenn, William
THE HUMAN COMPASS	Kennedy, Bart
THE HUMANOIDS	Williamson, Jack
A HUMBLE ROMANCE	Wilkins, Mary E.
A HUNDRED YEARS HENCE	Moresby, Lord
THE HUNGER	Beaumont, Charles
THE HUNGRY STONES	Tagore, Rabindranath
HUNTERS FROM SPACE	Silverberg, Robert
HUNTERS OF SPACE	Kelleam, Joseph E.
THE HUNTSMAN AT THE GATE	Jenks, Almet
HURTLERS THROUGH SPACE	Burrage, A. Harcourt
HUSH-A-BY BABY	Drake, Burgess
THE HUT IN THE FOREST	Bremner, Blache Irbe
I DIE POSSESSED	O'Sullivan, J. B.
I DOUBTED FLYING SAUCERS.	Layne, Stan
I, GOVERNOR OF CALIFORNIA	Sinclair, Upton
I KILLED STALIN	Noel, Sterling
I REMEMBER LEMURIA	Shaver, Richard
I, ROBOT	Asimov, Isaac
"I WILL NOT CEASE	Cousins, E. G.
I, YAHWEH	Grey, Robert Malory
ICEWORLD	Clement, Hal
IF CHRIST CAME TO CHICATO	Stead, William T.
IF CHRIST CAME TO CONGRESS	Howard, M. W.
IF I WERE YOU	Green, Julian
IF THE DEVIL CAME TO CHICAGO	Granville, Austyn and Knott, William W.
THE ILLUSTRATED MAN	Bradbury, Ray
THE IMAGE OF A DRAWN SWORD	Brooke, Jocelyn
IMAGINATION UNLIMITED	Bleiler, E. F. and Dikty, T. E.
IMAGINOTIONS	Jenks, Tudor
IMMORTAL ATHALIA	Haley, Harry F.
THE IMMORTAL ERROR	Trevor, Elleston
IMMORTALITY DELIVERED	Sheckley, Robert

THE IMMORTALS	Garner, Rolf
IN A TRANCE: AN HYPNOTIC MYSTERY	St. Clair, Vivian B.
IN ADAM'S FALL	Dodge, Constance W.
IN GHOSTLY COMPANY	Northcote, Amyas
IN JEOPARDY	Sutphen, Van Tassel
IN RE: SHERLOCK HOLMES	Derleth, August
IN REALMS UNKNOWN	Bell, Robert
IN THE BATTLE FOR NEW YORK	Hancock, H. Irving
IN THE CLOSED ROOM	Burnett, Frances Hodgson
IN THE DARK BACKWARD	Nevinson, Henry W.
IN THE FROCK OF A PRIEST	Gavassa, M.
IN THE GREAT WHITE LAND	Stables, W. Gordon
IN THE LAND OF THE GODS	Bacon, Alice Muriel
IN THE LAND OF THE LIVING DEAD	Tucker, Prentiss
IN THE PALE	Illiowizi, Henry
IN THE PENAL SETTLEMENT	Kafka, Franz
IN THE REALM OF TERROR	Blackwood, Algernon
IN THE SHADOW OF PA-MANKH	Langlois, Dora
IN THE THREE ZONES	Stimson, F. J.
IN THE WET	Shute, Nevil
IN WHAT STRANGE LAND?	Very, Pierre
INCARNATE ISIS	Desmond, Shaw
THE INCA'S RANSOM	MacCreagh, Gordon
THE INCREDIBLE PLANET	Campbell, John W.
THE INDESTRUCTIBLE	Garner, Rolf
INDEX TO SIBYL	Sturm, Justin
INDIA MOSAIC	Channing, Mark
THE INFINITE BRAIN	Long, Charles
THE INHABITANTS OF MARS	Mitchell, Prof. W.
INHERIT THE NIGHT	Christie, Robert
THE INN OF FIVE LOVERS	Saint-Laurent, Cecil
THE INNOCENCE OF PASTOR MULLER	Beuf, Carlo
THE INNOCENT EVE	Nathan, Robert
AN INTERNATIONAL INTERLUDE	Anonymous
INTERPLANETARY HUNTER	Barnes, Arthur K.
INTERRUPT THE MOON	Lesser, Edward John
INTERRUPTION	Mills, G. H. Saxon
INTO THIN AIR	Winslow, Horation and Quirk, Winslow
THE INVADER	Woods, Margaret L.
INVADER FROM RIGEL	Pratt, Fletcher
INVADERS FROM THE INFINITE	Campbell, John W.
INVADERS FROM EARTH	Conklin, Groff
INVASION FROM SPACE	Mackenzie, Nigel
THE INVASION OF THE UNITED STATES	Hancock, H. Irving
INVISIBLE BARRIERS	Osborne, David
THE INVISIBLE GUIDE	Hind, C. Lewis
THE INVISIBLE HOST	Bristow, Gwen and Manning, Bruce
INVISIBLE SCARLETT O'NEILL	Stamm, Russell
THE INVISIBLE SHIPS	"Sea-Lion"
THE INVOLUNTARY IMMORTALS	Phillips, Rog
IRON AND GOLD	Vaughan, Hilda
THE IRON STAR	True, John Prestoh

ISLAND	Huxley, Aldous
ISLAND IN THE SKY	Wellman, Manly Wade
THE ISLAND OF ATLANTIS	Anonymous
THE ISLAND OF LOST WOMEN	Stacpoole, H. de Vere
THE ISLAND OF SURPRISE	Brady, Cyrus Townsend
ISLAND TWILIGHT	Trantner, Nigel
ISLANDS IN THE SKY	Clarke, Arthur C.
ISLANDS OF SPACE	Campbell, John W.
THE ISLES WERE DISTURBED	Fenwick, Kenneth
THE ISOTOPE MAN	Maine, Charles Eric
IT HAPPENED TOMORROW	Williams, Francis
IT HAPPENS EVERY SPRING	Davies, Valentine
IT HOWLS AT NIGHT	Berrow, Norman
JACK OF EAGLES	Blish, James
JACK PUMPKINHEAD OF OZ	Baum, L. Frank
JAGUAR AND THE GOLDEN STAG	Allen, Dexter
JANICE IN TOMORROW-LAND	Thompson, Ruth Plumly
A JAPANESE MESCELLANY	Hearn, Lafcadio
JENNY VILLIERS	Priestley, J. B.
THE JEWELER OF BAGDAD	Wittels, Fritz
John CARSTAIRS, SPACE DETECTIVE	Long, Frank Belknap
JOHN INGLESANT	Shorthouse, J. Henry
JOHN PARMALEE'S CURSE	Hawthorne, Julian
JOHN WHOPPER, THE NEWSBOY	Anonymous
JOHNNY FORSAKEN	Stern, G. B.
JONAH	Nathan, Robert
JONAH AND THE VOICE	Tandrup, Harold
JONATHAN	O'Neill, Russell
JONLYS THE WITCH	Troubetskoy, Princess Paul
JOSHUA BEENE AND GOD	Gibson, Jewel
A JOURNALIST AND TWO BEARS	Edmund, James
JOURNEY INTO SPACE	Chilton, Charles
JOURNEY THROUGH SPACE	Williams, Speedy
JOURNEY THROUGH UTOPIA	Berneri, Marie Louise
JOURNEY TO INFINITY	Greenberg, Martin
A JOURNEY TO THE INTERIOR	Newby, P. H.
JOURNEYS IN SCIENCE FICTION	Loughlin, Richard J. and Popp, Lilian M.
THE JOY WAGON	Hadley, Arthur T.
JOYCE OF THE SECRET SQUADRON	Winterbotham, R. R.
THE JOYOUS ADVENTURER	Barnett, Ada
THE JUDGE OF JERUSALEM	Bloom, Ursula
THE JUDGE WILL CALL IT MURDER	Lott, S. Makepeace
JUDGMENT EVE	Harwood, H. C.
JUDGMENT NIGHT AND OTHER STORIES	Moore, C. L.
JUDGMENT ON JANUS	Norton, Andre
THE JUNGLE GODDESS	Sackville, Orme
JUPITER IN THE CHAIR	Fraxer, Ronald
THE KA OF GIFFORD HILARY	Wheatley, Denis
KAPPA	Akutagawa, Ryunosuke
KARMA	Hearn, Lafcadio
KATHY'S VISIT TO MARS	Collier, Dwight A.
KEMLO AND THE CRAZY PLANET	Eliott, E. C.
KEMLO AND THE MARTIAN GHOSTS	Eliott, E. C.
KEMLO AND THE SKY HORSE	Eliott, E. C.
KEMLO AND THE ZONES OF SILENCE	

THE KEY OF LIFE	Gibbs, (Sir) Philip
THE KEY TO THE GREAT GATE	Gottlieb, Hinko
KEY OUT OF TIME	Norton, Andre
KHAMBUNI. A MYSTERY OF THE SECRET SERVICE	Soutar, Andrew
THE KID FROM MARS	Friend, Oscar J.
THE KIDNAPPED MILLIONAIRES	Adams, Frederick Upham
KILLER TO COME	Merwin, Samuel
THE KING AND QUEEN OF MALLEBUSCH	Ebers, George
KING CONAN	Howard, Robert A.
KING JULIAN	Gatch, Tom
THE KING OF ANDAMAN	Cobban, James Maclaren
THE KING OF MEN	Miller, Alan
THE KING OF SCHNORRERS	Zangwill, Israel
KING OF THE WORLD	Morton, Guy
THE KING WAS IN HIS COUNTING HOUSE	Cabell, James Branch
THE KINGDOM OF A THOUSAND ISLANDS	Farrere, M.
THE KING'S ASSEGAI	Mitford, Bertram
THE KING'S MISSAL	Beamish, Noel de Vic
KINGS OF SPACE	Johns, Capt. W. E.
THE KINGSLAYER	Hubbard, L. Ron
KINSMEN OF THE DRAGON	Mullen, Stanley
KISS ME AGAIN, STRANGER	du Maurier, Daphne
THE KISS OF ISIS AND THE MYSTERY OF CASTLEBOURNE	Haggard, Capt. Arthur
THE KISS OF THE PHARAOH	Goyne, Richard
KNICKERBOCKER'S HISTORY OF NEW YORK	Irving, Washington
KNIGHT'S CASTLE	Eager, Edward
KONGO, THE GORILLA MAN	Orndorff, Frank
KWAIDAN	Hearn, Lafcadio
LA BRUJO THE WITCH	Markophrates
LADY ATHLYNE	Stoker, Bram
THE LADY DECIDES	Keller, David H.
THE LADY OF LOWFORD	Author of "The Holiday Book"
LADY OF THE TERRACES	Vivian, E. Charles
THE LADY WITH FEET OF GOLD	Dwyer, James Francis
THE LAIRD AND THE LADY	Grant, Joan
THE LAMP STILL BURNS	Wherry, Edith
LANCELOT BIGGS: SPACEMAN	Bond, Nelson F.
THE LAND OF ESA	Charles, Neil
THE LAND OF FORGOTTEN WOMEN	Webster, F. A. M.
THE LAND OF OZ	Baum, L. Frank
THE LAND WHICH LOVETH SILENCE	Sornicoli, Davide
THE LANGUAGES OF PAO	Vance, Jack
THE LAST ADAM	Duncan, Ronald
THE LAST CRUISE OF THE ELECTRA	Chipman, Charles P.
THE LAST EGYPTIAN	Anonymous
THE LAST ENEMY	Strong, L. A. G.
THE LAST FOOL	Lundstrom, Emil Ferdinand
THE LAST OF SIX: TALES OF AUSTRALIAN TROPICS	Favenc, Ernest
LAST OF THE GIANT KILLERS	Atkinson, T. C.
THE LAST OF THE VAMPIRES	Upton, Smyth
THE LAST OF THE WONDER CLUB	Halidom, M. Y.
THE LAST PRINCESS	Locke, Charles O.
THE LAST REFUGE OF A SCOUNDREL	Howard, Wendall

THE LAST REVOLUTION	Dunsany, Lord
THE LAST SPACE SHIP	Leinster, Murray
THE LAST WHITE MAN	Gandon, Yves
LATE FINAL	Gibbs, Lewis
LAUNCELOT, MY BROTHER	Roberts, Dorothy J.
LAURIE'S SPACE ANNUAL: 1953	Anonymous anthology
LAZARUS #7	Sale, Richard
LAZARUS OF BETHANY	Holcombe, William Henry
LEGENDS OF THE CITY OF MEXICO	Janvier, Thomas A.
LEGENDS OF THE PATRIARCHS AND PROPHETS	Baring-Gould, S.
THE LEGION OF TIME	Williamson, Jack
LENTALA OF THE SOUTH SEAS	Morrow, W. C.
LESLIE'S FATE AND HILDA	Haggard, Capt. Andrew
LET'S ALL GO TO HEAVEN	Day, Millard, F.
LETTERS FROM A LIVING DEAD MAN	Barker, Elsa
LEVEL 7	Roshwold, Mordecai
THE LIBERATION OF MANHATTAN	Demaitre, Edmund and Appleman, Mark J.
LIFE BEGINS TOMORROW	Parkman, Sydney
LIFE COMES TO SEATHORPE	Bell, Neil
LIFE EVERLASTING	Keller, David H.
A LIFE FOR THE STARS	Blish, James
LIFE MARCHES ON	Magor, Nancy and Woods, Margaret Murray
THE LIGHT OUT OF THE EAST	Crockett, S. R.
THE LIGHTS IN THE SKY ARE STARS	Brown, Fredric
LIMBO	Wolfe, Bernard
THE LINCOLN HUNTERS	Tucker, Wilson
LINKED LIVES	Ingalese, Isabella
LION MAN	Cripps, A. S.
THE LION, THE WITCH, AND THE WARDROBE	Lewis, C. S.
THE LION'S BROOD	Osborne, Duffield
LISTENING HANDS	Hope, Coral
LITERARY REMAINS OF THE LATE HENRY NEELE	Neele, Henry
THE LITTLE BLUE MAN	Hill, Dorothy
LITTLE BRONZE PLAYFELLOWS	Perry, Stella and Stern, George
A LITTLE CONFAB WITH SOCRATES	Simpkins, J. M.
THE LITTLE GLASS MAN	Hauff, Wilhelm
LITTLE JOURNEYS WITH MARTIN LUTHER	Harley, William Nicholas
THE LITTLE LAUNDRESS AND THE FEARFUL KNIGHT	Bloch, Bertram
THE LITTLE MEN	Kelleam, Joseph E.
A LITTLE NORTH OF EVERYWHERE	Norman, James
THE LITTLE TALES OF SMETHERS	Dunsany, Lord
LITTLE WIZARD STORIES OF OZ	Baum, L. Frank
THE LITTLE WORLD OF DON CAMILLO	Guareschi, Giovanni
LIVES IN A BOX	Grant, Richard
LIVING ON	Wilcox, F. W.
THE LIVING WOOD	de Wohl, Louis
LLANA OF GATHOL	Burroughs, Edgar Rice
LOAVES & FISHES	Capes, Bernard
THE LOCUST HORDE	Shaw, Stanley
LODESTAR—ROCKET SHIP TO MARS	Branley, Franklyn M.
THE LODGE IN THE WILDERNESS	Poor, Katherine Hillwood
THE LODGER	Lowndes, Belloc
THE LOG OF THE ARK BY NOAH	Gordon, I. L. and Frueh, A. J.

LONDON AFTER MIDNIGHT	Coolidge-Rask, Marie
LONE ELM	Prior, Anthony
THE LONELIEST GIRL IN THE WORLD	Fearing, Kenneth
LONESOME PLACES	Derleth, August
THE LONG LOUD SILENCE	Tucker, Wilson
THE LONG NIGHT	Caidin, Martin
THE LONG SHIPS	Bengtsson, Frans G.
THE LONG TOMORROW	Brackett, Leigh
THE LONG WAY BACK	Bennett, Margot
THE LONG WINTER	Christopher, John
LOOK BEHIND YOU	Burks, Arthur J.
LOOKING BEYOND	Lin Yutang
LOOKING FORWARD	Lesser, Milton
LOOKING FURTHER BACKWARD	Vinton, Arthur Dudley
THE LOOSE BOARD IN THE FLOOR	Miller, R. DeWitt
THE LOOTED GOLD	Westerman, John F. C.
LORD ADRIAN	Dunsany, Lord
LORD BLACKSHIRT	Graeme, Bruce
LORD OF THE DARK RED STAR	Lee-Hamilton, Eugene
LORD OF THE FLIES	Golding, William
LORD OF THE HORIZON	Grant, Joan
LORD OF THE LEOPARDS	Webster, F. A. M.
LORD OF THUNDER	Norton, Andre
LORDS OF ATLANTIS	West, Wallace
THE LORDS OF CREATION	Binder, Eando
LORDS OF THE EARTH	Mills, J. M. A.
LORE OF PROSERPINE	Hewlett, Maurice
LOST: A MOON	Capon, Paul
THE LOST CAVERN	Heard, Gerald
LOST CITY OF LIGHT	Webster, F. A. M.
THE LOST CITY OF THE AZTECS	Lath, J. A.
LOST IN SPACE	Smith, George O.
THE LOST ISLAND	Gilson, Major Charles
LOST ISLAND	McInnes, Graham Campbell
THE LOST PLANET	Dallas, Paul
THE LOST PLANET	MacVicar, Angus
THE LOST PRINCESS OF OZ	Baum, L. Frank
THE LOST QUEEN OF EGYPT	Morrison, Leslie
LOST RACE OF MARS	Silverberg, Robert
LOST SPRINGTIME	Dana, Julian
THE LOST STAR AND OTHER STORIES	Chapin, Maud Hudnut
THE LOST TRIBE	Aronin, Ben
THE LOST VIOL	Shiel, M. P.
THE LOST WORLD OF EVEREST	Gray, Berkeley
THE LOST YEARS	Lewis, Oscar
LOT'S WIFE	Ley-Piscator, Maria
THE LOTTERY	Jackson, Shirley
LOVE AMONG THE RUINS	Waugh, Evelyn
THE LOVE LIFE OF A FROG	Clander, D. V.
LOVE OF SEVEN DOLLS	Gallico, Paul
THE LOVERS	Winsor, Kathleen
LUCIFER AND THE CHILD	Mannin, Ethel
LUCIUS SCARFIELD	Revermort J A.

LUCKY STARR AND THE BIG SUN OF MERCURY	French, Paul
LUCKY STARR AND THE MOONS OF JUPITER	French, Paul
LUCKY STARR AND THE OCEANS OF VENUS	French, Paul
LUCKY STARR AND THE PIRATES OF THE ASTEROIDS	French, Paul
LUCKY STARR AND THE RINGS OF SATURN	French, Paul
THE LUNATIC REPUBLIC	Mackenzie, Compton
MACH I: A STORY OF THE PLANET IONUS	Adler, Allen
THE MACHINE GOD LAUGHS	Pragnell, Festus
MADAM JULIA'S TALE	Royde-Smith, Naomi
MADAM MARGOT	Bennett, John
MADMAN'S DRUM	Ward, Lynd
THE MADRONE TREE	Duncan, David
THE MAGIC BALL FROM MARS	Biemiller, Carl L.
MAGIC BY THE LAKE	Eager, Edward
MAGIC CASEMENTS	Day, Langston
MAGIC HOURS	Peacey, Howard
MAGIC LANTERNS	Saunders, Louise
MAGIC MATING	James, Wentworth
THE MAGIC OF OZ	Baum, L. Frank
MAGIC OR NOT?	Eager, Edward
THE MAGIC PICTURES	Ayme, Marcel
THE MAGIC PRESENCE	King, Godfre Ray
MAGIC SHADOW SHOW	Earnest, Olga D. A.
THE MAGIC TALE OF HARVANGER AND YOLANDE	Baker, G. P.
THE MAGIC TOOTH	Eels, Elsie S.
THE MAGICIAN	Beaton, David C.
THE MAGICIANS	Priestley, J. B.
THE MAGICIANS OF CHARNC	Williams, Geoffrey
THE MAGICIAN'S NEPHEW	Lewis, C. S.
MAGNIFICENT HORIZONS	Sabini, Ronaldo
THE MAGNIFICENT MCINNES	Mead, Shepherd
THE MAHATMA	Anonymous
THE MALACHITE CASKET	Bazhov, Pavel
MALICE IN KULTURLAND	Wyatt, Horace
THE MALLACCA CANE	Kemp, Robert
MAN ABROAD	Anonymous
MAN AND SUPERMAN	Shaw, George Bernard
A MAN DIVIDED	Stapledon, Olaf
A MAN FROM THE PAST	Fleischman, Theo
THE MAN FROM THE TUNNEL	Benson, Theodore
THE MAN IN GREY	Smith, Eleanor
THE MAN IN THE HIGH CASTLE	Dick, Philip K.
THE MAN IN THE MOON AND OTHER STORIES	Raymond, R. W.
THE MAN IN THE MOON IS TALKING	Orb, Clay
THE MAN IN THE TOP HAT	Jaeger, Cyril K.
MAN INTO BEAST	Spectorsky, A. C.
MAN OF MANY MINDS	Evans, E. E.
MAN OF MIRACLES	Leblanc, Maurice
THE MAN WHO ATE THE PHOENIX	Dunsany, Lord
THE MAN WHO CANNOT DIE	Williamson, Thames
THE MAN WHO COULDN'T SLEEP	Maine, Charles Eric
THE MAN WHO KILLED HITLER	Anonymous
THE MAN WHO KNEW	Webster, F. A. M.

THE MAN WHO KNEW THE DATE	Kerr, Sophie
THE MAN WHO LIVED BACKWARDS	Ross, Malcolm
THE MAN WHO LOST HIMSELF	Sitwell, Osbert
THE MAN WHO MET HIMSELF	Crawshay-Williams, Eliot
THE MAN WHO MISSED THE WAR	Wheatley, Dennis
THE MAN WHO SHOOK THE EARTH	HORLER, Sydney
THE MAN WHO SOLD THE MOON	Heinlein, Robert A.
THE MAN WHO SURVIVED	Marbo, Camille
THE MAN WHO WAS EMPEROR	Sowden, Lewis
THE MAN WHO WENT BACK	Barrow, Percy James
THE MAN WITH ABSOLUTE MOTION	Water, Silas
THE MAN WITH ONLY ONE HEAD	Barr, Densil Neve
THE MAN WITH THIRTY LIVES	Pym, Herbert
THE MAN WITH TWO BODIES	Fitz-Gibbon, Ralph
THE MAN WITH TWO SHADOWS	Maugham, Robin
THE MAN WITHOUT A NAVEL	Palmer, Cuthbert
THE MANATITLANS	Smile, R. Elton
MANDRAGORA	Estival
MANDRAKE	Sherry, Oliver
MANY ENCHANTMENTS	Segal, Lesley Keen
MANY MANSIONS	Dowding, Air Chief Marshall Lord
THE MARBLE FOREST	Durant, Theo
THE MARK OF THE MOON	Gerard, Francis
MAROONED ON MARS	del Rey, Lester
A MARRIAGE OF SOULS	Mathieson, Una Cooper
MARS MOUNTAIN	Key, Eugene G.
MARSHLANDS, AND PROMETHEUS MISBOUND	Gide, Andre
MARSHUNA	Watson, H. B. Marriot
THE MARTIAN	Du Maurier, George L.
THE MARTIAN CHRONICLES	Bradbury, Ray
THE MARTIAN MISSILES	Grinnell, David
A MARTIAN ODYSSEY	Weinbaum, Stanley G.
THE MARTIAN WAY	Asimov, Isaac
MARTIANS, GO HOME	Brown, Fredric
MARTIN AND HIS FRIEND FROM OUTER SPACE	Duka, Ivo and Kolda, Helena
THE MARVELLOUS EXPERIENCE OF JOHN RYDAL	Scott, Edward
THE MARVELLOUS LAND OF OZ	Baum L, Frank
MARY'S COUNTRY	Mead, Harold
THE MASK OF CTHULHU	Derleth, August W.
THE MASK OF SATAN	Lavonda, Marsha
THE MASK OF WISDOM	Clewes, Howard
THE MASTER	White, T. H.
A MASTER OF FORTUNE	Hyne, C. J. Cutliffe
MASTER OF SHADOWS	Lawrence, Margery
THE MASTER OF SOULS	Hansom, Mark
THE MASTER OF THE MACABRE	Thorndyke, Russell
THE MASTER OF THE MOON	Moore, Patrick
MASTER OF THE WORLD	Sylvester, John
THE MASTER SINNER	A well Known Author
MASTERLESS SWORDS	Suddaby, Donald
MASTERPIECES OF ADVENTURE	Braddy, Nolla
MASTERPIECES OF MYSTERY. RIDDLE STORIES	French, Joseph Lewis
MASTERS OF TIME	van Vogt, A. E.

THE MATHEMATICAL AND PHILOSOPHICAL WORKS	Wilkins, (Rev.) John
A MATTER OF LIFE AND DEATH	Warman, Eric
MAUT	Leonis, Sheila
MAYA	Foulke, William Dudley
McGARRITY & THE PIGEONS	Holm, John Cecil
McGILLICUDDY McGOTHAM	Wibberly, Leonard
A MEDICINE FOR MELANCHOLY	Bradbury, Ray
A MEETING OVER TUSCARORA	Efremov, I.
THE MEETING PLACE	Beresford, J. D.
MEL OLIVER AND SPACE ROVER ON MARS	Morrison, William
MELBOURNE AND MARS	Frazer, Joseph
MELCHIOR'S DREAM	Ewing, Mrs. Juliana Horatia
THE MEMOIRS OF A GHOST	Stonier, G. W.
MEMOIRS OF A MIDGET	de la Mare, Walter
THE MEMOIRS OF SOLAR PONS	Derleth, August W.
THE MEMORY BANK	West, Wallace
MEN AGAINST THE STARS	Greenberg, Martin
THE MEN FROM ARCTURUS	Winterbotham, Russ
MEN, MARTIANS AND MACHINES	Russell, Eric Frank
MEN WHO WOULDN'T STAY DEAD	Clarke, Ida Clyde
THE MENACE FROM EARTH	Heinlein, Robert A.
THE MENACE FROM THE MOON	Lynch, Bohun
THE MERGING OF RONALD LETHERIDGE	Marks, Percy L.
THE MERMAID	Dougall, L.
THE MERMAID OF ZENNOR	Moloney, Eileen
THE MERRY MIRACLE	Mian, Mary
THE MESMERISTS	Farjeon, Benjamin Leopold
THE MESMERIST'S SECRET	Dormer, Daniel
MESSAGE FROM A STRANGER	Mannes, Marya
A MESSAGE FROM SPACE	Goodchild, George
MESSIAH	Vidal, Gore
MESSIAH ON THE HORIZON	Cruso, Solomon
THE METAL EATER	Sheldon, Roy
METHUSELAH'S CHILDREN	Heinlein, Robert A.
THE MIDNIGHT HOUR AND AFTER	Naish, Reginald T.
THE MIDNIGHT PATIENT	Nostovsky, Egon
MIDSUMMER SANITY	Ingram, Kenneth
THE MIDWICH CUCKOOS	Wyndham, John
A MIGHTY EMPIRE	Barlow, J. Swindle
A MILE BEYOND THE MOON	Kornbluth, C. M.
THE MIND CAGE	van Vogt, A. E.
MIND OUT OF TIME	Tonks, Angela
MIND PARTNER	Gold, H. L.
THE MIND READER	Phillips, L. M.
THE MIND READER	Roghenberg, Alan Baie
THE MINDWORM	Kornbluth, C. M.
MINIATURE ROMANCES FROM THE GERMAN	Anonymous anthology
MINIONS OF THE MOON	Beyer, William Grey
A MIRACLE FOR CAROLINE	Feiner, Ruth
MIRACLE IN BRITTANY	Jordan, Mildred
MIRACLE IN THE RAIN	Hecht, Ben
A MIRACLE OF ST. ANTHONY	Maeterlinck, Maurice
THE MIRACLE ON 34th STREET	Davies, Valentine
MIRANGO THE MANEATER	

A MIRROR FOR OBSERVERS	Pangborn, Edgar
A MIRROR OF SILVER	Bridges, Roy
MISS PICKERELL GOES TO MARS	MacGregor, Ellen
MISS PIM'S CAMOUFLAGE	Stanley, Dorothy
MISSING MEN OF SATURN	Latham, Philip
MISSION ACCOMPLISHED	Walker, Jerry
MISSION OF GRAVITY	Clement, Hal
MISSION TO THE MOON	del Rey, Lester
MR. ARROW	Russell, Austin
MR. BASS'S PLANETOID	Cameron, Eleanor
MR. BREMBLE'S BUTTONS	Langley, Dorothy
MR. CHANG'S CRIME RAY	Apple, A. A.
MR. GEORGE AND OTHER ODD PERSONS	Grendon, Stephen
MR. KRONION	Kerby, Susan Alice
MR. MUDGE CUTS ACROSS	Sanborn, R. A.
MISTER PIMNEY	Wyman, Justus E. and Surendorf, Charles
MR. PRETRE	Belloc, Hillaire
MR. PUNCH'S PRIZE NOVELS	Lehman, R. C.
MR. THEOBALD'S DEVIL	Keown, Anna Gordon
MR. WHITTLE AND THE MORNING STAR	Nathan, Robert
MRS. CANDYAND SATURDAY NIGHT	Tallant, Robert
MRS. CANDY STRIKES IT RICH	Tallant, Robert
MRS. SEARWOOD'S SECRET WEAPON	Wibberley, Leonard
MISTS OF DAWN	Oliver, Chad
THE MIXED MEN	van Vogt, A. E.
MOG, THE MOUND BUILDER	Crump, Irving
MOKEANNA	Burnand, F. C.
MOMENT OF DECISION	Hough, S. B.
THE MOMENT OF TRUTH	Jameson, Storm
THE MONIKINS: A LAND OF CIVILIZED MONKEYS	Cooper, J. Fenimore
THE MONK AND THE HANGMAN'S DAUGHTER	Bierce, Ambrose
MONKEY	Wu Cheng-En
MONKEY FACE	Gilbert, Stephen
MONSTER-LAND	Quiz
MOON AHEAD	Greener, Leslie
THE MOON CHILDREN	MacNaughton, Donald
THE MOON IS HELL!	Campbell, John W.
THE MOON MAKER	Train, Arthur and Wood, Robert W.
THE MOON MAN	Steiger, Andrew Jacob
MOON OVER THE BACK FENCE	Carlson, Esther
MOONBEAMS FROM THE LARGER LUNACY	Leacock, Stephen
MOONFLEET	Falkner, John Meade
MOONFLOWER	Peterson, Margaret
MOONFOAM & SORCERIES	Mullen, Stanley
MOONLIGHT IN UR	Watson, E. L. Grant
MOONRAKER	Fleming, Ian
THE MOOR'S GOLD	Aronin, Ben
MORAG, THE SEAL	Brodie-Innes, J. W.
MORE THAN HUMAN	Sturgeon, Theodore
MORE THINGS IN HEAVEN	Owen, Walter
MORE UNCANNY STORIES	Anonymous anthology
MORGAN ROCKEFELLER'S WILL	Clarke, Francis H.
MORNING FOR MR. PROTHERO	Oliver, Jane

MORTAL SUMMER	Van Doren, Mark
MOSTYN STEYNE: A NOVEL	Quinn, Roderick Joseph
THE MOTH MEN	Rochester, George E.
MOTHER-IN-LAW INDIA	Sinderby, Donald
MOUNT KESTREL	Pilibin, A.
MOUNTAIN BRIDE	Coatsworth, Elizabeth
THE MOUNTAIN OF GOLD	Winch, E.
THE MOUNTAIN OF MYSTERY	Langley, Kenlis
THE MOUNTAIN SPIRITES KINGDOM	Knatchbull-Hugessen, E. H.
THE MOUSE THAT ROARED	Wibberley, Leonard
MUBENDI GIRL	Webster, F. A. M.
MURDER IN MILLENIUM VI	Gray, Curme
MURDER ON THE WAY	Roscoe, Theodore
MUTANT	Padgett, Lewis
THE MUTINOUS WIND	Reynard, Elizabeth
MY BEST SCIENCE FICTION STORY	Margulies, Leo and Friend, Oscar J.
MY FLIGHT TO VENUS	Howard, Dana
MY JOURNEYS WITH ASTARGO	Barnhouse, Perl T.
MY LADY OF THE NILE	Egbert, H. M.
MY LIFE IN THE BUSH OF GHOSTS	Tutuola, Amos
MY LIFE IN TIME	Newton, Bertha
MY LIFE WITH BORLEY RECTORY	Turner, James
MY ONLY MURDER AND OTHER TALES	Favenc, Ernest
MYSTERIES OF THE COSMOS	Taney, Ahmet Raif
THE MYSTERIOUS CHINESE MANDRAKE	Ekbergh, Ida Diana
THE MYSTERIOUS FIVE	Taylor, Marie E.
MYSTERIOUS HAPPENINGS	Lewis, Maurice
MYSTERIOUS PLANET	Wright, Kenneth
MYSTERY	Anonymous anthology
THE MYSTERY OF ARTHUR GORDON PYM	Poe, Edgar Allan and Verne, Jules
THE MYSTERY OF BURNLEIGH MANOR	Livingston, Walter
THE MYSTERY OF LUCIEN DELORME	De Taramond, Guy
THE MYSTERY OF MADELINE LE BLANC	Ehrmann, Max
THE MYSTERY OF MAR SABA	Hunter, James H.
THE MYSTERY OF THE GREEN RAY	Le Queux, William
THE MYSTERY OF THE HIDDEN CITY	Bull, Albert E.
MYSTERY OF THE THIRDMINE	Lowndes, Robert W.
THE MYSTERY OF WO-SING	Hales, A.G.
THE NAKED SUN	Asimov, Isaac
A NAME FOR EVIL	Lytle, Andrew
THE NAMELESS ONES	Scott, R. T. M.
THE NATURAL MAN	Miller, Patrick
NAZER(A ZIGZAG PHILOSOPHY)	Joyce, John A.
NECROMANCER	Dickson, Gordon R.
NEEDLE	Clement, Hal
NEIGHBORS	Houghton, Claude
NEILA SEN AND MY CASUAL DEATH	Connelly, J. H.
NERO, AND OTHER POEMS	Smith, Clark Ashton
NERVES	del Rey, Lester
NEUROOMIA: A NEW CONTINENT	McIver, G.
NEVER BY CHANCE	Tate, Sylvia
A NEW ALICE IN THE OLD WONDERLAND	Anonymous
A NEW MESSIAH	Cromie, Robert

THE NEW PANJANDRUM	Farrow, G. E.
NEW TALES OF SPACE AND TIME	Healy, Raymond J.
THE NEW TERROR	Leroux, Gaston
THE NEW WIZARD OF OZ	Baum, L. Frank
A NEW WONDERLAND	Baum, L. Frank
NEWBURY IN ORM	Williams, Islwyn
NEXT DOOR TO THE SUN	Coblentz, Stanton A.
NEXT OF KIN	Russell, Eric Frank
NEXT STOP--MARS	Edwards, David
NIGHT DRUMS	Abdullah, Achmed
THE NIGHT I DIED	Irish, William
NIGHT IN BABYLON	Wellard, James H.
NIGHT IN NO TIME	Crawshay-Williams, Eliot
NIGHT OF THE AUK	Oboler, Arch
NIGHT ON THE RIVER AND OTHER STORIES	Freyer, Dermot
NIGHTMARES OF EMINENT PERSONS	Russell, Bertrand
NIGHT'S YAWNING PEAL	Derleth, August W.
NINE HORRORS	Brennan, Joseph Payne
"998"	Hyams, Edward S.
THE NINE POINTED STAR	Sykes, Claude W.
NINE TALES OF SPACE AND TIME	Healy, Raymond J.
NINE TOMORROWS	Asimov, Isaac
1984	Orwell, George
NO BLADE OF GRASS	Christopher, John
NO BOUNDARIES	Kuttner, Henry and Moore, C. L.
NO MAN FRIDAY	Gordon, Rex
NO OTHER GODS	Penfield, Wilder
NO PLACE LIKE EARTH	Carnell, D. J.
NO PLACE ON EARTH	Charbonneau, Louis
NO REFUGE	Boland, John
NOAH'S ARK	Zanuck, Darryl and de Haas, Arline
NOAH'S STOWAWAY	Martin, Lester
NOBODY KNOWS WHAT THE STORK WILL BRING	Criswell, Charles
NOBODY SAY A WORD	Van Doren, Mark
NOCTURNAL REVELS	Anonymous
NOMAD	Smith, George O.
NONE SO BLIND	Baker, Gordon
NORTH OF THE STARS	Stoddard, Charles
NORTH SEA MONSTER	Spencer, D. A. and Randerson, W.
NORTHWEST OF EARTH	Moore, C. L.
NOT IN OUR STARS	Hyams, Edward S.
NOT IN SOLITUDE	Gantz, Kenneth F.
NOT LONG FOR THIS WORLD	Derleth, August W.
NOT THIS AUGUST	Kornbluth, C. M.
THE NOTARY'S NOSE	About, Edmond
NOTES FOR A NEW MYTHOLOGY	Long, Haniel
NOUR-EDODYN, OR THE LIGHT OF FAITH	Murray, Sir Charles D.
A NOVEL, A NOVELLA AND FOUR SHORT STORIES	Lytle, Andrew
NOVELS AND TALES	Wilde, Oscar
NOVELS, SKETCHES, AND ESSAYS	Anonymous anthology
NOW TO THE STARS	Johns, Capt. W. E.
No. 56 AND OTHER STORIES	Mandes, Catulle
NUMBER NINE, OR, THE MIND SWEEPERS	Herbert, A. P.

NUTRO 29	Norris, Frank
NYMPHS OF THE VALLEY	Gibran, Kahlil
O KING, LIVE FOREVER	Myers, Henry
O MEN OF ATHENS	Malcolm, A. C.
O'CALLAGHAN THE SLAVE TRADER	Lampen, Charles Dudley
OCCAM'S RAZOR	Duncan, David
THE OCTOBER COUNTRY	Bradbury, Ray
THE ODIOUS ONES	Sohl, Jerry
OF ALL POSSIBLE WORLDS	Tenn, William
OF CASTLE TERROR	Inman, Arthur Crew
OF LUNAR KINGDOMS	Wilson, Henry Lovejoy
OF THE NIGHT WIND'S TELLING	David, E. Adams
O'HALLORAN'S LUCK AND OTHER SHORT STORIES	Benet, Stephen Vincent
THE OLD BOAT ROCKER	Mudd, William S.
THE OLD DIE RICH	Gold, H. L.
OLD JUNK	Tomsinson, H. M.
THE OLD LION	de la Mare, Walter
THE OLDEST LAND	Stanton, Coralie and Hosken, Heath
THE OMNIBUS OF SCIENCE FICTION	Conklin, Groff
THE OMNIBUS OF TIME	Farley, Ralph Milne
ON SATAN'S MOUNT	Tilton, Dwight
ON THE BEACH	Shute, Nevil
ON THE MARBLE CLIFFS	Juenger, Ernst
ON THE TRAIL OF 1960	Wiley, Ray H.
THE ONCE AND FUTURE KING	White, T. H.
ONCE AROUND THE PARK	Shannon, Frank
ONCE IN ALEPPO	Barton, Donald R.
ONCE UPON A STAR	Crossen, Kendall Foster
ONE	Karp, David
ONE DOLLAR'S WORTH	Brown, F. H.
ONE HALF THE WORLD	Barlow, James
ONE IN THREE HUNDRED	McIntosh, J. T.
THE ONE WHO IS LEGION	Barney, Natalie Clifford
THE ONYX RING	Sterling, John
THE OPAL MATRIX	Chambers, W. Jerome
THE OPEN SECRET	A Priest
OPERATION: OUTER SPACE	Leinster, Murray
OPERATION SPACE	Ball, John Jr.
OPERATION SPRINGBOARD	Ball, John Jr.
OPERATION SUPERMAN	Hawton, Hector
ORCHARD OF TEARS	Rohmer, Sax
ORIGINAL STORY: A TALE OF A WORLD	Smith, James
OSSIAN'S RIDE	Hoyle, Fred
THE OTHER END	Roberts, R. Ellis
THE OTHER HALF OF THE PLANET	Capon, Paul
THE OTHER MRS. JACOBS	Praed, Campbell
THE OTHER ONE	Turney, Catherine
THE OTHER PLACE	Priestley, J. B.
THE OTHER SIDE OF THE MOON	Derleth, August W.
THE OTHER SIDE OF THE SKY	Clarke, Arthur C.
THE OTHER SIDE OF THE SUN	Capon, Paul
THE OTHER SIDE OF THE UNIVERSE	Dreifuss, KUrt
OTHER STORIES	Knatchbull-Hugessen E. H.
OTHER VOICES, OTHER ROOMS	

OUR COMING WORLD	Michaud, A. C.
OUR GHOSTS	Leigh, Edmund
OUT OF MY MIND	Bilbo, Jack
OUT OF THE AGES	Pryce, Devereux
OUT OF THE DEEPS	Wyndham, John
OUT OF THE EVERYWHERE	Dinnis, Enid
OUT OF THE PAST	Spurrell, H. S. F
OUT OF THE SILENCE	Mahoney, Patrick
OUT OF THE UNKNOWN	van Vogt, A. E. and Hull, E. Mayne
OUT OF THIS WORLD	Leinster, Murray
THE OUTCASTS	Fraser, William Alexander
THE OUTER DARKNESS	Wright, R. H.
THE OUTER REACHES	Derleth, August W.
THE OUTLAWS OF MARS	Kline, Otis Adelbert
OUTPOST MARS	Judd, Cyril
OUTPOST OF JUPITER	del Rey, Lester
OUTPOSTS IN SPACE	West, Wallace
THE OUTWARD ROOM	Brand, Millen
OVERSHADOWED	Yulee, C. Wickliffe
OZMA OF OZ	Baum, L. Frank
P. X.	Taylor, Malcolm
PACK RAT	Kelley, Francis Clement
A PAD IN THE STRAW	Woodforde, Christopher
PAINTED FACE, AND OTHER GHOST STORIES	Onions, Oliver
THE PALE MOUNTAINS	Wolff, Carl Felix
THE PALM-WINE DRINKARD	Tutuola, Amos
PAN AND THE LITTLE GREEN GATE	Brett, Sylvia
PAN AND THE YOUNG SHEPHERD	Hewlett, Maurice
PANDORA'S SHOCKS	Wildig, Laura
PANIC AMONG PURITANS	Laver, James
PANORAMA OF MODERN LITERATURE	Anonymous anthology
THE PANTHER, A TALE OF TEMPTATION	Warner, Anne W.
THE PARALYZED KINGDOM	Nizzi, Guido
PARK; A FANTASTIC STORY	Gray, John
A PARODY OUTLINE OF HISTORY	Stewart, Donald Ogden
THE PASS OF THE GREY DOG	Noy, John
THE PASSING OF OUL-I-BUT	Sullivan, Alan
THE PASSIONATE CLOWNS	Marvell, W. Holt
THE PATCHWORK GIRL OF OZ	Baum, L. Frank
THE PATH OF THE GREAT	Gargilis, Stephen
PATH OF UNREASON	Smith, George O.
PATTERN FOR CONQUEST	Smith, George O.
PATTERN OF SHADOWS	Burke, Jonathan
PAWN OF TIME	Carson, Robin
PAWNS IN ICE	Gibbs, Henry
PEACE, MY DAUGHTERS	Barker, Shirley
THE PEACEMAKERS	Casewit, Curtis W.
THE PEACEMAKERS	Hayes, Hiram W.
PEBBLE IN THE SKY	Asimov, Isaac
PECKOVER	Beresford, J. D.
THE PENCIL OF GOD	Marcelin, Philippe Thoby and Pierre
PEOPLE MINUS X	Gallun, Raymond Z.
PEOPLE OF THE COMET	Hall, Austin

THE PEOPLE ON OTHER PLANETS	Fox, Richard A.
THE PERFECT PLANET	Smith, Evelyn E.
THE PERFUME OF EGYPT	Leadbetter, C. W.
PERIL ON THE AMAZON	Duff, Douglas V.
THE PERILOUS DESCENT	Carter, Bruce
PERSEVERANCE ISLAND	Frazer, Douglas
PERTURBED SPIRITS	Bull, R. C.
THE PERVERTED VILLAGE	Soutar, Andrew
PETER DOWN THE WELL	Low, A. M.
PETER PAN AND WENDY	Barrie, James
PETER SCHLEMIHL IN AMERICA	Anonymous
PETER THE BRAZEN	Worts, George F.
THE PETRIFIED PLANET	Pratt, Fletcher and Piper, H. Bean & Merril
THE PHANTOM ARMY	Pemberton, Max
PHANTOM FLEET	"Sea-Lion"
THE PHANTOM FUTURE	Merriman, H. S.
THE PHANTOM LADY	Irish, William
A PHANTOM LOVER	Lee, Vernon
THE PHANTOMS OF A PHYSICIAN	Miller, Alan
THE PHARAOH AND THE PRIEST	Glovatsky, Alexander
PHARAOH'S DAUGHTER AND OTHER STORIES	Astor, W. W.
THE PHILOSOPHER'S STONE	Larsen, J. Anker
THE PHILOSOPHICAL CORPS	Cole, Everett B.
PHYLLIS	Cunningham, E. V.
THE PICNIC	de la Mare, Walter
PICTURES IN THE FIRE	Collier, John
THE PIDGEON	Galsworthy, John
PILGRIM SORROW	Sylva, Carmen
PILGRIMAGE: THE BOOK OF THE PEOPLE	Henderson, Zenna
THE PILGRIMAGE OF STRONGSOUL AND OTHER STORIES	Davidson, John
PILLAR OF FIRE	Borodin, George
PIPE DREAMS AND TWILIGHT TALES	Jackson, Birdsall
PITIFUL DUST	Knowles, Vernon
PITTED AGAINST ANARCHISTS	Kemble, W. F.
THE PLACE OF DREAMS	Barry, W.
THE PLANET MAPPERS	Evans, E. E.
PLANET OF LIGHT	Jones, Raymond F.
THE PLANETS: A MODERN ALLEGORY	Kreymborg, Alfred
PLANETS FOR SALE	Hull, E. Mayne
PLANETS OF ADVENTURE	Wells, Basil
PLAYER PIANO	Vonnegut, Kurt Jr.
THE PLAYS OF J. B. PRIESTLEY	Priestley, J. B.
PLEASANT DREAMS	Bloch, Robert
PLUTONIA	Obruchev, V. A.
PODKAYNE OF MARS	Heinlein, Robert A.
THE POINT OF NO RETURN	Verron, Robert
POINT ULTIMATE	Sohl, Jerry
POISONOUS MIST	MacCreagh, Gordon
POLICE YOUR PLANET	Van Lhin, Eric
POLIOPOLIS AND POLICLAND	Chaney, J. M.
THE PORCELAIN MAGICIAN	Owen, Frank
PORT OF PERIL	Kline, Otis Adelbert
PORTALS OF TOMORROW	Derleth, August W.

PORTLAND, OREGON, A. D. 1999	Hayes, Jeff W.
POSSIBLE WORLDS OF SCIENCE FICTION	Conklin, Groff
POST MORTEM	Cullingford, Guy
POST WAR PIRATE	King-Hall, Stephen
THE POT OF GOLD	Wilkins, Mary E.
THE POWER	Robinson, Frank M.
POWER FOR SALE	Knittel, John
A FRANKISH FAIR	Davenport, Gentry
PREFERRED RISK	McCann, Edson
PRELUDE TO SPACE	Clarke, Arthur C.
PREMATURE ANGEL	Osler, William
THE PREMIER AND THE PAINTER	Zangwill, Israel
PRESTER JOHN	Buchan, John
THE PREVALENCE OF WITCHES	Menen, Aubrey
PRIESTESS AND QUEEN	Reader, E. E.
PRINCE CASPIAN	Lewis, C. S.
PRINCE GODFREY	Gorska, Halina
PRINCE LUCIFER	Staughton, Simon
THE PRINCE OF ARGOLIS	Smith, J. Moyr
PRINCE OF DARKNESS	Verner, Gerald
PRINCE OF PARADISE	Gerard, Francis
A PRINCE OF THE EAST	Harkins, James W.
THE PRINCESS OF BABYLON	Voltaire, Francois Marie
THE PRINCESS OF THE ATOM	Cummings, Ray
PRISONER IN THE SKULL	Dye, Charles
PRISONERS OF SATURN	Suddaby, Donald
PRIZE SCIENCE FICTION	Wollheim, Donald A.
THE PROFESSIONAL & OTHER STORIES	Goodrich-Freer, A.
PROFESSOR PECKAM'S ADVENTURES IN A DROP OF WATER	Malcolm-Smith, George
THE PROFESSOR'S POISON	Gordon, Neil
THE PROJECT	Sinclair, Andrew
THE PROPHET AND THE MIRACLE	Prokopoff, Stephen
THE PROPHET OF BARKELEY SQUARE	Hichens, Robert S.
PROSE AND POETRY	Baudelaire, Charles
PROVIDENCE ISLAND	Hawkes, Jacquetta
THE PROWLERS OF THE DEEP	Kelsey, Franklyn
PRUE AND I	Curtis, George William
THE PUPPET MASTERS	Heinlein, Robert A.
THE PURCELL PAPERS	Le Fanu, J. Sheridan
THE PURGATORY OF PETER THE CRUEL	Greenwood, James
PURGATORY OF THE CONQUERED	Whatley, Joseph L.
PURPLE ISLANDS	Carter, Dee
THE PURPLE LEGION	Eliot, George Fielding
THE PURPLE MIST	Locke, G. E.
THE PURPLE PROPHET	Cox, William Edward
THE PURPLE SHADOW	Snell, Edmund
THE PURPLE TWILIGHT	Groom, Pelham
PURSUIT THROUGH TIME	Burke, Jonathan
Q'S MYSTERY STORIES	Quiller-Couch, A. T.
THE QUARTZ EYE	Webster, Henry Kitchell
THE QUEEN OF THE EXTINCT VOLCANO	Lampen, Charles Dudley
QUEEN OF THE JESTERS	Pemberton, Max
QUEEN OF THE WORLD	Weston, George

QUEEN ZIXI OF IX	Baum, L. Frank
THE QUEST	van Eeden, Frederik
QUEST FOR PAJARO	Maxwell, Edward
THE QUEST FOR UTOPIA	Negley, Glenn and Patrick, J. Max
THE QUEST OF THE ABSOLUTE	Balzac, Honore de
THE QUEST OF THE SPIDER	Robeson, Kenneth
THE QUEST OF THE WHITE MERLO	Gask, Lillian
THE QUICK AND THE DEAD	Peterkiewicz, Jerzy
R IS FOR ROCKET	Bradbury, Ray
RABBITS	Phillip, Alex J.
THE RADIO MAN	Farley, Ralph Milne
THE RADIUM POOL	Repp, Ed Earl
THE RADIUM REBELS	Meredith, George
RAIDERS FROM THE RINGS	Nourse, Alan E.
RAMAYANA	Menen, Aubrey
RANDALL'S ROUND	Scott, Eleanor
RANDOM SHOTS	Adeler, Max
RANGERS OF THE UNIVERSE	Law, Winifred
THE RAPE OF MAN	Cowie, Donald
RASHOMON AND OTHER STORIES	Akutagawa, Ryunosuke
RASSELAS, PRINCE OF ABISSINIA	Johnson, Samuel
THE RAT RACE	Franklin, Jay
REACH FOR TOMORROW	Clarke, Arthur C.
THE REALM OF THE WIZARD KING	Gilson, Charles
THE REBEL PASSION	Burdekin, Kay
RE-BIRTH	Wyndham, John
THE RED BUTTON	Irwin, Will
THE RED COURT	Vale, Rena M.
THE RED HOT DOLLAR	Umbstaetter, H. D.
THE RED JOURNEY BACK	Cross, John Keir
THE RED PERI	Weinbaum, Stanley G.
THE RED PLANET	Campbell, H. J.
THE RED PLANET	Heinlein, Robert A.
THE RED ROOM	Dennis, Geoffrey
THE REFUGEE CENTAUR	antoniorrobles
THE REMARKABLE LIFE OF DR. FAUSTUS	Anonymous
REMINISCENCES OF SOLAR PONS	Derleth, August W.
THE REMNANTS OF 1927	Long, Paul and Wye, Alan
RENNAISANCE	Jones, Raymond F.
THE RENT IN THE VEIL	Lawrence, Magery
REPEAT PERFORMANCE	O'Farrell, William
REPORT FROM PARADISE	Twain, Mark
REPORT ON THE STATUS QUO	Roberts, Terence
REPRIEVE FROM PARADISE	Elliott, H. Chandler
RESEARCHES INTO THE UNKNOWN	Row, Arthur
THE RESOLUTE MR. PANSY	Trowbridge, John
RESURGENT DUST	Garner, Rolf
RESURRECTION	Gerhardi, William
THE RETURN OF CONAN	Nyberg, Bjorn and de Camp, L. Sprague
THE RETURN OF ERICA	Vilmorin, Louise de
THE RETURN OF FURSEY	Wall, Mervyn
RETURN OF THARN	Browne, Howard
THE RETURN OF THE KING	Tolkien, J. R. R.
RETURN TO ELYSIUM	

RETURN TO MARS	Johns, Capt. W. E.
RETURN TO THE LOST PLANET	MacVicar, Angus
REVOLT IN 2100	Heinlein, Robert A.
REVOLT ON ALPHA C	Silverberg, Robert
THE REVOLT ON VENUS	Rockwell, Carey
THE RICHARDSON STORY	Williams, Francis
RIDAN THE DEVIL	Becke, Louis
RIDERS TO THE STARS	Siodmak, Curt
THE RIFT IN THE LUTE	Langley, Noel
THE RIM OF SPACE	Chandler, A. Bertram
RIM OF THE PIT	Talbot, Hake
RING AROUND THE SUN	Simak, Clifford D.
THE RING OF THE AGES	Klimbach, Sophie Mann
THE RING OF UG, AND OTHER WEIRD TALES	Stock, E. Elliot
RINGSTONES	"Sarban"
RINKITINK IN OZ	Baum, L. Frank
THE RIVER OF DARKNESS; OR, UNDER AFRICA	Graydon, William Murray
THE ROAD TO OZ	Baum, L. Frank
ROAD UNCONVENTIONAL	Gilmore, Louis
ROADS	Quinn, Seabury
THE ROARING DOVE	Kerby, Susan Alice
ROBIN RITCHIE	Haynes, Dorothy K.
ROBINSON THE GREAT	Anonymous
THE ROBOT AND THE MAN	Greenberg, Martin
ROBOT HUNT	Vernon, Roger Lee
ROBOTS HAVE NO TAILS	Padgett, Lewis
ROCKET JOCKEY	St. Joh, Philip
ROCKET MAN	Correy, Lee
ROCKET TO LIMBO	Nourse, Alan E.
ROCKET TO LUNA	Marsten, Richard
ROCKET RIDER	MacLaren, Evelyn
THE ROCKETS	Edmonds, Harry
ROCKETS TO NOWHERE	St. John, Philip
ROGUE IN SPACE	Brown, Fredric
ROGUE QUEEN	de Camp, L. Sprague
ROLLA; OR, THE VIRGIN OF THE SUN	Kotzebue, Augustus Von
THE ROLLING STONES	Heinlein, Robert A.
ROMANCE OF ELAINE	Reeve, Arthur B.
THE ROMANCE OF PALOMBRIS AND PALLOGRIS	Baker, G. P.
THE ROMANCE OF THE STARS	Leo, Bessie
THE ROOM BEYOND	Carr, Robert Spencer
THE ROOTS OF THE MOUNTAINS	Morris, William
THE ROSE BATH RIDDLE	Rud, Anthony
ROUND TRIP TO HELL IN A FLYING SAUCER	Michael, Cecil
THE ROYAL BOOK OF OZ	Baum, L. Frank
THE RUNAWAY WORLD	Coblentz, Stanton A.
RUSTY'S SPACE SHIP	Lampman, Evelyn Sibley
ST. DINGAN'S BONES	Callender, Julian
THE SACK OF MONTE CARLO	Frith, Walter
THE SACRED FIRE	Sydmort, Theodore
THE SAINT AND THE DEVIL	Winwar, Frances
SAINT ERRANT	Charteris, Leslie
ST. GEORGE AND THE WITCHES	Dunne, J. W.
THE SALAMANDER	

THE SALAMANDER	Smith, E. Oakes
THE SALAMANDER TOUCH	Roe, Ivan
SAMUEL BOYD OF CATCHPOLE SQUARE	Farjeon, Benjamin Leopold
THE SAND OF NISON	Regnas, C.
THE SANDS OF MARS	Clarke, Arthur C.
THE SANYASI	Penny, F. E.
SARAH HALL'S SEA GOD	Du Boice Theodora
THE SARAGOSSA MANUSCRIPT	Potocki, Jan
SARGASSO OF SPACE	North, Andrew
SARISKA BENORI	Smith, Barbara Dale
SATAN IN THE SUBURBS	Russell, Bertrand
SATAN, LTD.	Evans, Gwyn
SATAN WAS A MAN	Bierstadt, E. H.
THE SATANIST	Wheatley, Dennis
SATELLITE E ONE	Castle, Jeffery Lloyd
SATIRIC TALES	Lunatic, Nicholas
THE SATURDAY EVENING POST TREASURY	Butterfield, Roger
THE SAUCER PEOPLE	Garver, Ronald G.
SAVAGE CLUB PAPERS FOR 1869	Halliday, Arthur
THE SCAPEGOAT	Brooke, Jocelyn
THE SCARCROW OF OZ	Baum, L. Frank
THE SCARF	Bloch, Robert
SCAVENGERS IN SPACE	Nourse, Alan E.
A SCENT OF NEW-MOWN HAY	Blackburn, John
THE SCHOOL IN SPACE	Browne, Reginald
SCIENCE AND SORCERY	Ford, Garret
SCIENCE FICTION ADVENTURES IN DIMENSION	Conklin, Groff
SCIENCE FICTION ADVENTURES IN MUTATION	Conklin, Groff
SCIENCE FICTION CARNIVAL	Brown, Fredric and Reynolds, Mack
SCIENCE FICTION SHOWCASE	Kornbluth, Mary
SCIENCE FICTION STORIES	Pohl, Frederick
THE SCIENCE FICTION SUBTREASURY	Tucker, Wilson
SCIENCE FICTION TERROR TALES	Conklin, Groff
SCIENCE FICTION THINKING MACHINES	Conklin, Groff
THE SCIENCE FICTIONAL SHERLOCK HOLMES	Anonymous
SCOTTISH GHOST STORIES	O'Donnell, Elliott
THE SCREAMING GHOST	Carmer, Carl Lanson
THE SCREAMING SKULL	Horler, Sydney
THE SEA FAIRIES	Baum, L. Frank
THE SEA GHOULS	Spanner, E. F.
SEA GODS	Baumgartl, I.
SEA HORSES	Young, Francis Brett
THE SEA OF DREAMS	Bennett, Alfred Gordon
THE SEA PEOPLE	Lukens, Adam
THE SEA PEOPLE	Sizemore, Julius C. and Wilkie G
SEA SIEGE	Norton, Andre
SEALED ENTRANCE	Voss-Bark, C.
SEALSKIN TROUSERS	Linklater, Eric
THE SEANCE AT RADLEY MANOR	Drake, Catherine
THE SEARCH FOR ZEI	de Camp, L. Sprague
SEARCH THE SKY	Pohl, Frederick J. and Kornbluth, C. M.
THE SECOND ARMADA	Anonymous
THE SECOND CONQUEST	De Wohl, Louis

THE SECOND FACE	Ayme, Marcel
SECOND FOUNDATION	Asimov, Isaac
THE SECOND GALAXY READER	Gold, H. L.
THE SECOND GHOST BOOK	Asquith, Cynthia
THE SECOND MAN	Roberts, C. B.
SECOND SATELLITE	Richardson, Robert S.
SECOND SIGHT	Gunn, Neil M.
SECOND STAGE LENSMAN	Smith, Edward Elmer
THE SECOND TIGRESS	"Ganpat"
SECRET BOMBER	Powell, "Sandy" H. P.
THE SECRET COMMONWEALTH OF ELVES, FAUNS AND FAIRIES	Kirk, Robert
THE SECRET LIFE OF MISS LOTTINGER	Bell, Neil
THE SECRET MASTERS	Kersh, Gerald
THE SECRET OF A STAR	Martin, Eva M.
THE SECRET OF SATURN'S RINGS	Wollheim, Donald A.
THE SECRET OF THE CRATER	Hill, H. Haverstock
THE SECRET OF THE LEAGUE	Bramah, Ernest
THE SECRET OF THE MARTIAN MOONS	Wollheim, Donald A.
SECRET OF THE NINTH PLANET	Wollheim, Donald A.
SECRET OF THE SACRED LAKE	Gammon, David
THE SECRET OF THE SARGASSO	MacDonald, Robert M.
THE SECRET OF THE ZODIAC	Sterne, Julian
THE SECRET PEOPLE	Jones, Raymond F.
THE SECRET SCIENCE BEHIND THE MIRACLES	Long, Max Freedom
SECRET WEAPON	Newman, Bernard
THE SEDAN CHAIR AND SIR WILFRED'S SEVEN FLIGHTS	Chatelain, Madame de
SEE WHAT I MEAN?	Brown, Lewis
THE SEEDLING STARS	Blish, James
SEEDS OF LIFE	Taine, John
THE SEEDS OF TIME	Wyndham, John
THE SEERESS	Lissenden, George B.
SEETEE SHIP	Stewart, Will
SEETEE SHOCK	Stewart, Will
SELECTED SHORT STORIES OF FRANZ KAFKA	Kafka, Franz
SELECTED STORIES BY Q	Quiller-Couch, A. T.
SENRAC, THE LION MAN	Langford, George
A SENSATIONAL TRANCE	Dawson, Forbes
SENTINELS FROM SPACE	Russell, Eric Frank
SEVEN DAY MAGIC	Eager, Edward
SEVEN DAYS IN NEW CRETE	Graves, Robert
7 DAYS TO NEVER	Frank, Pat
SEVEN DAYS WHIPPING	Biggs, John
SEVEN DREAMERS	Slosson, Annie Trumbull
SEVEN MODERN COMEDIES	Dunsany, Lord
SEVEN OUT OF TIME	Zagat, Arthur Leo
SEVEN SONS OF BALLYHACK	Spivey, T. S.
SEVEN STARS FOR CATFISH BEND	Burman, Ben Lucien
SEVEN TIMES PROVEN	"Ganpat"
THE SEVEN WHO WERE HANGED	Andreyev, Leonid
17 AND BLACK	Waer, Jack
THE SEVENTH ANNUAL OF THE YEARS BEST S F	Merrill, Judith
THE SEVENTH DAY	Kirst, Hans Helmut
THE SEVENTH VIAL	Sleath, Frederick

THE SEX WITHOUT SENTIMENT	Winslow, Thyra Samter
S F: YEAR'S GREATEST SCIENCE FICTION	Merrill, Judith
S F '57: YEAR'S GREATEST SCIENCE FICTION	Merrill, Judith
S F '58: YEAR'S GREATEST SCIENCE FICTION	Merrill, Judith
S F '59: YEAR'S GREATEST SCIENCE FICTION	Merrill, Judith
THE SHADE OF TIME	Duncan, David
SHADOW FORMS	Hall, Manly P.
THE SHADOW OF A DREAM	Haldane, Charlotte
THE SHADOW OF ARVOR	Rinder, Edith W.
THE SHADOW OF FEAR	Toye, Nina
SHADOW OF FU MANCHU	Rohmer, Sax
SHADOW ON THE HEARTH	Merrill, Judith
SHADOW OVER THE EARTH	Wilding, Philip
SHADOWINGS	Hearn, Lafcadio
THE SHADOWS AROUND US	Morrison, Arthur
SHADOWS IN THE SUN	Oliver, Chad
SHADOWS MOVE AMONG THEM	Mittelholzer, Edgar
SHADOWS WAITING	Chilton, Eleanor Carroll
SHAMBLEAU & OTHERS	Moore, C. L.
SHANE LESLIE'S GHOST BOOK	Shane, Sir Leslie
SHE WHO SLEEPS	Rohmer, Sax
SHEBA VISITS SOLOMON	Eliat, Helene
SHEYKH HASSAN: THE SPIRITUALIST	Hillam, S. A.
THE SHINING SWORD	Coleman, Charles G. Jr.
THE SHIP OF DEATH	Stilgebaurer, Edward
SHIP OF DESTINY	Slater, Henry J.
THE SHIP OF FLAME	Stone, William S.
SHOOT!	Newman, Bernard
THE SHORT REIGN OF PIPPIN IV	Steinbeck, John
SHORT STORIES	Pain, Barry
THE SHREIKING HANDS	Warwick, Anne
THE SHRINE OF LOVE	Dilke, Lady
THE SHROUDED PLANET	Randall, Robert
THE SHROUDED WOMAN	Bombal, Maria-Louisa
SHUFFLEY WANDERERS	Pudney, John
THE SHUTTERED ROOM	Lovecraft, H. P.
SIDEWISE IN TIME	Leinster, Murray
SIGHT UNSEEN & THE CONFESSION	Rinehart, Mary Roberts
THE SIGN OF THE SEVEN SEAS	Dawson, Carley
SILENCE IN HEAVEN	Erlanger, Michael
SILENT GUESTS	Forrest, A. E.
THE SILICA GEL PSEUDOMORPH	Hart, Edward
THE SILVER CHAIR	Lewis, C. S.
THE SILVER DEATH	Gibbs, George
THE SILVER THORN	Walpole, Hugh
SILVERLOCK	Myers, John Myers
SIMON BLACK IN SPACE	Southall, Ivan
THE SIN OF SALOME	Harris, A. L.
SINBAD AND HIS FRIENDS	Strunsky, Simeon
THE SINGER	Taine, John
THE SINISTER RESEARCHES OF C P RANSOM	Nearing, H.
SINX OF SEVERAC BABLON	Rohmer, Sax
SINS OF SUMURU	Rohmer, Sax

SIR HENRY	Nathan, Robert
SIR PETER'S ARM.	Cobb, Michael
THE SIRENS OF TITAN	Vonnegut, Kurt Jr.
SIRIUS AND OTHER STORIES	Fowler, Ellen Thorneycroft
SIX FANTASIES	Brighouse, Harold
SIX LIVES AND A BOOK	Houghton, Claude
THE SIXTH ANNUAL YEAR'S BEST SCIENCE FICTION	Merrill, Judith
THE SIXTH COLUMN	Fleming, Peter
SIXTH COLUMN	Heinlein, Robert A.
THE SIXTH GALAXY READER	Gold, H. L.
THE SIXTH SPEED	Rath, E. J.
THE SKY BLOCK	Frazee, Steve
SKY ISLAND	Baum, L. Frank
THE SKYLARK OF VALERON	Smith, Edward Elmer
SKYLARK THREE	Smith, Edward Elmer
SKYPORT	Siodmak, Curt
THE SKYSTONE	Hilzinger, J. George
THE SLAVE OF SILENCE	White, Fred M.
SLAVES OF SLEEP	Hubbard, L. Ron
THE SLAVES OF SUMURU	Rohmer, Sax
SLAVES OF THE LAMP	Howard, George Bronson
SLEEP HAS HIS HOUSE	Kavan, Anna
SLEEP NO MORE	Holt, L. T. C.
THE SLEEPING QUEEN	Brand, Neville
SLOW BURNER	Haggard, William
A SMALL ARMAGEDDON	Roshwold, Mordecai
THE SMALL BACK ROOM	Balchin, Nigel
THE SMASHED WORLD	Slater, Henry J.
THESMILER WITH THE KNIFE	Blake, Nicholas
SMUGGLER'S RIDE	Woodiwiss, John C.
THE SNAKE LADY	Lee, Vernon
SNAPDRAGON	Savill, Mervyn
SNARE FOR WITCHES	Chamberlain, Elinor
SNOW FURY	Holden, Richard Cort
SO MANY STEPS TO DEATH	Christie, Agatha
SOJOURNERS BY THE WAYSIDE	Mulier
THE SOLITARY FARM	Hume, Fergus
THE SOLITARY HUNTERS & THE ABYSS	Keller, David H.
SOLO	Tabori, Paul
SOLOMON'S STONE	de Camp, L. Sprague
SOLUTION T-25	Du Bois, Theodora
THE SOLVENT	Goldring, Douglas and Nepean, Hubert
SOME CHINESE GHOSTS	Hearn, Lafcadio
SOME FANTASIES OF FATE	Welborne, M. W.
SOMEONE LIKE YOU	Dahl, Roald
SOMETHING ABOUT CATS	Lovecraft, H. P.
SOMETHING OCCURRED	Farjeon, Benjamin Leopold
SOMETHING TERRIBLE, SOMETHING LOVELY	Sansom, William
SOMETHING WICKED THIS WAY COMES	Bradbury, Ray
SOMETIME NEVER	Dahl, Roald
SOMETIME—NEVER	Leighton, Clare
THE SON OF A STAR	Richardson, Benjamin Ward
SON OF A TINKER	Walsh, Maurice

THE SON OF MARY BETHEL	Barker, Elsa
SON OF POWER	Comfort, Will L. and Ki Dost, Zamin
A SON OF THE GODS	Lodge, Mrs.
SON OF THE MORNING	Frankau, Gilbert
SON OF THE STARS	Jones, Raymond F.
SON OF TI-COYO	Richer, Clement
THE SONNET IN THE BOTTLE	Fennessey, J. C.
SONS OF THE OCEAN DEEPS	Walton, Bryce
SONS OF THE SWORDMAKER	Walsh, Maurice
SONS OF THE WOLF	Lukens, Adam
SORCERER'S SHAFT	Gerard, Francis
THE SOTEN MONOPLANE	Westerman, John F. C.
THE SOUL OF MARSHALL GILLES DA RAIZ	Lewis, D. B. Wyndham
A SOUL ON FIRE	Marryat, Florence
THE SOUND OF HIS HORN	"Sarban"
A SOUR APPLE TREE	Blackburn, John
SOUTH	Sansom, William
SPACE CADET	Heinlein, Robert A.
SPACE CAPTIVES OF THE GOLDEN MEN	Patchett, Mary Elwyn
SPACE CAT	Todd, Ruthven
SPACE CAT AND THE KITTENS	Todd, Ruthven
SPACE CAT VISITS VENUS	Todd, Ruthven
THE SPACE EGG	Winterbotham, Russ
SPACE HAWK	Gilmore, Anthony
SPACE LAWYER	Schachner, Nat
THE SPACE MERCHANTS	Pohl, Frederick and Kornbluth, C.M.
SPACE ON MY HANDS	Brown, Frederic
SPACE PIONEERS	Norton, Andre
SPACE PLATFORM	Leinster, Murray
SPACE POLICE	Norton, Andre
SPACE SERVICE	Norton, Andre
SPACE SHIP TO VENUS	Nicholson, John
THE SPACE SHIP UNDER THE APPLE TREE	Slobodkin, Louis
SPACE, SPACE, SPACE	Sloane, William
SPACE TO LET	Butler, Joan
SPACEFLIGHT VENUS	Wilding, Philip
SPACEMEN, GO HOME	Lesser, Milton
SPACE-TIME TASK FORCE	Yorke, Preston
SPACE TUG	Leinster, Murray
SPACEWARD BOUND	Brown, Slater
SPACEWAYS SATELLITE	Maine, Charles Eric
THE SPAEWIFE	Anonymous
SPANISH LEGENDARY TALES	Middlemore, S. G. C.
THE SPARROWS OF PARIS	Pei, Mario
SPAWN OF THE VORTEX	Gayle, Harold
THE SPECTRE LOVER	Southworth, Mrs. EDEN
THE SPECTRE OF THE PRIORY	Anonymous
SPECTRUM	Amis, Kingsley and Conquest, Robert
SPECTRUM II	Amis, Kingsley and Conquest, Robert
A SPELL FOR OLD BONES	Linklater, Eric
SPELLS AND PHILTRES	Smith, Clark Ashton
SPIDER'S WAR	Wright, S. Fowler
SPIRIT LAKE	Heming, Arthur
THE SPIRIT WAS WILLING	

SPLIT IMAGE	De Rouen, Reed R.
SPOOKS DELUXE	Walker, Danton
SPOOKS OF THE VALLEY	Jones, Louis C.
THE SPOTTED PANTHER	Dwyer, James Francis
SPRAGUE DE CAMP'S NEW ANTHOLOGY	de Camp, L. Sprague
THE SPREADING DAWN	King, Basil
SPURIOUS SUN	Borodin, George
THE SQUARE ROOT OF VALENTINE	Fleming, Berry
STAND BY FOR MARS	Rockwell, Carey
THE STAR BEAST	Heinlein, Robert A.
STAR BORN	Norton, Andre
STAR BRIDGE	Williamson, Jack and Gunn, James E.
THE STAR CONQUERORS	Bova, Ben
STAR DUST	Vivian, E. Charles
THE STAR DWELLERS	Blish, James
STAR GATE	Norton, Andre
STAR GUARD	Norton, Andre
THE STAR KINGS	Hamilton, Edmond
STAR LADY	Webster, F. A. M.
STAR MAN'S SON	Norton, Andre
THE STAR OF ILL OMEN	Wheatley, Dennis
THE STAR OF LIFE	Hamilton, Edmond
STAR OF STARS	Pohl, Frederik
THE STAR OF THE INCAS	Blundell, Peter
THE STAR RAIDERS	Suddaby, Donald
STAR RANGERS	Norton, Andre
STAR SCIENCE FICTION STORIES	Pohl, Frederik
STAR SCIENCE FICTION STORIES #2	Pohl, Frederik
STAR SHIP ON SADDLE MOUNTAIN	Hallam, Atlantis
STAR SHORT NOVELS	Pohl, Frederik
STAR SURGEON	Nourse, Alan E.
STAR WAYS	Anderson, Poul
STARBOY	Biemiller, Carl L.
STARHAVEN	Jorgenson, Ivor
STARMAN	McWilliams, J. A.
STARMAN JONES	Heinlein, Robert A.
STARMAN'S QUEST	Silberberg, Robert
THE STARMEN	Brackett, Leigh
THE STARS ARE OURS	Bulmer, H. K.
THE STARS ARE OURS	Norton, Andre
THE STARS ARE TOO HIGH	Bahnson, Agnew H. Jr.
THE STARS LIKE DUST	Asimov, Isaac
STARSHIP	Aldiss, Brian
STARSHIP THROUGH SPACE	Correy, Lee
STARSHIP TROOPERS	Heinlein, Robert A.
STELLA RADIUM DISCHARGE	Luna, Kris
THE STELLAR MISSILES	Repp, Ed Earl
STEP TO THE STARS	del Rey, Lester
STEPPENWOLF	Hesse, Hermann
A STIR OF ECHOES	Matheson, Richard
STOLEN SOULS	Le Queux, William
THE STOLEN SPHERE	Cross, John Keir
THE STONE AXE OF BURKAMUKK	Bruce, Mary Grant

STONES OF ENCHANTMENT	Martyn, Wyndham
STORIES	Yefremov, I.
STORIES AND FANTASIES FROM THE JEWISH PAST	Cohn, Emil Bernhard
STORIES BY AMERICAN AUTHORS Vol. 5	Anonymous anthology
STORIES BY AMERICAN AUTHORS Vol. 8	Anonymoug anthology
STORIES BY ENGLISH AUTHORS--IRELAND	Anonymous anthology
STORIES BY ENGLISH AUTHORS--THE SEA	Anonymous anthology
STORIES BY FOREIGN AUTHORS--FRENCH	Anonymous anthology
STORIES FOR TOMORROW	Sloane, William
STORIES WEIRD AND WONDERFUL	Nisbet, Hume
STORIES, WEIRD AND WONDERFUL	Muddock, J. E. P.
STORM AND ECHO	Prokosch, Frederic
A STORM IS RISING	Mackenzie, Nigel
STORM OVER WARLOCK	Norton, Andre
STORY OF A FEATHER	Jerrold, Douglas William
THE STORY OF COSTA BERLING	Lagerlof, Selma
THE STORY OF DOCTOR DOLITTLE	Lofting, Hugh
THE STORY OF KASTAN	Ekberg, C. Whitworth
THE STORY OF MY DICTATORSHIP	Anonymous
STOWAWAY TO THE MUSHROOM PLANET	Cameron, Eleanor
STRANDED IN HEAVEN	Crottet, Robert
A STRANGE ADVENTURE IN THE LIFE OF MISS LAURA MILDMAY	Le Fanu, J. Sheridan
STRANGE ADVENTURE STORIES FOR BOYS	Thompson, Ames
THE STRANGE ADVENTURES OF ISRAEL PENDRAY	Hocking, Silas K.
STRANGE ADVENTURES OF MR. COLLIN	Heller, Frank
THE STRANGE AND SURPRISING ADVENTURES OF GOOROO SIMPLE	Crowquill, Alfred
THE STRANGE BEDFELLOWS OF MONTAGUE AMES	Parker, Norton
STRANGE CARAVAN	Lawrence, Margery
THE STRANGE CASE OF MR. PELHAM	Armstrong, Anthony
A STRANGE DESTINY	Dawe, Carlton
STRANGE DOINGS IN STRANGE PLACES	Anonymous anthology
ASTRANGE ENCHANTMENT	Farjeon, Benjamin Leopold
STRANGE ENDS AND DISCOVERIES	Housman, Laurence
STRANGE EVIL	Gaskell, Jane
A STRANGE EXPERIENCE	Holcombe, William Henry
STRANGE EXPERIENCE OF TINA MALONE	Paige, Ethel C. M.
STRANGE GIFT	Bushnell, Adelyn
THE STRANGE JOURNEYS OF COLONEL POLDERS	Dunsany, Lord
STRANGE LIFE OF IVAN OSOKIN	Ouspensky, P. D.
STRANGE MEMORIES	O'Reilly, Rev. A. J.
STRANGE PORTS OF CALL	Derleth, August W.
STRANGE TALES FROM BLACKWOOD	Anonymous anthology
STRANGE TALES OF THE BORDERS	Boyd, Halbert J.
STRANGE TALES OF THE SEVEN SEAS	Lockhart, J. G.
THE STRANGE THIRTEEN	Gamon, Richard B.
STRANGE TRANSFIGURATION OF HANNAH STONE	Marryat, Florence
THE STRANGE WORLD OF PLANET X	Ray, Rene
STRANGER FROM SPACE	Adair, Hazel and Marriott, Ronald
STRANGER IN A STRANGE LAND	Heinlein, Robert A.
STRANGER THAN TRUTH	Caspary, Vera
STRANGERS IN THE UNIVERSE	Simak, Clifford D.
THE STRANGEST STORY EVER TOLD	Colp, Harry D.
STRAWS AND PRAYERBOOKS	Cabell, James Branch

STRAYERS FROM SHEOL	Wakefield, H. Russell
STRINGER'S FOLLY	Pilkington, Roger
SUB COOLUM--SKY BUILT HUMAN WORLD	Russell, Addison P.
SUBI: THE VOLCANO	Cole, Burt
SUBMARINE CITY	Collins, Errol
THE SUBMARINE GIRL	Turner, Edgar
SUMMER WILL SHOW	Warner, Sylvia Townsend
SUN IN SCORPIO	Fraser, Ronald
THE SUN QUEEN	Kaner, Hyman
THE SUNKEN WORLD	Coblentz, Stanton A.
THE SUNLESS SEA	Burnshaw, Stanley
THE SUPERHUMAN LIFE OF GESAR OF LING	David-Neel, Alexandra and the Lama Yongden
SUPERNATURAL STORIES	Timbs, John
THE SUPER-WOMAN	Sutter, A. Oliver
THE SUPERNATURAL READER	Conklin, Groff and Lucy
THE SURGEON'S STORIES--SECOND CYCLE	Topelius, Z.
THE SURGEON'S STORIES--FIFTH CYCLE	Topelius, Z.
THE SURGEON'S STORIES--SIXTH CYCLE	Topelius, Z.
THE SURPRISING ADVENTURES OF THE MAGICAL MONARCH OF MO	Baum, L. Frank
SURPRISING TRAVELS AND ADVENTURES OF BARON MUNCHAUSEN	Anonymous
THE SURVIVOR AND OTHERS	Lovecraft, H. P. and Derleth, August W.
THE SURVIVORS	Godwin, Tom
SWEAR BY APOLLO	Barker, Shirley
THE SWORDSMAN OF MARS	Kline, Otis Adelbert
SYLVIE AND BRUNO	Carroll, Lewis
SYLVIE AND BRUNO CONCLUDED	Carroll, Lewis
THE SWORD OF CONAN	Howard, Robert E.
TAKE ME TO YOUR PRESIDENT	Wibberly, Leonard
TAKEOFF	Kornbluth, C. M.
A TALE OF TWO CLOCKS	Schmitz, James H.
TALE OF TWO FUTURES	Hayne, William P.
TALES AT TEA TIME	Knatchbull-Hugossen, E. H.
TALES FROM GAVAGAN'S BAR	de Camp, L. Sprague and Pratt, Fletcher
TALES FROM JOKAI	Jokai, Maurus
TALES FROM TIMBUKTU	Smedley, Constance
TALES FROM UNDERWOOD	Keller, David H.
TALES GROTESQUE AND CURIOUS	Akutagawa, Ryunosuke
TALES IN THE SPEECH HOUSE	Grindrod, E. E.
TALES OF A TRAVELER	Irving, Washington
TALES OF ADVENTURERS	Household, Geoffrey
TALES OF CONAN	Howard, Robert E. and de Camp, L. Sprague
TALES OF HORROR AND THE SUPERNATURAL	Machen, Arthur
TALES OF MYSTERY AND ADVENTURE	Anonymous anthology
TALES OF MYSTERY AND REVENGE	Langley, Noel
TALES OF THE DEAD	Anonymous anthology
TALES OF THE ENCHANTED ISLANDS OF THE ATLANTIC	Higginson, Thomas Wentworth
TALES OF THE FAIRIES AND OF THE GHOST WORLD	Curtin, Jeremiah
TALES OF THE MONKS FROM THE GESTA ROMANORUM	Komroff, Manuel
TALES OF THE UNCANNY AND SUPERNATURAL	Blackwood, Algernon
TALES OF TUSITALA	Stevenson, Robert Louis
TALES OF THE TWO BORDERS	O'Meara, Walter
TALES TO BE TOLD IN THE DARK	Davenport, Basil
TALES TOLD BY SIMPSON	Sinclair May

TALK OF THE DEVIL	Butler, Ewan
TALL SHORT STORIES	Duthie, Eric
TALL STORIES	Thomas, Lowell
TAM, SON OF THE TIGER	Kline, Otis Adelbert
TAN MING	Stormont, Lan
TARZAN AND THE FOREIGN LEGION	Burroughs, Edgar rice
TEDDY IN DARKEST AFRICA	Coggs, Dr.
TEDIOUS BRIEF TALES OF GRANTA AND GRAMARYE	Ingulphus
TEEN-AGE SCIENCE FICTION STORIES	Elam, Richard M.
TEEN-AGE SUPER SCIENCE STORIES	Elam, Richard M.
THE TEMPLE OF SAEHR	Pearson, W. T.
TEN TALES	Maginn, William
TEN TRAILS TO TYBURN	Graeme, Bruce
THE TERRIBLE AWAKENING	Desmond, Shaw
TERROR IN THE MODERN VEIN	Wollheim, Donald A.
THE TERROR OF THE AIR	Le Queux, William
THE TERROR OF THE SHAPE	Jude, Christopher
TESSSIE, THE HOUND OF CHANNEL ONE	Mead, Shepherd
THANKS TO CLAUDIUS	Looming, John F.
THERE IS ANOTHER HEAVEN	Nathan, Robert
THERE WAS A LITTLE MAN	Jones, Buy P and Constance B.
THERE WERE TWO PIRATES	Cabell, James Branch
THEY BLOCKED THE SUEZ CANAL	Divine, Arthur D.
THEY SHALL HAVE STARS	Blish, James
THEY'D RATHER BE RIGHT	Clifton, Mark and Riley, Frank
THINGS THAT GO BUMP IN THE NIGHT	Jones, Louis C.
THE THIRD FORCE	Matheson, Hugh
THE THIRD GALAXY READER	Gold, H. L.
THE THIRD LEVEL	Finney, Jack
THE THIRTEEN CLOCKS	Thurber, James
13 STRANGE STORIES	Kennedy, Douglas
THE THIRTIETH PIECE OF SILVER	Hayes, Lillian
31st OF FEBRUARY	Bond, Nelson F.
THIRTY MILLION GAS MASKS	Campbell, Sarah
THIS CREEPING EVIL	"Sea-Lion"
THIS DELICATE CREATURE	O'Leary, Con
THIS FORTRESS WORLD	Gunn, James E.
THIS INWARD HORROR	Warren, J. Russell
THIS ISLAND EARTH	Jones, Raymond F.
THOMAS BOOBIG	Marshall, Luther
THOU HAST A DEVIL	Hutchinson, R. C.
THOU MUST WRITE: A BUSHMAN'S STORY	Faucett, Francis
THOU SHALT NOT SUFFER A WITCH	Haynes, Dorothy K.
THE THOUSAND AND SECOND NIGHT	Heller, Frank
THREE HEARTS AND THREE LIONS	Anderson, Poul
THREE THOUSAND YEARS	McClary, Thomas Calvert
THREE TO CONQUER	Russell, Eric Frank
THRILLS, CRIMES AND MYSTERIES	Anonymous anthology
THE THRONE OF SATURN	Wright, S. Fowler
THROUGH A GLASS DARKLY	McCloy, Helen
THROUGH A GLASS DARKLY	Norris, Kathleen
THE THUNDERBOLT MEN	MacArthur, David S.
THUNDERBOLT OF THE SPACEWAYS	Ohlson, Hereward

TI-COYO AND HIS SHARK	Richer, Clement
THE TIDE	Sheean, V.
TIGER BY THE TAIL	Nourse, Alan E.
THE TIGER GIRL	Casserly, Gordon
TIGER IN THE KITCHEN	Sorenson, Villy
TIGER, TIGER	Bester, Alfred
TIK-TOK OF OZ	Baum, L. Frank
TIME AND AGAIN	Simak, Clifford D.
TIME BOMB	Tucker, Wilson
TIME FLIGHT	Longstreth, Thomas Morris
TIME FOR THE STARS	Heinlein, Robert A.
THE TIME GARDEN	Eager, Edward
TIME IS THE SIMPLEST THING	Simak, Clifford D.
TIMELINER	Maine, Charles Eric
TIME MARCHES SIDEWAYS	Finn, Ralph L.
THE TIME MASTERS	Tucker, Wilson
TIME OUT OF JOINT	Dick, Philip K.
TIME TO COME	Derleth, August W.
THE TIME TRADERS	Norton, Andre
TIME TRANSFER	Sellings, Arthur
THE TIN WOODMAN OF OZ	Baum, L. Frank
THE TITAN	Miller, P. Schuyler
TITANIA HAS A MOTHER	Brahms, Caryl and Simon, S. J.
TITUS ALONE	Peake, Mervyn
TO LIVE FOREVER	Vance, Jack
TO OUTER SPACE	Johns, Capt. W. E.
TO THE DEVIL: A DAUGHTER	Wheatley, Dennis
TO THE END OF TIME	Stapledon, Olaf
TO WHOM IT MAY CONCERN	Borgese, Elizabeth
TO WORLDS UNKNOWN	Johns, Capt. W. E.
TOAD	Cronin, Edward
THE TOE AND OTHER TALES	Harvey, Alexander
THE TOKEN	Anonymous anthology
TOLD AT TWILIGHT	Everitt, Nicholas
THE TOLTEC SAVIOR	Graham, (Mrs.) John Ellsworth
TOM SWIFT AND HIS ATOMIC EARTH BLASTER	Appleton, Victor II
TOM SWIFT AND THE COSMIC ASTRONAUTS	Appleton, Victor II
TOM SWIFT AND HIS DEEP SEA HYDRODOME	Appleton, Victor II
TOM SWIFT AND HIS DIVING SEACOPTER	Appleton, Victor II
TOM SWIFT AND HIS ELECTRONIC RETROSCOPE	Appleton, Victor II
TOM SWIFT AND HIS FLYING LAB	Appleton, Victor II
TOM SWIFT AND HIS GIANT ROBOT	Appleton, Victor II
TOM SWIFT AND JETMARINE	Appleton, Victor II
TOM SWFIT AND HIS OUTPOST IN SPACE	Appleton, Victor II
TOM SWIFT AND ROCKET SHIP	Appleton, Victor II
TOM SWIFT AND HIS SPACE SOLARTRON	Appleton, Victor II
TOM SWIFT AND HIS SPECTROMARINE SELECTOR	Appleton, Victor II
TOM SWIFT AND HIS ULTRASONIC CYCLOPLANE	Appleton, Victor II
TOM SWIFT AND THE PHANTOM SATELLITE	Appleton, Victor II
TOM SWIFT AND THE VISITOR FROM PLANET X	Appleton, Victor II
TOM SWIFT IN THE CAVES OF NUCLEAR FIRE	Appleton, Victor II
TOM SWIFT IN THE RACE TO THE MOON	Appleton, Victor II
TOMATO CAIN AND OTHER STORIES	Kneale, Nigel
THE TOMB OF THE DARK ONES	Mills, [illegible]

TOMORROW	Wylie, Philip
TOMORROW AND TOMORROW	Eldershaw, M. Bernard
TOMORROW AND TOMORROW & THE FAIRY CHESSMEN	Padgett, Lewis
TOMORROW ALWAYS COMES	Bartlett, Vernon
TOMORROW IS A NEW DAY	Hubbard, T. O'B.
TOMORROW SOMETIMES COMES	Rayer, F. G.
TOMORROW THE STARS	Heinlein, Robert A.
TOMORROW'S COMET	Sowden, Lewis
TOMORROW'S HORIZON	Meagher, George E.
TOMORROW'S SPECTACLES	Elliott, William J.
TOMORROW'S WORLD	Collins, Hunt
TOMORROW'S YESTERDAY	Stanley, Alfred M.
THE TORCH	Bechdolt, Jack
THE TORTURE CHAMBER	Van der Elst, Violet
A TOUCH OF STRANGE	Sturgeon, Theodore
TOWARD THE STARS	Bradley, H. Dennis
THE TOWER OF ZANID	de Camp, L. Sprague
THE TOYMAKER	Jones, Raymond F.
TRAFALGAR REFOUGHT	Clowes, W. Laird and Burgoyne, Alan H.
THE TRAGEDY BEHIND THE CURTAIN	Bayldon, Arthur A. D.
THE TRAIL OF CTHULHU	Derleth, August W.
THE TRAIL OF PHARAOH'S TREASURE	Reid, C. Lestock
TRANCE BY APPOINTMENT	Trevelyan, G. E.
THE TRANSCENDENT MAN	Sohl, Jerry
THE TRANSFORMATION OF UNCLE PARKER	Thatcher, A and Hogarth, C. J.
TRAVELERS OF SPACE	Greenberg, Martin
THE TRAVELLER'S RETURN	Bozman, E. F.
TRAVELER'S TALES	Adams, H. C.
THE TRAVELLING GRAVE	Hartley, L. P.
TRAVELS BY SEA AND LAND	Alethitheras
TRAVELS IN THE INTERIOR	Courtney, L. T.
TREACHERY IN OUTER SPACE	Rockwell, Carey
THE TREASURE OF THE RED TRIBE	Gilson, (Major) Charles
THE TREASURE TRAIN	Reeve, Arthur B.
A TREASURY OF AMERICAN FOLKLORE	Botkin, B. A.
A TREASURY OF FRENCH TALES	Pourrat, Henri
A TREASURY OF GREAT SCIENCE FICTION	Boucher, Anthony
A TREASURY OF SCIENCE FICTION	Conklin, Groff
THE TREASURY OF SCIENCE FICTION CLASSICS	Huebler, Harold W.
A TREE OF NIGHT	Capote, Truman
TREES OF GHOSTLY DREAD	O'Donnell, Elliott
TREVY THE RIVER	Reid, Leslie
TRIANGLE	Asimov, Isaac
TRIPLANETARY	Smith, Edward Elmer
TRITON	Hubbard, L. Ron
THE TRITONIAN RING	de Camp, L. Sprague
TROUBLE ON TITAN	Nourse, Alan E.
TROUBLED STAR	Smith, George Ol
TROUT'S TESTAMENT	Fraser, Ronald
TROYANA	Meek, Col. S. P.
THE TRUE LEGEND OF ST. DUNSTAN AND THE DEVIL	Flight, Edward G.
TUNNEL IN THE SKY	Heinlein, Robert A.
TUSSLES WITH TIME	Romaine, Jules

TWENTY FOUR HOURS	Charles, Neil
THE TWENTY SECOND CENTURY	Christopher, John
THE 27th DAY	Mantley, John
TWENTY TWO GOBLINS	Ryder, Arthur W.
TWICE IN TIME	Wellman, Manly Wade
TWILIGHT DREAMS	Carpenter, Bishop W. B.
THE TWILIGHT OF MAGIC	Lofting, Hugh
TWILIGHT ON THE BETZY	Dinesen, Thomas
TWILIGHT WORLD	Anderson, Poul
TWIN OF THE AMAZON	Fearn, John Russell
TWINKLE, TWINKLE LITTLE STAR	Barzman, Ben
TWO CAME TO TOWN	Strunsky, Simeon
TWO RUBLES TO TIMES SQUARE	Richards, Guy
TWO SOUGHT ADVENTURE	Leiber, Fritz
TWO TICKETS FOR TANGIER	Mason, Van Wyck
THE TWO TOWERS	Tolkien, J. R. R.
TWO WORLDS	Lorraine, Paul
TYPEWRITER IN THE SKY & FEAR	Hubbard, L. Ron
[illegible]'S [illegible]	V[illegible]sour, John
TYRANT OF TIME	Eshbach, Lloyd Arthur
UARDA	Ebers, Georg
UBIQUE, THE SCIENTIFIC BUSHRANGER	Martin, Clarence W.
"UGLY" A HOSPITAL DOG	Dabbs, George
ULRIC THE JARL	Stoddard, William O.
ULTRA, A STORY OF PRE-NATAL INFLUENCE	Hunt, Laura shellabarger
UNBORN TOMORROW	Frankau, Gilbert
UNCANNY STORIES	Anonymous anthology
UNCANNY STORIES	Giraud, S.Louis
THE UNCERTAIN ELEMENT	Scott, Jeremy
UNCHARTED SEAS	Wheatley, Dennis
UNCLE ARTHUR AND OTHER STORIES	Pudney, John
AN UNCONVENTIONAL FAIRY TALE	Hayes, Herbert E. E.
UNDER THE BRUCHSTONE	Denwood, J. M. and Wright, S. Fowler
UNDER THE INFLUENCE	Kerr, Geoffrey
UNDER THE LABEL	Tombleson, J. B.
UNDER THE LINDEN TREE	Williamson, Thames
UNDER THE SUN	Buck, Charles W.
UNDER THE TRIPLE SUNS	Coblentz, Stanton A.
UNDERGROUND CITY	Verne, Jules
UNDERSEA CITY	Pohl, Frederik and Williamson, Jack
UNDERSEA FLEET	Pohl, Frederik and Williamson, Jack
UNDERSEA QUEST	Pohl, Frederik and Williamson, Jack
THE UNDESIRED PRINCESS	de Camp, L. Sprague
THE UNDYING FIRE	Pratt, Fletcher
UNHOLY ALLIANCE	Wheeler, Francis
THE UNICORN	Buchanan, Thomas G.
THE UNKNOWN DEPTHS	O'Donnell, Elliott
THE UNKNOWN DICTATOR	Ingham, L. H.
THE UNPLEASANT PROFESSION OF JONATHAN HOAG	Heinlein, Robert A.
THE UNQUIET SPIRIT	Steen, Marguerite
UNSEEN ARRAY	Peck, Winifred
UNTOUCHED BY HUMAN HANDS	Sheckley, Robert
UNVEILED MYSTERIES	King, Godfre Ray
UNWISE CHILD	

UP JENKINS!	Hingley, Ronald
UP THE MATTERHORN IN A BOAT	Pope, Marion M.
THE UPAS TREE	Barclay, Florence L.
UTHER AND IGRAINE	Deeping, Warwick
THE UTMOST ISLAND	Myers, Henry
UTOPIA (THE VOLCANO ISLAND)	Dimondstein, Boris
UTOPIA 239	Gordon, Rex
THE UTTERMOST	Stallard, (Mrs.) Arthur
VALLEY BEYOND TIME	Wilkins, Vaughan
VALLEY OF LIGHT	Patterson, Glennie V.
VAN WAGONER'S WAYS	Alden, W. L.
VANDALS OF THE VOID	Vance, Jack
VANDOVER AND THE BRUTE	Norris, Frank
VANGUARD TO VENUS	Castle, Jeffery Lloyd
THE VANISHING ISLAND	O'Connell, Charles C.
VAULT OF THE AGES	Anderson, Poul
THE VEIL, A ROMANCE OF TUNISIA	Stevens, E. S.
THE VELVET WELL	Gearon, John
THE VENGEANCE OF MYNHEER VAN LOK	Stacpoole, H. de Vere
THE VENGEANCE OF SCIENCE	Delmaine, James
VENOM	Hastings, A. C. G.
THE VENOM-SEEKERS	Berry, Bryan
VENUS BOY	Sutton, Lee
VENUS: ONE WORLD VEARER PARADISE	Paterson, Arthur elliott
VENUS: THE LONELY GODDESS	Erskine, John
VERDICT OF THE GODS	Ghosh, Sarah Kumar
VERE VEREKER'S VENGEANCE	Hood, Thomas
THE VERGE OF TWILIGHT	Carolin, Q. C.
THE VICTORIAN CHAISE LOUNGE	Laski, Marghanita
VIKRAM AND THE VAMPIRE	Burton, Richard F.
THE VILLA JANE	Laing, Janet
THE VILLAGE THAT WANDERED	Smith, Surrey
THE VINTAGE	West, Anthony
VIRGIN IN FLAMES	Rohmer, Sax
VIRGIN PLANET	Anderson, Poul
VISIT OF THE PRINCESS	Mottram, R. H.
A VISIT TO TAPOS	Little, William
THE VISITANT	Tugel, Ludwig
THE VOICE OF THE DOLPHINS	Szilard, Leo
VOICE OF THE MURDERER	Walsh, Goodwin
VOODOO	Esteven, John
THE VORTEX BLASTER	Smith, Edward Elmer
VOYAGE INTO THE UNKNOWN	Kittelle, P. Wayne
THE VOYAGE OF ITHOBAL	Arnold, Edwin
THE VOYAGE OF THE DAWN TREADER	Lewis, C. S.
THE VOYAGE OF THE LUNA I	Craigie, David
THE VOYAGE OF THE SPACE BEAGLE	van Vogt, A. E.
A VOYAGE TO LITHO	Cock, Capt. Samuel
VOYAGE OF WILL ROGERS TO THE SOUTH POLE	Spotswood, Christopher
THE VOYAGES OF DOCTOR DOLITTLE	Lofting, Hugh
VROUW GROBELAAR AND HER LEADING CASES	Gibbons, Perceval
THE VULTURE	Noy, John
WALDO & MAGIC, INC.	Heinlein, Robert A.

WALK UP THE SKY	Williams, Robert Moore
WALKING ON BORROWED LAND	Owens, William A.
WALL OF SERPENTS	de Camp, L. Sprague and Pratt, Fletcher
THE WANTING SEED	Burgess, Anthony
THE WAR AGAINST THE RULL	van Vogt, A. E.
WAR AND THE WEIRD	Phillips, Forbes and Hopkins, R. Thurston
THE WAR OF THE WIRELESS WAVES	Westerman, Percy F.
THE WAR OF THE WORLDS	Robinson, Frederick
WARDERS OF THE DEEP	Silver, R. Norman
'WARE WOLF	Forester, E. Lascelles
A WARNING FROM MARS	Whiteside, Edward
WARNINGS FROM BEYOND	Giraud, S. Louis
WASP	Russell, Eric Frank
A WATCHER OF THE SKIES	Mertins, Gustave F.
THE WAX IMAGE AND OTHER STORIES	Rhodes, Kathryn
A WAY HOME	Sturgeon, Theodore
WAY STATION	Simak, Clifford D.
WAYS THAT ARE WARY	de Bra, Lemuel
WE ALWAYS LIE TO STRANGERS	Randolph, Vance
WE ARE FOR THE DARK	Howard, Elizabeth Jane and Aickman, Rob.
WE HAVE ALWAYS LIVED IN THE CASTLE	Jackson, Shirley
WE, PEOPLE OF AMERICA AND HOW WE ENDED POVERTY	Sinclair, Upton
WE, THE FEW	Hawkinson, John L.
THE WEAPON SHOPS OF ISHER	van Vogt, A. E.
THE WEATHER IN MIDDENSHOT	Mittelholzer, Edgar
THE WEB OF EASTER ISLAND	Wandrei, Donald
WEDDING DANCE	de Tourville, Anne
THE WEEK-END BOOK OF GHOST STORIES	Carrington, Hereward
THE WEIRD IDOL OF PENANG TOWERS	Wells, George
WEIRD ISLANDS	Bosschere, Jean de
THE WEIRD OF "THE SILKEN THOMAS"	Manifold-Craig, R.
THE WEIRD ORIENT	Illiowizi, Henry
THE WEIRD SISTERS	Blyth, James
WEIRD TALES BY AMERICAN WRITERS	Anonymous anthology
THE WELL OF THE UNICORN	Fletcher, George U.
THE WELL WISHERS	Eager, Edward
THE WEREWOLF OF PONKERT	Munn, H. Warner
WEREWOLVES	O'Donnell, Elliott
WEST COUNTRY STORIES	Rowse, A. L.
WEST OF THE SUN	Pangborn, Edgar
WEST WIND DRIFT	McCutcheon, George Barr
WHAT HAS FOUR WHEELS AND FLIES?	Wallop, Douglas
WHAT MAD UNIVERSE?	Brown, Frederic
WHAT NEVER HAPPENED	"Ropshin"
WHAT TIMMY DID	Lowndes, Belloc
THE WHEELS OF IF	de Camp, L. Sprague
WHEN AND IF	Reynolds, Philip
WHEN HE SHALL APPEAR	Kampf, Harold
WHEN THE DEVIL WAS SICK	Ross, Charles
WHEN THE GREAT WAR CAME	Navarchus
WHEN THE KISSING HAD TO STOP	Fitzgibbon, Constantine
WHEN THE MOON DIED	Savage, Richard
WHEN THE MOUNTAIN FELL	Ramuz, C. F.
WHEN THEY CAME BACK	

WHEN THEY COME FROM SPACE	Clifton, Mark
WHERE THE STARS ARE BORN	Spaull, George T.
WHIMS	Wanderer
WHIMS AND ODDITIES	Hood, Thomas
THE WHISPERING BUDDHA	Cowles, John C.
THE WHISPERING CHORUS	Sheehan, Perley Poore
WHITE AUGUST	Boland, John
THE WHITE BULL	Voltaire, Francois Marie
THE WHITE FACED PRIEST	Hume, Fergus
THE WHITE FAKIR	Huddleston, George
THE WHITE FLAME	Cornelius, Mary R.
THE WHITE OWL	Smithson, Annie M. P.
THE WHITE WIDOWS	Merwin, Samuel
THE WHITE WIFE	Bede, Cuthbert
THE WHITE WITCH	Buchanan, Muriel
WHO BLOWED UP THE CHURCH HOUSE?	Randolph, Vance
WHO GOES THERE?	Campbell, John W.
THE WHOOPING CRANE	Kreisheimer, H. C.
WHY NOT NOW?	St. John, Arthur
WILD AND WEIRD	Campbell, Gilbert
WILD TALENT	Tucker, Wilson
THE WILES OF WOMEN	Decourdemanche, J. A.
WILLIAM AND THE MOON ROCKET	Crompton, Richmal
WILSON'S TALES OF THE BORDERS	Wilson
WIND FROM THE NORTH	O'Neill, Joseph
THE WIND ON THE MOON	Linklater, Eric
THE WINDS OF TIME	Oliver, Chad
WINDWAGON SMITH	Schramm, Wilbur
WINE OF THE DREAMERS	MacDonald, John D.
A WINE OF WIZARDRY	Sterling, George
WINGED VICTORY	MacFarlane, Claire
WINGED WORLD	Harper, Harry
THE WINGS OF DR. SMIDGE	Philbrook, Rose
WINGS OF REVOLUTION	Holden, J. Railton
THE WINTER SWAN	Youd, Christopher
A WISH A DAY	Ruck, Berta
WISHING SMITH	Hyne, C.J. Cutliffe
THE WISHING STAR	Galgano, Ruth H.
WITCH IN THE MILL	Peel, Alfreda Marion
THE WITCH OF WITHYFORD	Chanter, Granville
THE WITCH QUEEN OF KHAM	Fitzgerald, Ena
THE WITCH WOMAN	Cabell, James Branch
THE WITCHBOWL	Squires, Marjorie
WITCHCRAFT	Sleigh, Bernard
THE WITCHES	Williams, Jay
WITCHES THREE	Leiber, Blish, Pratt
WITCHES, WARLOCKS AND GHOSTS	Mason, J. Edward
THE WITCHING NIGHT	Cody, C. S.
WITHOUT SORCERY	Sturgeon, Theodore
THEWIZARD'S MANTLE	Halidom, M. Y.
THE WOLF FROM THE WEST	Crawshay-Williams, Eliot
A WOMAN AS GREAT AS THE WORLD	Hawkes, Jacquetta
THE WOMAN OF DESTINY	Warshawsky, Samuel Jesse

THE WOMAN WHO WAS NO MORE	Boileau, Pierre and Narcejac, Thomas
A WOMAN'S UTOPIA	Daughter of Eve
WONDER TALES FROM CHINA SEAS	Olcott, Frances Jenkins
THE WONDERFUL ADVENTURES OF SIR JOHN MAUNDEVILLE, KNIGHT	Layard, Arthur
THE WONDERFUL FARM	Ayme, Marcel
THE WONDERFUL FLIGHT TO THE MUSHROOM PLANET	Cameron, Eleanor
THE WONDERFUL GOATSKIN	MacDonald, Greville
THE WONDERFUL VOYAGES OF CAP'N PENN	Shumway, Harry Irving
THE WONDERFUL WIZARD OF OZ	Baum, L. Frank
THE WONDERLAND OF JOHN DEVLIN	Milligan, Clarence P.
THE WORLD AT BAY	Capon, Paul
A WORLD BEWITCHED	Graham, James M.
WORLD IN ECLIPSE	Dexter, William
THE WORLD OF A	van Vogt, A. E.
A WORLD OF DIFFERENCE	Conquest, Robert
WORLD OF WONDER	Pratt, Fletcher
WORLD OUT OF MIND	McIntoch, J. T.
THE WORLD THAT COULDN'T BE	Gold, H. L.
THE WORLD WITHIN	Aswell, Mary Louise
THE WORLD WITHIN	Lukens, Adam
WORLD WITHOUT END	Mackenzie, Nigel
WORLD WITHOUT RAIMENT	Dardanelle, Louise
THE WORLD'S DOUBLE	Horner, Donald M.
WORLD'S GREAT ADVENTURE STORIES	Anonymous anthology
THE WORLD'S GREAT FOLK TALES	Foster, James R.
THE WORLDS OF CLIFFORD SIMAK	Simak, Clifford D.
THE WORLDS OF SCIENCE FICTION	Mills, Robert P.
WORLDS OF TOMORROW	Derleth, August W.
THE WORLD'S STRANGEST GHOST STORIES	Hopkins, R. Thurston
WORLDS WITHOUT END	Baker, Denys Val
THE WORSTED VIPER	Mitchell, Gladys
THE WRATH TO COME	Mackenzie, Nigel
WRAXTON MARNE	Ray, Rene
WRECKERS MUST BREATHE	Innes, Hammond
WRITTEN IN SAND	Ewers, John
WRITTEN WITH MY LEFT HAND	Barker, Nugent
WRONG SIDE OF THE MOON	Ashton, Francis and Stephen
YANKEE VIKING	Hartley, Livingston
THE YEAR AFTER TOMORROW	del Rey, Lester
THE YEAR OF THE COMET	Christopher, John
THE YEAR THE YANKEES LOST THE PENNATN	Wallop, Douglas
THE YEAR WHEN STARDUST FELL	Jones, Raymond F.
YEAR'S BEST SCIENCE FICTION NOVELS: 1952	Bleiler, E. F. and Dikty, T. E.
YEAR'S BEST SCIENCE FICTION NOVELS; 1953	Bleiler, E. F. and Dikty, T. E.
YEAR'S BEST SCIENCE FICTION NOVELS: 1954	Bleiler, E. F. and Dikty, T. E.
THE YELLOW HAND	Upward, Allen
THE YELLOW LORD	Comfort, Will L.
A YELLOW NAPOLEON	Southon, Arthur E.
THE YELLOW PEOPLE	Peterson, Margaret
YEW TREES FROM THE WINDOWS	Idle, Doreen
YOU DO TAKE IT WITH YOU	MacDonald, Donald K. and Roberts, A. J.
YOU SHALL KNOW THEM	Vercors
YOU WOULDN'T BELIEVE IT	Goodrich, Arthur

YOUNG ART AND OLD HECTOR	Gunn, Neil M.
YOUNG VISITOR TO MARS	Elam, Richard M.
YOUR SINS AND MINE	Caldwell, Taylor
YOUR STORY, ZALEA	Langdon, Norman E.
THE ZEIT-GEIST	Dougall, L.
ZENITH D	Lorraine, Paul
ZOTZ!	Karig, Walter

SCIENCE FICTION

An Arno Press Collection

FICTION

About, Edmond. **The Man with the Broken Ear.** 1872

Allen, Grant. **The British Barbarians:** A Hill-Top Novel. 1895

Arnold, Edwin L. **Lieut. Gullivar Jones:** His Vacation. 1905

Ash, Fenton. **A Trip to Mars.** 1909

Aubrey, Frank. **A Queen of Atlantis.** 1899

Bargone, Charles (Claude Farrere, pseud.). **Useless Hands.** [1926]

Beale, Charles Willing. **The Secret of the Earth.** 1899

Bell, Eric Temple (John Taine, pseud.). **Before the Dawn.** 1934

Benson, Robert Hugh. **Lord of the World.** 1908

Beresford, J. D. **The Hampdenshire Wonder.** 1911

Bradshaw, William R. **The Goddess of Atvatabar.** 1892

Capek, Karel. **Krakatit.** 1925

Chambers, Robert W. **The Gay Rebellion.** 1913

Colomb, P. et al. **The Great War of 189—.** 1893

Cook, William Wallace. **Adrift in the Unknown.** n.d.

Cummings, Ray. **The Man Who Mastered Time.** 1929

[DeMille, James]. **A Strange Manuscript Found in a Copper Cylinder.** 1888

Dixon, Thomas. **The Fall of a Nation:** A Sequel to the Birth of a Nation. 1916

England, George Allan. **The Golden Blight.** 1916

Fawcett, E. Douglas. **Hartmann the Anarchist.** 1893

Flammarion, Camille. **Omega:** The Last Days of the World. 1894

Grant, Robert et al. **The King's Men:** A Tale of To-Morrow. 1884

Grautoff, Ferdinand Heinrich (Parabellum, pseud.). **Banzai!** 1909

Graves, C. L. and E. V. Lucas. **The War of the Wenuses.** 1898

Greer, Tom. **A Modern Daedalus.** [1887]

Griffith, George. **A Honeymoon in Space.** 1901

Grousset, Paschal (A. Laurie, pseud.). **The Conquest of the Moon.** 1894

Haggard, H. Rider. **When the World Shook.** 1919

Hernaman-Johnson, F. **The Polyphemes.** 1906

Hyne, C. J. Cutcliffe. **Empire of the World.** [1910]

In The Future. [1875]

Jane, Fred T. **The Violet Flame.** 1899

Jefferies, Richard. **After London; Or, Wild England.** 1885

Le Queux, William. **The Great White Queen.** [1896]

London, Jack. **The Scarlet Plague.** 1915

Mitchell, John Ames. **Drowsy.** 1917

Morris, Ralph. **The Life and Astonishing Adventures of John Daniel.** 1751

Newcomb, Simon. **His Wisdom The Defender:** A Story. 1900

Paine, Albert Bigelow. **The Great White Way.** 1901

Pendray, Edward (Gawain Edwards, pseud.). **The Earth-Tube.** 1929

Reginald, R. and Douglas Menville. **Ancestral Voices:** An Anthology of Early Science Fiction. 1974

Russell, W. Clark. **The Frozen Pirate.** 2 vols. in 1. 1887

Shiel, M. P. **The Lord of the Sea.** 1901

Symmes, John Cleaves (Captain Adam Seaborn, pseud.). **Symzonia.** 1820

Train, Arthur and Robert W. Wood. **The Man Who Rocked the Earth.** 1915

Waterloo, Stanley. **The Story of Ab:** A Tale of the Time of the Cave Man. 1903

White, Stewart E. and Samuel H. Adams. **The Mystery.** 1907

Wicks, Mark. **To Mars Via the Moon.** 1911

Wright, Sydney Fowler. **Deluge: A Romance** *and* **Dawn.** 2 vols. in 1. 1928/1929

SCIENCE FICTION

NON-FICTION:
Including Bibliographies,
Checklists and Literary Criticism

Aldiss, Brian and Harry Harrison. **SF Horizons.** 2 vols. in 1. 1964/1965

Amis, Kingsley. **New Maps of Hell.** 1960

Barnes, Myra. **Linguistics and Languages in Science Fiction-Fantasy.** 1974

Cockcroft, T. G. L. **Index to the Weird Fiction Magazines.** 2 vols. in 1 1962/1964

Cole, W. R. **A Checklist of Science-Fiction Anthologies.** 1964

Crawford, Joseph H. et al. **"333": A Bibliography of the Science-Fantasy Novel.** 1953

Day, Bradford M. **The Checklist of Fantastic Literature in Paperbound Books.** 1965

Day, Bradford M. **The Supplemental Checklist of Fantastic Literature.** 1963

Gove, Philip Babcock. **The Imaginary Voyage in Prose Fiction.** 1941

Green, Roger Lancelyn. **Into Other Worlds:** Space-Flight in Fiction, From Lucian to Lewis. 1958

Menville, Douglas. **A Historical and Critical Survey of the Science Fiction Film.** 1974

Reginald, R. **Contemporary Science Fiction Authors,** First Edition. 1970

Samuelson, David. **Visions of Tomorrow:** Six Journeys from Outer to Inner Space. 1974